The Reformers and the American Indian

The REFORMERS *and the* AMERICAN INDIAN

Robert Winston Mardock

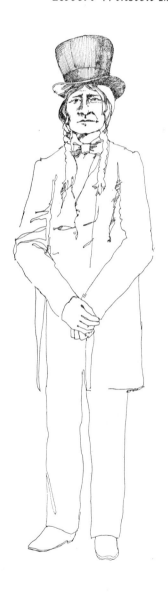

University of Missouri Press, 1971

ISBN 0–8262–0090–7

Library of Congress Card Number 79–113815

Printed and bound in the United States of America

Copyright © 1971 by The Curators of the University of Missouri

University of Missouri Press, Columbia, Missouri 65201

To Martha, my wife

Acknowledgments

Without the assistance of friends, colleagues, and others who were willing to give their time and abilities, I could not have written this book. To Robert G. Athearn, Professor of History at the University of Colorado, I extend my deep appreciation for his supervision of the first draft. To John Brennan, Director of Colorado University's Western History Collections, my thanks for helping me locate frontier material. I am especially grateful to Robert W. Richmond, Archivist at the Kansas State Historical Society, who not only came up with many useful documents but also read the original manuscript and offered valuable suggestions. My gratitude also goes to John Alden, Keeper of Rare Books at the Boston Public Library, and to William H. Bond, Director of the Houghton Library, Harvard University, for their cooperation in my research in the correspondence of several reformers.

Archibald Hanna, Director of the Western Americana Collection, Yale University Library, helped to locate important papers of the humanitarians, and the Washburn University Sweet Summer research grant provided much-needed financial aid. The materials in the Library of Congress and the National Archives and the kindly cooperation of David C. Mearns, Chief of the Library's Manuscript Division, and W. Neil Franklin, Jane F. Smith, Jose D. Lizardo, and Edward E. Hill of the Archives were indispensable. Finally, I thank my father, Lester E. Mardock, who made helpful suggestions about the early chapters, and my wife, Martha, who typed both the original and final manuscripts. Many others gave assistance at various times, and they also receive my sincere appreciation. The Houghton Library's Lydia Maria Child and Helen Hunt Jackson materials are used by permission of the Harvard College Library.

R.W.M.
Millikin University
June, 1970

Contents

Introduction

Most of the men and women who took up the cause of Indian rights during the post-Civil War years had previously been involved with the antislavery movement. Their work for the liberation of the Negro slaves had helped to prepare them for action in the movement to improve the condition of the Indians. The expansion of humanitarian reform was a natural transition to a broader area of activity that eventually affected the civil rights of nearly all racial minorities within the United States. Working as individual writers and lecturers or as members of organizations, those who tried to reform the Indian policy represented a number of Christian denominations. Their personal beliefs ranged from orthodoxy to a liberal free religion, but most could be described as social-gospel Christian humanists because they were deeply concerned with the improvement of the well-being of their fellowmen.

Some concentrated on Indian-rights work, while others became involved in a multitude of reform causes. The political sympathies of nearly all were with the Republicans, the antislavery party and the party that would inaugurate the reformed Indian policy. Most of them lived in Massachusetts, Pennsylvania, and New York, but a few had migrated to the Far West, where firsthand observation had converted them to work for Indian rights. Among them were congressmen, teachers, ministers, businessmen, Indian agents, Federal Government officials, farmers, journalists and writers, and several who could be called professional reformers. Nearly all were middle-class idealists who believed in the basic right of all men to freedom from oppression and who felt an obligation to bring this belief to reality.

In their day, most of the reformers were considered social radicals by their critics, and probably the majority of people in the United States held a similar opinion. Ideas of progressive transition and change did guide their thoughts and actions on most significant social issues, but they were not revolutionaries or truly utopian thinkers. They had no desire to overturn the basic social, political, or economic structure of the nation, and most of them were too experienced and too realistic to expect social perfection. Like the Transcendentalists before them, they condemned extreme materialism as an evil and insisted that religion should be the soul of society. Thus, they rejected the current European communistic theories as a worship of materialism. On the other hand, they were certain that a key to Indian civilization was individual ownership of land, a concept that was a basic part of their American heritage. They were optimists who believed that real improvements could be achieved and that a much better world for all men could become a reality within the existing framework of society. The idea that the new era must embody the principles of universal justice, freedom, and humanity was to them reasonable, possible, and essential.

The reformers appealed to two authorities to justify their demands for change. One was religious, documented by the New Testament; the other was political, documented by the Declaration of Independence and the Bill of Rights. The political authority was the legal framework, and the religious authority provided the basic foundation for the entire structure of human rights—the pervading power of love and the brotherhood of mankind. Practical and rational on one hand, mystical and pietistic on the other, they assumed that what they were doing was right and just. Wendell Phillips called it a "working reform Christianity" that he believed would regenerate the world.

The reformers were not the kind of evangelist associated with the second Great Awakening of the early part of the century, but they were evangelists in their own way. Buttressed by Christian principles, they directed their campaign specifically at saving a race from earthly extinction rather than saving souls. However, their religious leaders, and to a large degree all of the reformers, believed that saving the Indians would involve converting them to Christianity as an integral part of the civilizing process. Christianization would at the least enhance the possibility of saving souls. Although the government emphasized that integrity and peace were the objectives when it assigned reservation agencies to churchmen during the 1870's, the work of saving Indian souls was probably considered part of the over-all effort. Few reformers objected to conversion of the Indians, but a significant minority expressed alarm at any attempt to force the tribes to accept Christianity on the grounds they, too, should be allowed the freedom of choice.

On the other hand, the white people's practice of Christian principles would save the Indians from extermination and civilize them. The reformers considered this task an obligation of all people who professed Christianity. If they heeded its tenets, they would bring the rewards of peace and prosperity to the nation. Furthermore, this approach would help to allay the national guilt of the crime against a weaker race, and finally, it would spare the nation the consequences of God's wrathful judgment. The reformers thought the solution to the problem was a national responsibility, for the Indians were an integral part of the national community. John Greenleaf Whittier expressed this viewpoint when he said, "The more we do, in the true spirit of the Gospel, for others [the freedmen and the Indians] the more we shall really do for ourselves." To the reformers, it was a question of whether the people of the United States would be saved or damned together. The nation had already taken an important step in redeeming itself by eliminating the sin of Negro slavery. The eradication of the sins against the Indians must come next, and the brotherhood of the human race must be made a reality.

Christian principles demanded the elimination of injustice of all kinds and the extension of civil rights and privileges of a liberal democracy to everyone. The failure to do so had produced the great inequity that the reformers maintained was the primary cause of all the Indian wars. Conversely, the waging of war by either race could not bring about true justice. A few years earlier, when many of the Indian-rights advocates had been engaged in the abolition crusade, they had reluctantly condoned military action against the Southern slave system as the lesser of the two evils. But on the frontier, the Army was attacking the oppressed racial minority, not the oppressors.

A social-gospel form of Christianity not only provided the reform impulse but also shaped the reformers' views of the Indians and their place in the total scheme of things. God had "made of one blood all nations of men," they insisted, and therefore the Indians were the white men's brothers. By the same token, no basic differences separated the races, and human nature must be essentially the same in all of them. However, they believed that the Indians possessed more abundantly such innate traits as integrity, loyalty, and bravery. Not many reformers openly referred to the Indians as noble savages, but the views of some were influenced by Rousseau. Pre-Civil War romanticism undoubtedly affected reform writers like John Greenleaf Whittier, whose poem "The Funeral Tree of the Sokokis," published in 1843, depicted the "bronzed forms of the wilderness" as nature's noblemen. However, forty years later, Helen Hunt Jackson's novel *Ramona* presented much the same characterization.

The reformers did not make an issue of the explosive idea that intermarriage between the Indians and white people would be the ultimate solution to the Indian problem, as Thomas Jefferson had once theorized and as one young reformer suggested after observing the progress of the mixed-blood Cherokees. Acceptance of miscegenation was as alien to people in the nineteenth century as would have been John Collier's twentieth-century concept of individual cultural societies existing within the structure of the national society. Assimilation was almost always relegated to the political and economic realm rather than the social. The social organization that seemed most realistic at the time was multiracial, where all enjoyed equal rights and opportunities within close conformity to the culture of the majority.

Because the Indians' culture obviously was at a much lower stage of development than the expanding Euro-American civilization, the humanitarians recognized that elevating the Indians—in a broad cultural sense—was their primary task. Although they rarely mentioned it by name, they accepted the Darwinian concept of the survival of the most fit, in a social context, as a working hypothesis. The reformers did not think that the red *race* was inherently inferior; they believed the Indians were capable of cultural advancement to the national level. Such advancement was also a necessity, for if the Indians remained uncivilized primitives, they would be unable to compete successfully in the struggle for existence.

Most reformers explained the reasons for the Indians' condition by referring to the social evolutionary theories of the day and the conditioning the Indians had received from their civilizers. Unfortunately, they had acquired more of the vices than the virtues of civilization. As Wendell Phillips put it, "all the good the Indian has is his own; most of his vices he can rightfully charge to the white man." From these analyses, the reformers concluded that they should work for a massive but carefully controlled educational program that would bring a rapid acculturation and an enforced evolutionary change. Within a generation or two, the Indians would be a civilized and assimilative people. The belief that the Indians were products of their environment who had been educated by circumstances permitted reformers to accept the theory that the Indians could be changed to culturally acceptable members of society by restructuring their environment in an acceptable pattern. The new way of life would be based on the values of idealized middle-class, nineteenth-century Easterners—law-abiding, morally Christian, and politically democratic. The new Indians would be industrious, self-supporting landowners who had all the rights and duties of citizenship.

When the reformers tried to explain the Indians' native traits and culture, they were on the defensive, because prejudice existed everywhere in the nation. The lingering romanticized views of a superior order of aboriginal primitives were often overshadowed by lurid tales of past and present savage torture and butchery. At the popular level, the Indian-rights publications were smothered by an increasing flow of books, dime novels, and frontier newspaper reports depicting the Indians as bloodthirsty red devils. The reformers reacted to the challenge by overpraising the Indians' good traits and overlooking their defects. This reaction was often apparent in their attitudes about the white people who were in frequent contact with the Indians—the Army, the agents and post traders, and the border frontiersmen in general. They criticized the Army because they believed it represented unnecessary force and a policy of extermination, and they thought the agents and post traders were corrupt scoundrels who cheated the Indians. The border people generally came off somewhat better. They could be either lawless ruffians and greedy land speculators or peaceful agricultural settlers, the forefront of civilization. Even when they were pictured as peaceful pioneers, the border people were not as romanticized as they had been in the early nineteenth century. Rather, they were innocent victims of the perfidy of the ruffians and speculators who actually provoked the Indian outrages.

The reformers saw a direct cause and effect relationship; injustice to the Indians led to retaliation that hurt innocent frontier settlers. Although they often excused the violence of the Indians on grounds that they were more sinned against than sinning, the reformers did draw a line. Raw violence, in any form and for any reason, repelled them. Pacifist in principle, they envisioned democratic, legislative, and legal means to help the Indians. For that reason, some reformers stressed the need for punishing those Indians who were guilty of the attacks on peaceful settlements in the same way other lawbreakers were punished. This view posed a dilemma: When were the Indians fighting to preserve what was rightfully theirs and when were the attacks simply unprovoked savagery? The reformers seem to have resolved this dilemma by giving the Indians the benefit of the doubt. Underlying the reform viewpoint was a tacit belief that much of the Plains and Rocky Mountain West was, or at least should be, a gigantic Indian preserve upon which all white men were, in effect, illegal trespassers. The threatened extinction of the Indians in the West was not a consequence of manifest destiny; it was mainly a product of the cruel cupidity of white men. The burden of the responsibility for all the frontier problems rested upon the shoulders of white people and the government's Indian policy. In the final analysis, God would hold the entire nation guilty for the blood of all the innocent victims.

Many reformers thought criminal behavior on the part of the frontier population, military or civilian, was unusually prevalent, and they strongly condemned it. People on the frontier should know that obedience to a higher moral law, as well as man-made law, was an integral part of a civilized society. Those who had abused and outraged the Indians had broken both kinds of law and, according to Wendell Phillips, had violated the indefeasible purpose of New Englanders "that the law shall be as potent on the prairies as it is in State street." The reformers do not appear to have made the law-abiding frontier farmer the victim of a conscious class bias. They considered the majority peaceful yeomen pioneers who were close to the earth and absorbing its honest virtues like their neighbors, the Indians. All would be well if the greedy, criminal elements were either controlled or converted to righteousness. The reformers' devoted belief in the brotherhood of man and in equality under the law led to their separating the good from the bad, regardless of class or occupation. However, they sometimes forgot this high-principled outlook, which the general public in the East Coast states apparently did not share. During a lecture tour in 1875, Alfred Meacham was struck by the "almost universal prejudice against border men by eastern people, who speak of them as a class devoid of character." Unfortunately, this attitude strengthened frontier opposition to a movement that seemed willing to sacrifice civilized lives and property to save savage barbarians.

In Congress, the East-West division of opinion on the characteristics of the frontier people and the Indians, and their relationships to each other, was more clearly defined. The legislators were divided, often along political and geographical lines, into two emotion-filled enemy camps when they considered legislation of Indian policy during the 1860's and 1870's. Despite the division, and the fact that Congress was sometimes singled out as the real obstacle to the solution of the Indian problem, there were enough dedicated reformers in that body to legislate a humanitarian Indian policy. Without Congress and the national Administration behind them, the reformers would have made little progress.

The terms "humanitarian," "reformer," and "Indian-rights worker" have been used throughout the book to describe those actively involved in the movement. They were all humanitarian in the sense that they believed that all men, regardless of race, deserved humane treatment because all were children of God. Thus, all were brothers and had to live together as members of the human family in a world of order, harmony, peace, and happiness. They were all reformers because their goals were not only to change Indian policy to a peaceful, humanitarian one but also to uplift the total culture of the Indians and to improve upon the morals of white citizens so that the nation would be able to peacefully assimilate the Indians. All were working for the recognition and legalization of what they believed to be the natural rights of the Indians in a liberal, democratic America.

Without exception, the reformers were unsparing in their criticism of the government's Indian policy, but they did not stop at that. Both as individuals and as members of organizations, they presented positive plans for a new program to solve the Indian problem for all time. The incorporation of many of the reform ideas into the body of Indian policy from 1869 to 1890 suggests the significance of their work.

1

The Seeds of Reform

The official policy of the United States Government, announced by President James Monroe in December, 1824, called for the voluntary removal of the Indian tribes in the East to the territories of the trans-Mississippi West. Peace on the frontier, the education of the Indians in the arts of civilization, and the opening of tribal lands for settlement were primary objectives.[1] However, the attainment of peace and civilization proved to be elusive, for the subsequent enforced removal during the 1830's and 1840's failed to bring a permanent solution to the Indian problem. Although removing the tribes from the immediate paths of westward-moving settlement merely delayed a real solution for thirty or forty years, it did provide a respite for Indian policy makers, and it permitted humanitarians to concentrate on their attempts to end Negro slavery.

Most of the antislavery humanitarians were well aware that the Indians were often victims of flagrant injustices. In December, 1829, a young convert to abolitionism, William Lloyd Garrison, wrote an editorial in the *Genius of Universal Emancipation* strongly denouncing the Federal Government's policy of removing the Indians. Six months later, in the same journal, he attacked the "refusal" of Democratic party senators to observe the faith of Indian treaties as the "climax of party depravity, which, in this instance, is one degree *below* total depravity." In *The Liberator*'s engraved heading, Garrison portrayed a slave auction, but he showed trampled copies of Indian treaties in the dust at the feet of the auctioneers.[2]

Like Garrison, Lydia Maria Child, the Massachusetts editor of *The National Anti-Slavery Standard*, thought that a close correlation existed between enslavement of the Negroes and mistreatment of the Indians. Both races were the unfortunate victims of contact with the white race, she concluded in 1843. "Rum, gunpowder, the horrors of slavery, the unblushing knavery of trade" had been their teachers, and because these had failed to produce a high degree of moral and

---

1. James D. Richardson, ed., *A Compilation of the Messages and Papers of the Presidents*, 1897–1917 ed., II, 830.
2. Wendell P. Garrison and Francis J. Garrison, *William Lloyd Garrison, 1805–1879: The Story of His Life Told by His Children*, I, 156, 182–83, 232.

intellectual cultivation, "we coolly declare that the negroes are made
for slaves, that the Indians cannot be civilized; and that when either
of the races come in contact with us, they must either consent to be
our beasts of burden, or be driven to the wall, and perish!" She was
convinced that only an attitude of equality and brotherly love on the
part of the white race would solve the slavery problem and bring
justice to the Indians.[3]

By the beginning of the 1840's, Quaker abolitionist Lucretia
Mott believed that racial rights had become a question of priority.
She found an inconsistency in dissolving the Friends Committee on
Slavery and continuing the Indian Committee. She wrote in 1841
about "the Indian, who is injured and abased enough truly, but
whose oppression and suffering at the hand of the whites has not
been a tithe of those of the downtrodden negro." She continued, "If
the wrongs of the Indian are seven-fold, surely those of the negro are
seventy and seven."[4]

The conviction among reformers that they must first concentrate
all their efforts on eliminating the great evil of slavery was crystal-
lizing during the 1840's, and it had become a reality by the 1850's. At
the Philadelphia lyceums during the 1850's, where both the Negro
and the Indian questions were often discussed, Lucretia and James
Mott directed the attention of the participants to the subject of
abolitionism.[5] By this time, Mrs. Child observed, the evils of slavery
seemed closer and much more degrading and vicious than any other
wrongs of the day. She later recalled that "a death-grapple with
slavery was then coming upon the republic, and all felt that one or
the other must die. There was too much excitement and anxiety to
admit of attention to any other topic."[6]

When the great majority of humanitarians were devoting their
energies to the antislavery struggle, two men—Henry Benjamin
Whipple, an Episcopalian bishop, and John Beeson, an Oregon
farmer—had turned their attention to the Indians.

As a youth, Whipple had displayed strong convictions about
the "unrighteousness of an unequal fight," but his college experience
at Oberlin failed to convert him to active abolitionism. However,
during the 1840's, his mind turned toward the truths of the Gospels
and to the needs of the Indians—a "dying race." He was ordained
in 1849, and after ten years of ministerial work in the East and Mid-

3. Lydia Maria Child, *Letters from New York, 1st and 2d Series*, 160–61.
4. Anna Davis Hollowell, ed., *James and Lucretia Mott. Life and Letters*, 218–19.
5. *Ibid.*, 384.
6. Lydia Maria Child, *An Appeal for the Indians*, 15.

west, he was elected the first Episcopalian bishop of the frontier diocese of Minnesota.[7]

Through his ready compassion and persuasive oratory, Bishop Whipple soon gained the confidence of the Chippewa and eastern Sioux tribes as he toured his wilderness diocese in 1859 and 1860. He was shocked by the demoralized condition of his native charges and became intensely concerned with the injustice and inhumanity of the Federal Indian system. In a letter to President Buchanan in April, 1860, he insisted that the only hope for the Indians was in their civilization and Christianization. He warned that a Sioux uprising was inevitable unless immediate steps were taken to halt the illegal sale of liquor and to reform the corrupt trade system, for "a nation which sowed robbery would reap a harvest of blood."[8]

Bishop Whipple's reform efforts paralleled those of John Beeson. Like Whipple, Beeson was motivated by religious conviction. In 1860, he wrote that his conversion to Methodism at the age of fourteen left him with the lifelong desire "to be good and useful in the world." After he had settled on a farm in northern Illinois in 1834, he was able to put his humanitarian beliefs into practice. During his nineteen-year residence in Illinois, Beeson worked for the temperance cause and aided fugitive slaves along the Underground Railroad. After 1850, he experienced "an intense desire to cross the Rocky Mountains," so in the spring of 1853, he set out for Oregon with his wife and son. He stated a few years later, "We had no sooner got west of the Mississippi river than I had a foreshadowing of a work to do for the Indians."[9] The Beeson family had just settled on their farm in Oregon's Rogue River valley when they found themselves in the midst of a war between the Rogue River Indian tribes of southeastern Oregon and white settlers. During this war, which broke out in 1853 and lasted until 1856, Beeson became convinced that the Indians were being wrongfully deprived of their homes and that the corruption and destruction that he saw in the Rogue River War was "rampant throughout the nation." After the Indians were defeated by troops and placed on reservations, he became even more deeply concerned about the "national injustice towards the weaker races." He was overwhelmed by the callous treatment of the Indians and "vowed before God to risk property and life . . . to plead for the Indians until justice was done."[10]

7. Henry Benjamin Whipple, *Lights and Shadows of a Long Episcopate*, 2, 5–6.
8. *Ibid.*, 50–51, 105.
9. *The Calumet*, I, 1 (February, 1860), 7.
10. *Ibid.*, 8.

He began by writing letters to the civil and military authorities and to the newspaper editors and clergy of Oregon and California. His blunt exposés of wrongs done to the Indians during the Rogue River War brought a violent reaction from his Oregon neighbors, who not only failed to sympathize with his cause but also feared that the federal payments of their claims for damages would be jeopardized. Warned that his life was in danger, Beeson fled to Fort Lane for protection. From there, he traveled to the East Coast, where he wasted no time in his new calling. Within a few weeks after his arrival in New York City, Beeson had put into circulation 3000 copies of his first pamphlet on Indian rights and had enlisted the aid of a number of churches and sympathizers.[11] He also proposed that a national convention be called to discuss the Indian question so that the "best political party" could include an Indian-rights plank in its 1856 platform. This proposal met with less response.

Determined to see justice done, Beeson delivered to Congress sufficient evidence to influence that body to reduce greatly the reparations claims for losses allegedly suffered by settlers during the Rogue River War.[12] He claimed that this evidence saved the Federal Government nearly three million dollars, but his success almost cost him his life. Shortly after his return to Oregon, he was twice fired upon from ambush, and a gang of night riders burned his home. Beeson returned to the East in 1856 to join the fight for Indian rights—"a moral war against moral wrongs."[13]

Beeson's pre-Civil War crusade reached its climax on October 9, 1859, at a public meeting in Boston's Faneuil Hall, when his appeals for the Indians were supplemented by speeches from Edward Everett, Wendell Phillips, and other Boston reformers who had taken time out from the antislavery fight. A few months later, Beeson published the first and only issue of *The Calumet*, a journal intended to be the voice of the Indians, the new National Indian Aid Association, and others interested in improving the Indians' situation.[14] By that time, however, the public's attention was on the secession crises and the slavery issue, and the underfinanced journal died a quick death.

The coming of the Civil War only served to aggravate the In-

11. *Ibid.*, 8, 9, 25, 26.
12. John Beeson, letter to Hiram Price, Commissioner of Indian Affairs, May 19, 1885, Bureau of Indian Affairs, Letters Received; John Beeson, "Statement Relating to Indian Matters in Oregon," October 3, 1856, *ibid.*
13. *Ibid.*
14. *The Calumet*, I, 1 (February, 1860), 13, 29–30.

dian problem. A reduction in appropriations and troops for Indian affairs, an increased migration of white settlers across and into Indian territories, and a growing corruption in the agency and annuity system brought a series of bloody frontier conflicts. But it took the gory uprising of the Minnesota Sioux in August, 1862, to jolt the nation's attention to the nearly forgotten Indian question.

Solving the immediate problem of the Minnesota Sioux fell upon the already overburdened Federal Government and the citizens of the sparsely settled frontier state. By September, Colonel Henry H. Sibley's volunteers had taken 1700 Sioux prisoners, and a military commission had sentenced more than 300 to death.

Despite physical fatigue and a severe infection resulting from his efforts to aid the victims of that war, Bishop Whipple drew up a six-point plan embodying a thorough overhaul of the government's Indian policy. To provide the document with greater authority, he secured the signatures of thirty-eight Episcopalian bishops, rectors, and prominent laymen and sent it to President Lincoln.[15] In the fall of 1862, Whipple, whose Indian name was "Straight Tongue," traveled to Washington and reported personally to the President on the causes of the Minnesota outbreak. The President was deeply moved and later told a friend that Whipple's description of the "rascality of this Indian business" made him feel it "down to my boots." Lincoln added, "If we get through this war, and I live, this Indian system shall be reformed."[16]

Bishop Whipple won the respect of both white men and Indians. His earnest letters and memorials to Presidents, Indian Bureau officials, and congressmen, which he continued to send until the early 1890's, were emotional appeals for justice and practical suggestions for reforming Indian policy. As his experience and wisdom on Indian affairs became known, people in Washington often asked for his advice and aid. His personal appeals to Eastern philanthropists kindled much interest in Indian rights and brought generous financial assistance for his missionary work on the White Earth Chippewa Reservation and his Sioux mission in Minnesota.

After the outbreak of the Civil War, John Beeson came to believe that the nation's calamities were caused not by slavery but actually by "an extension of the unneighborly, unChristian, and destructive practice which for generations has been operating against the Aborigines." Wrongdoing to the Indians preceded the enslavement of the Negroes; the annihilation of the Indians and the usurpation of their lands had prepared the way for the introduction of

15. *Ibid.*, 138–41.
16. *Ibid.*, 136–37.

slavery. Furthermore, the Indian Bureau had been for many years under the control of the "Slave Power," whose attitude toward the Indians had been "as secret and as cruel as was the Inquisition in the dark ages." Thus, he concluded, because the wrong to the Indians was the first of the nation's sins and the beginning of national demoralization, "their redress is of right and necessity the first step in the order of national reform and of self preservation."[17]

In November, 1862, Beeson, who was then living in New York City, wrote President Lincoln that his contacts with persons living in all parts of the country indicated the presence of a deep, though latent, desire for justice for the Indians. He then suggested to the President that no reform measure he could recommend would meet with more general approval than reform of the Indian Bureau.[18] The overburdened Chief Executive talked with Beeson on several occasions during the most trying war years. In 1862, Beeson's charges of "robbery and fraud" in three Western Indian superintendencies brought a presidential order for an investigation.[19] In their last meeting in 1864, Lincoln told him that, having heard Beeson's arguments several times, he wanted Beeson to "rest assured that as soon as the pressing matters of this war is [sic] settled the Indians shall have my first care and I will not rest untill [sic] Justice is done to their and to your Sattisfaction [sic]."[20]

Besides meeting with Lincoln, Beeson had frequent interviews with other national leaders, and Senator Thaddeus Stevens once secured him an audience with Congress. In a memorial to the Senate, the reformer proposed that a special committee be appointed to examine the "treatment of the Indians in general . . . the Sioux in particular."[21] In addition to his work in Washington, Beeson organized public meetings in the churches and public halls of most of the other principal cities in the East. During seven years of Indian-rights work in that part of the country, Beeson helped to initiate reform of Indian policy and worked to arouse the dormant sympathy for Indians that he confidently believed to exist. He returned to Oregon in 1865 only because his funds were exhausted. In 1867, after

17. John Beeson, letter to President Lincoln, November 18, 1862, Secretary of the Interior, Letters Received.

18. John Beeson, letter to President Lincoln, November 11, 1862, ibid.

19. As quoted by John Beeson, letter to Edward P. Smith, Commissioner of Indian Affairs, July 29, 1873, Bureau of Indian Affairs, Letters Received.

20. John Beeson, letter to Edward P. Smith, June 25, 1873, ibid.

21. John Beeson, Memorial to Congress, May 2, 1864, Senate, Letters Received.

nearly three years of "rigid economy and persistant [sic] labor," he again was ready for the work in which, he wrote Indian Commissioner Taylor, "my head and heart is [sic] most deeply interested."[22]

The efforts of Bishop Whipple and John Beeson, and the bloody Minnesota Sioux uprising, suggested to President Lincoln that, despite the exigencies of the Civil War, an overhaul of the Indian system could not wait much longer. In his second annual message to Congress, on December 1, 1862, Lincoln asked that Congress give special consideration to such a reorganization and added, "Many wise and good men have impressed me with the belief that this can be profitably done."[23]

Congress failed to respond to the President's request, and nothing was accomplished toward reorganization in 1863. This omission prompted Lincoln, in his annual message of that year, to insist upon the "urgent need for immediate legislative action" to carry out his earlier request for remodeling the Indian system. "Sound policy and our imperative duty to these wards of the Government demand our anxious and constant attention to their material well-being, to their progress in the arts of civilization, and, above all, to that moral training" that would bring them under the Christian faith.[24] Congress did act upon this recommendation, but it limited its reorganization provisions to the State of California. Nevertheless, it had taken the first cautious step toward reform of national Indian affairs.[25]

Lincoln's embryo Indian policy, which emphasized material, spiritual, and intellectual progress, embodied the very essence of the program that the humanitarian reformers would advocate shortly after the war. The influence of Lincoln's humanism, the strong impetus given to the idea of equality by freeing the slaves, and the feeling that the war was a just punishment for an erring nation provided the stimulus for postwar reform. The experience of the war years inspired a vigorous movement for a humanitarian Indian policy. Its members envisioned a permanent solution to the enigma that had been haunting the national conscience for nearly a century. As *The National Anti-Slavery Standard* observed in 1869, the movement to improve the condition of the Indians was one of the "good results of

22. John Beeson, letter to Nathaniel G. Taylor, Commissioner of Indian Affairs, August 20, 1867, Bureau of Indian Affairs, Letters Received.

23. Richardson, *Messages and Papers*, VII, 3333.

24. *Ibid.*, 3388.

25. Commissioner of Indian Affairs, *Annual Report of the Commissioner of Indian Affairs*, 1864, *Annual Report of the Secretary of the Interior*, 38th Cong., 2d sess., 1864–1865, House Exec. Doc. No. 1 (Serial 1220), 156.

the abolition of chattel slavery, and of the increasing recognition of the equal rights of the victims of that iniquitous system, that a more just policy is now sought and recommended in relation to the Indians."[26]

The crusades for the abolition of slavery and then for the rights of the Negro freedmen seemed only a short step removed from a broader movement that would encompass all oppressed races in the United States. A direct connection probably existed between abolitionism and efforts to secure Indian rights as reform movements. Those antislavery humanitarians who became involved in work for Indian rights after the war frequently associated the two movements. They considered the fight for the rights of Indians an extension of the struggle for the freedom and civil rights of Negroes.

In the spring of 1865, when the war was almost ended and emancipation practically accomplished, Lydia Maria Child suggested in a letter to John Greenleaf Whittier that the nation's humanitarians make strong and persistent efforts to protect the Indians from encroachments in the future. "Their wrongs," she declared, "have been almost equal to those of the black race; and the government ought to be made to feel that the eye of the people is on them and their agents, in this matter."[27] The idea that reform was a mutual responsibility of both citizens and government had become accepted in the United States before the Civil War. This approach was by 1865 successfully righting the worst of the wrongs done to the Negroes; there was no reason to believe that it could not do the same for the Indians.

In 1865, Mrs. Child was a respected humanitarian who was best known for her antislavery books and pamphlets and her writings for *The National Anti-Slavery Standard*, an abolitionist journal that she edited for eight years during the 1840's. She had been a pioneer in the abolitionist movement, joining the New England Anti-Slavery Society in 1831 shortly after her marriage to David Lee Child, a Boston lawyer who shared her views. "She was wise in counsel," observed John Greenleaf Whittier, "and men like Charles Sumner, Henry Wilson, Salmon P. Chase, and Governor Andrew availed themselves of her foresight and sound judgment of men and measures."[28]

On the other hand, she had been criticized for her "innocent

26. *The National Anti-Slavery Standard*, April 10, 1869, 2.
27. Lydia Maria Child, letter to John Greenleaf Whittier, April or May, 1865, in Lydia Maria Child, Letters to John Greenleaf Whittier, 1857–1876.
28. Lydia Maria Child, *Letters of Lydia Maria Child*, viii, xiii.

audacity" in handling themes that required "larger equipment" than she could bring into service.[29] Like most of the social reformers of the time, she probably was deficient in anthropological knowledge, but her warm religious nature and her courageous belief in the universal brotherhood of all mankind lent determination and conviction to her reform efforts. "Nothing can ever change my belief that human nature is essentially the same in all races and classes of men, and that its modifications for good or evil are to be attributed to the education of circumstances," she wrote to Aaron Powell, retired editor of *The National Anti-Slavery Standard*. "My faith never wavers that men can be made just by being treated justly, honest by being dealt with honestly, and kindly by becoming objects of kindly sympathy."[30]

The Reverend Henry Ward Beecher took a similar view during his lecture tour of six East Coast cities in late 1866 and early 1867. "We have reached a stage of moral development in which we begin to see *unity* of race," he told his audiences. Furthermore, people of all races had their rights, and all must be educated to use them.[31] Reverend Beecher, a member of one of the nation's most prominent antislavery families, had been a leader in the movement. Thousands of people heard and read the sermons that this nationally known clergyman delivered each week at his Congregational Church in Brooklyn. He was a moderate in most ways, but he was at heart an active reformer whose views were dominated by his love of freedom and equality. He once said, "They are not reformers who simply abhor evil. Such men become in the end abhorrent themselves."[32]

Beecher's prewar concern with Indian rights was subordinate to his interest in the antislavery cause, but he recognized its necessity and importance. In 1859, when John Beeson came to New York City, the Reverend provided him with a lecture room and contributed a collection of forty dollars.[33] After the war, Reverend Beecher vigorously campaigned for universal suffrage and civil service reform as well as for Indian rights.

Equally well known for his antislavery work was the Boston abolitionist Wendell Phillips. Outspoken and sometimes aggressively

29. "Lydia Maria Child," *The Atlantic Monthly*, 1, 6 (December, 1882), 840, 844.

30. *The National Standard*, August 27, 1870, 4.

31. Henry Ward Beecher, "Universal Suffrage," Henry Ward Beecher, Papers, 1838–1878.

32. N. A. Shenstone, *Anecdotes of Henry Ward Beecher*, 422.

33. *The Calumet*, I, 1 (February, 1860), 26.

blunt, he was nevertheless a powerful and effective orator who had many followers among humanitarians. He was a professional reformer who hated evil and inequality and who believed that love and justice would solve most of humanity's problems, including racial strife. The small white cards that he often gave to his admirers bore the scrawled maxim: "Peace if possible. Justice at any rate. W. P."[34] When Daniel Webster had declared in 1850 that the Government of the United States "in all its history . . . has been beneficent," Phillips had answered, "witness all Indians, Negroes and Mexicans!"[35] His appearance on the platform with John Beeson at Faneuil Hall in 1859 had been prompted by his sympathy for a "just cause." Phillips had then predicted that, in a future age, "another Prescott would become famous by writing a history of the atrocious wrongs now done to the Indian race."[36]

Following the war, Phillips turned his seemingly inexhaustible energy and talents to freedmen's rights, temperance, woman suffrage, and labor reform. Despite this expansion of activity, he became a leading proponent of Indian rights in 1868 and, until his death in 1884, played a significant role in the movement. Always unyielding and uncompromising when principles of right and justice were at stake, Phillips continued to win both friends and enemies. *The New York Times* attacked him as an erratic radical who "as a matter of course, on every question that comes up . . . will try to take a view precisely opposite to that of everybody else."[37] He received a more favorable press in E. L. Godkin's *The Nation* and in such journals as *The National Anti-Slavery Standard* and its successors, where his editorial contributions frequently appeared.

Convinced that the treatment of Indians in the United States was "one of the foulest blots in our history," Phillips could clearly see the need to bring the issue of Indian rights into the struggle for universal racial equality. At a Boston celebration of the sixth anniversary of the emancipation of the slaves, he observed that he would have all races of men equal in every respect before the law.[38] At another time, he told a Boston audience that the Fifteenth Amendment had put the truth that all men are created equal into the Constitution. "But," he said, "it remains for this generation and the next to apply it. With infinite toil, at vast expense, sealing the charter

34. Wendell Phillips, Papers, 1843–1884.
35. Wendell Phillips, *Review of Webster's Speech on Slavery*, 44.
36. *Boston Journal*, reprinted in *The Calumet*, I, 1 (February, 1860), 30.
37. *The New York Times*, January 8, 1868.
38. *Ibid.*, January 2, 1869.

with 500,000 graves, we have made it true of the negro. With what toil, at what cost, with what devotion, you will make it true of the Indian and the Chinese, the coming years will tell."[39]

Not all of the antislavery humanitarians worked for Indian rights, and many of those who did failed to become deeply involved. Undoubtedly, there was some justification for one reformer who was interested in Indian policy to ask, "How can anti-slavery men and reformers generally be so indifferent?"[40] There were, however, valid reasons for what seemed to be a shirking of responsibility. Most of the social ills that reformers had attacked in the 1830's and 1840's still existed. Consequently, the reformers devoted themselves to a number of humanitarian activities. Soon after the war, they worked for temperance and prohibition, equality and suffrage for women, the rights of labor, and the abolition of war. In addition, there was the new problem of freedmen's rights, which would be especially important to antislavery workers, at least until the passage of the Fifteenth Amendment in 1870. As a result, a movement to help the Indians did not coalesce immediately, nor did it attract all of the reformers of the day. But in time, the Indian problem not only would test the abilities and try the patience of government and Army authorities but also would arouse a widespread humanitarian zeal almost equal to the fervor of the antislavery crusade itself.

39. Moncure D. Conway, "Wendell Phillips," *The Fortnightly Review*, XIV, 43 (July 1, 1870), 73.
40. Alfred H. Love, "The Indians," *The Bond of Peace*, I, 12 (December, 1868), 3.

2

Feed Them or Fight Them

The progress of Beeson and Whipple in Washington and steps taken by Lincoln to implement a semblance of change in the Indian policy had no perceptible effect on the frontier. The first legislative move of significance—the provision for reorganization in California—had little impact in the Great Plains region, where hostilities had intensified greatly during 1863 and 1864.

Cheyenne attacks on wagon trains and ranches in western Kansas caused *The Junction City Weekly Union* to call for five hundred troops to "subdue and chastise these Indians in a manner which will prevent a repetition of their outrages, and give peace and security to our border."[1] Many other Western newspaper editors, as well as state and territorial officials, military commanders, and settlers in the Plains country were expressing similar opinions.

No indications of a change in policy were forthcoming from Washington, and by the summer of 1864, military action seemed to be the only solution. In September, Major General Samuel R. Curtis, Commander of the Department of Kansas, ordered Colonel John M. Chivington of the Colorado militia to pursue and punish the hostile Indians. He reflected the prevailing attitude by adding, "I want no peace until the Indians suffer more." Two months later, Chivington's troops fulfilled the orders when they attacked Chief Black Kettle's Cheyenne and Arapaho village in southeastern Colorado Territory. The attack was so bloody that it acquired notoriety among critics of the Indian policy as the Sand Creek Massacre.[2] Also, in the summer and fall of 1864, Colonel Kit Carson led troops against raiding Kiowas and Comanches in the Texas Panhandle, and on November 25, 1864, he and his troops fought the first Battle of Adobe Walls.

The Plains tribes reacted to these assaults with such vengeance during the winter of 1864 and 1865 that travel and telegraph communication over the Platte Road, which ran through Nebraska, Wyoming, and Colorado, was completely disrupted. The cutting of the vital East-West link, the threat to future construction of the Union Pacific Railroad, which was then getting under way in Ne-

1. *The Junction City* (Kansas) *Weekly Union*, June 4, 1864.
2. Secretary of War, *Report on the Sand Creek Massacre*, 39th Cong., 2d sess., 1866–1867, Senate Exec. Doc. No. 26, 171, 173.

braska Territory, and the attacks in Kansas, Texas, New Mexico, and Arizona indicated complete loss of government control of the Plains Indian tribes.

This situation aroused Congress to take the second important step to change the Indian policy. On March 1, 1865, Senator James R. Doolittle (Republican, Wisconsin), a member of the Senate Committee on Indian Affairs, introduced a joint resolution directing an inquiry by a joint congressional committee into the "condition of the Indian tribes and their treatment by civil and military authorities."[3] In arguing the merits of such an investigation, Doolittle pointed out that, since the unscrupulousness of some Army officers and the fraudulent practices of the Federal Government's superintendents and agents were being blamed for the Indian uprisings, "it would be a matter of economy at least" to determine the "truth of these allegations." He then suggested that the joint committee be asked to report to the next Congress any conclusions for the better administration of Indian affairs that it might reach during the course of the investigation.[4]

Although the Platte Road was reopened by March 1, 1865, fear that the attacks might be repeated and genuine alarm over the status of Western Indian affairs eliminated any serious opposition to Doolittle's resolution, and it became law on March 3. After a thorough investigation, the joint committee of three senators and four representatives reported to the Congress on January 26, 1867. The report stated that the effects of disease, intemperance, wars, white emigration, and the "irrepressible conflict between a superior and inferior race when brought in contact" were rapidly decimating the Indians. Furthermore, most Indian wars could be traced to the aggressions of lawless whites, "always to be found on the frontier." It also rebuked the Army by strongly recommending that the Indian Bureau should remain in the Department of the Interior rather than be transferred to the War Department. Finally, the committee urged that five boards of inspection be appointed and given the authority to correct the abuses and the evils of the Indian system. Such a plan, it believed, would prevent useless wars with the Indians and result in greater efficiency and fidelity in all branches of the Indian service.[5] The recommendation for the boards of inspection had been submitted earlier to the Senate in a bill proposed by Senator Doolittle. The Senate passed it on March 19, 1866, but in 1867 the House sub-

3. *Congressional Globe,* 39th Cong., 1st sess., 1865–1866, Part 1, 158.
4. *Ibid.,* 327.
5. Congress, Joint Special Committee, *Condition of the Indian Tribes,* 39th Cong., 2d sess., 1866–1867, Senate Report No. 156, 3–10.

stituted a transfer proposal for the inspection boards and the Senate refused to concur.

Nevertheless, the findings and recommendations of the joint committee marked the germination of a new approach, a "peace policy," for handling Government-Indian relations. Its objectives were to preserve and civilize the Indians. The committee's sympathy for the Indians and its emphasis upon negotiation, instead of force, to settle frontier troubles indicated the existence in Congress of a small but active "peace party." Senators Doolittle and John B. Henderson (Republican, Missouri) and Representatives George W. Julian (Republican, Indiana) and William Windom (Republican, Minnesota) were becoming the more prominent congressional spokesmen for those humanitarians who were interested in Indian rights. Doolittle, a devoted friend of President Lincoln, was sympathetic to his desire to remodel the Indian system. Quaker extraction inclined Julian toward the peace policy. He kept in touch with the Society of Friends and knew its suggestions for reforms of the Indian policy. At times, he acted as an unofficial congressional spokesman for the Friends. Of the four, Julian was the most active reformer, championing such causes as woman suffrage and reform of land policy, in addition to reform of the Indian policy. Windom, another of Lincoln's friends and a descendant of Quakers, was convinced that the Sioux were incapable of civilization. However, he did believe that other tribes could be civilized, and he supported the peace approach as the best solution.

These four congressmen, all staunch opponents of slavery, had switched their political allegiance to the Republican party. Doolittle, Julian, and Windom were Northerners by birth and residence, but Henderson was a native Virginian who had grown up in Missouri. He was a strong Unionist who opposed both secession and radical abolitionism before the Civil War. After 1862, he underwent a political conversion, became a supporter of Lincoln's policies on emancipation and Reconstruction, and introduced the Thirteenth Amendment in the Senate. He also backed the President's plan for reorganizing the Indian system, and his membership on the Senate Committee on Indian Affairs gave him the opportunity to implement reforms.

In 1866, considerable pressure for a change in Indian policy was coming from the frontier West, where many newspaper editors favored solutions diametrically opposed to the peace policy. They supported a House amendment to the Indian appropriation bill for the fiscal year beginning July 1, 1866. It provided for the transfer of the Indian Bureau from the Department of the Interior to the War Department, the elimination of the Indian agencies, and the division of the Indian country into districts under control of Army officers. *The Leavenworth Daily Conservative* concluded that this plan would be "much less expensive to the government, and vastly more satisfactory to the Indians."[6] Editors in the Plains and Rocky Mountain regions, where Indian warfare was current, frequently spoke for a more permanent solution. As the *Kansas Daily Tribune* stated it in July, 1866, "There can be no permanent, lasting peace on our frontiers till these devils are exterminated. Our eastern friends may be slightly shocked at such a sentiment, but a few year's residence in the West, and acquaintance with the continued history of their outrages upon the settlers and travelers of the West, has dispersed the romance with which these people are regarded in the East."[7] Such sentiments, by contributing to Eastern opinion that all frontier people favored extermination, quickened the reform spirit in the East. Meanwhile, the House transfer amendment, strongly opposed by peace-policy senators, was defeated in the Senate by a vote of 21 to 12.[8]

Army officers serving in the Indian country proposed various measures, but General Sherman, who was in charge of the Division of the Mississippi, and Major General John Pope, who was over the Department of the Missouri, thought that a "reservation system," as well as War Department control of the Indian Bureau, would soon be necessary. Pope saw "both humanity and economy" in the plan, which two frontier experts, William Bent and Kit Carson, had suggested in 1865.[9] At the time, most of these military views had been acceptable to congressmen who wanted to reform Indian policy. The only one they might have questioned was transferring the Indian Bureau to the War Department. But when military activity in the West increased after 1866, they attacked the Army leaders' views as anti-Indian.

There was no strong opposition in Congress to a reform of Indian policy in 1866. The greatest barrier to change was the reformers' and the Government's ignorance about the necessity of new measures to meet the burgeoning crisis. Most congressmen, government officials, and citizens were absorbed in postwar politics and Reconstruction; to them, the Indian problem seemed remote and insignificant. President Johnson's only effort to remodel the Indian system was his

6. *The Leavenworth* (Kansas) *Daily Conservative*, July 1, 1866.
7. *Kansas Daily Tribune* (Lawrence), July 10, 1866.
8. *Congressional Globe*, 39th Cong., 1st sess., 1865–1866, Part 4, 3555.
9. Gen. John Pope, letter to Hon. J. Bright Smith and People of Colorado, Santa Fe, New Mexico, August 3, 1866, in Carl Schurz Papers, Vol. 7, 1865–1869; Robert G. Athearn, *William Tecumseh Sherman and the Settlement of the West*, 25, 42.

sanctioning the extension of the reservation system to the Plains tribes. Senator Doolittle, who was unsuccessfully pleading for the inspection boards, despaired of getting the "ear of Congress or the ear of the Senate on anything which concerns our Indian relations."[10]

However, a renewal of hostilities on the Plains during the fall of 1866 swept congressional apathy aside. The warfare was triggered by the Government's decision to construct military posts on the Bozeman Trail. John Bozeman had discovered it in 1863, and it had become a useful short cut from Fort Laramie, Dakota Territory, which was on the Platte Road—the old Oregon Trail—to the gold fields of western Montana Territory. But 170 miles of it traversed the choice hunting grounds of the western Sioux and their Northern Cheyenne and Arapaho allies. The Indians believed that the heavy travel over the trail was a serious threat to their food supply, the buffalo herds. In 1865, under the leadership of Sioux Chief Red Cloud, they demonstrated their opposition to Government plans to build a wagon road through their domain by attacking a Federal road-survey expedition and at the same time increasing their attacks on Bozeman Trail travelers. In June, 1866, Colonel Henry B. Carrington arrived at Fort Laramie with seven hundred troops and orders to fortify and garrison the trail, to avoid offensive warfare, and to concentrate on protecting travelers and keeping the peace.

The terms of the Fort Laramie Treaty of 1851 had given the Federal Government the right to construct roads and military posts on the Sioux reserve and had granted the tribe annuities for fifteen years. The Sioux reserve was a vast territory of 123,000 square miles that included most of present eastern Wyoming, northeastern Colorado, and western Nebraska. As drafted, the treaty had provided the annuities for fifty years, but before passage, the Senate had reduced the number of years to fifteen. Only part of the tribe had been notified of the change, and when the annuities were discontinued in 1866, most western Sioux bands believed that the government had defrauded them.

By June, 1866, Red Cloud had become convinced that military occupation of the Bozeman route meant a permanent road through the Sioux hunting grounds, which would be disastrous for the Indian way of life in that region. Believing, too, that in the termination of the annuities the Government had acted in bad faith, he angrily refused to sign a new Fort Laramie treaty that would have permitted unrestricted use of the road and the establishment of military posts. Red Cloud is reported to have told the commander of Fort Laramie

10. *Congressional Globe*, 39th Cong., 1st sess., 1865–1866, Part 3, 1712.

that if the Army carried out its fortification and occupation plans, the Indians would "mark every mile of that Bozeman Trail from the North Platte to the Yellowstone with the bodies of your soldiers."[11]

During the construction of the military posts—Forts Reno, Phil Kearney, and C. F. Smith—in the fall of 1866, the Indian leader proceeded to carry out his threat. After weeks of almost daily skirmishing, the Indians managed to execute a perfectly conceived ambush. They expertly decoyed Captain William Fetterman, a subordinate to Colonel Carrington at Fort Phil Kearney, and his command of eighty infantry and cavalry into a trap set by more than one thousand warriors. Captain Fetterman had once boasted that with eighty men he could ride through the entire Sioux nation, but there was no escape and no survivors.[12] The reports of this slaughter shocked the nation, brought scathing criticism upon the Indian policy, and forced the Government to take immediate action.

Both Congress and the Army responded. In February, 1867, Congress authorized the Sanborn-Sully Commission to investigate the causes of the Fetterman Massacre and to determine which tribes were friendly and which were hostile. The commission's instructions from Secretary of the Interior O. H. Browning indicated that the main objective was to prevent a general Indian war. However, the commissioners could not go beyond holding friendly talks, distributing presents, and finally ascertaining which tribes were willing to go on reservations.[13] While the commissioners performed their mission, the news of the Fetterman Massacre and reports of bloody Indian attacks from Montana to Texas spread panic among the border settlements. Also in February, General William T. Sherman tried to satisfy demands for military protection and to discourage the organization of volunteer civilian regiments of Indian fighters by ordering the punitive Hancock expedition against the Cheyennes of the central Plains. General W. S. Hancock's troops burned a Cheyenne and Arapaho village and one hundred Sioux lodges on the Pawnee River in western Kansas on April 19. But along the Union

11. Grenville M. Dodge, *The Battle of Atlanta and Other Campaigns*, 99–100; Margaret I. Carrington, *Ab-Sa-Ra-Ka, Land of Massacre*, 79–80; Lucy E. Textor, *Official Relations Between the United States and the Sioux Indians*, 109; see also Col. Henry B. Carrington, *History of Indian Operations on the Plains*, 50th Cong., 1st sess., 1887–1888, Senate Exec. Doc. No. 33 (Serial 2504).

12. Grace Raymond Hebard and E. A. Brininstool, *The Bozeman Trail*, I, 305.

13. Senate, *Report to the Senate on the Origin and Progress of Indian Hostilities on the Frontier*, 40th Cong., 1st sess., 1867, Senate Exec. Doc. No. 13 (Serial 1308), 55–56, 74.

Pacific Railroad and the Bozeman Trail, the undermanned western Army could take only defensive action against overwhelming numbers of determined Sioux warriors.

Meanwhile, a growing number of congressmen became discouraged by military reverses and disturbed about the heavy cost of seemingly fruitless frontier campaigns. They began to consider seriously the peace approach to the Indian problem. After the Sanborn-Sully Commission reported in early July that most of the Indians were ready for peace and recommended that aggressive warfare against them cease at once,[14] the House of Representatives organized a peace commission to confer with the hostile tribes. The only serious opposition to approval of the bill authorizing the new commission came from George Julian. He objected to hasty passage because he believed the next session of Congress could draw up a better measure, one that would incorporate provisions for complete reform of the Indian system. These provisions appeared in a memorial he had just received from the Society of Friends in Indiana. William Windom replied that the bill must be passed at once because, he said, "There are a great many peaceable bands of Indians who, though they belong to tribes that are disposed to go to war, . . . desire to leave those tribes and remain at peace with us." Also, the bill included an appropriation to feed and clothe those who chose peace; otherwise, they would "be compelled to take up arms against us." Julian made no further objections, and on July 20, 1867, the bill was passed. It was generally agreed that a new system of Indian policy would be devised later.[15]

Nathaniel G. Taylor, Commissioner of Indian Affairs, was chairman of the Peace Commission, and Senator Henderson, John B. Sanborn, Samuel F. Tappan, General Sherman, and Major Generals William S. Harney, Alfred H. Terry, and C. C. Augur were its members. They were directed to establish peace with the hostile tribes, to remove, "if possible," the causes of the war, and to secure the safety of the frontier settlements and the men who were building the transcontinental railroads. Also, they were to inaugurate a plan for civilizing the Indians.[16]

The commissioners represented several different points of view. Taylor, Henderson, and Tappan strongly believed that applying Christian principles would do much more to solve the Indian problem than would using military force. Sanborn, a Minnesota lawyer, was a brigadier general of volunteers during the Civil War and had

14. *Ibid.*, 74.
15. *Congressional Globe*, 40th Cong., 1st sess., 1867, 756.
16. *Ibid.*

conducted a successful campaign against the southwestern Plains Indians in 1865. His participation in the Sanborn-Sully Commission's investigation of hostilities on the northern Plains in February, 1867, had convinced him that most tribes were ready for peace but that military control must precede peacemaking. General Sherman best expressed the military representatives' views when he wrote to his brother that he would let the peacemakers assume the responsibility this year, for the Army could use a little time to prepare for the "inevitable war" that would follow their failure.[17] In view of the tremendous task imposed upon the commissioners, Sherman's blunt and at times ill-concealed skepticism could be excused.

Samuel Tappan had been appointed to the commission after William Windom, who had just been elected chairman of the House Committee on Indian Affairs, asked that he be excused and that Tappan be appointed in his place.[18] Tappan was another antislavery worker who became interested in the Indians. He was a Bostonian who had known William Lloyd Garrison and Wendell Phillips. In 1854, he joined the first contingent of the Massachusetts Emigrant Aid Company and traveled with it to Kansas, where he participated in the free-state struggle and covered that activity as a correspondent for Horace Greeley's *New York Tribune* and several other Republican journals. In 1860, he moved to Denver and worked for the Denver *Daily Herald*, and in 1861, he became a lieutenant colonel in the First Colorado Cavalry, which was active in the New Mexico campaign and the Plains Indian wars. Although he passionately criticized Colonel John Chivington and the Sand Creek Massacre of 1864, Tappan was appointed president of the military investigation commission that strongly censured the attack.[19] He expressed his concern for Indian rights in letters to fellow reformers and government officials during the immediate postwar years. When he was appointed to the Peace Commission, Senator Samuel Pomeroy (Republican, Kansas) called him "a good man . . . who understands the Indians, and understands this whole question."[20]

The commissioners had just started to work when several people

17. Athearn, *William Tecumseh Sherman*, 173.
18. Samuel F. Tappan, "Autobiography," Samuel F. Tappan Papers; Henry E. Fritz, *The Movement for Indian Assimilation, 1860–1890*, 48–49; William E. Connelley, *A Standard History of Kansas and Kansans*, I, 493; II, 692.
19. *Congressional Globe*, 40th Cong., 1st sess., 1867, 753.
20. Indian Peace Commission, Report to the President, January 7, 1868, *Annual Report of the Commissioner of Indian Affairs*, 1868, *Annual Report of the Secretary of the Interior*, 40th Cong., 3d sess., 1868–1869, House Exec. Doc. No. 1 (Serial 1366), 486.

from the Great Plains voiced the extreme opposition in that area to the peace approach. A Montanan wrote that the government seemed to be "pursuing the old policy of treating for peace, and sending out larger quantities of supplies for the Indians. As winter is coming on, and the Indians for that reason will soon be compelled to stop their hellish work of murder and plunder, no doubt, they will see fit to accept the treaties and presents, and trade for an abundant supply of the most approved arms and ammunition in the spring."[21] Kansas Governor Samuel Crawford said the Peace Commission represented a "wicked policy" that encouraged the Indians "in the most bloody and atrocious crimes." Real peace, he believed, would come only when prompt and decisive measures were used to punish the Indians, rather than reward their evil deeds with presents from peace commissioners.[22] Another Kansan described the mission of the peace commissioners as "the most senseless, the most ridiculous piece of business we have ever heard of."[23] This opposition, and the bloody war that the Plains Indians appeared to be winning, presented immediate and formidable obstacles.

The Peace Commission first directed its attention to the tribes of the northern Plains. In September, 1867, at North Platte, Nebraska, the commissioners held their first meeting with genuine hostiles—a delegation of Oglala and Brulé Sioux and Northern Cheyennes. These bands had agreed to come only after the commissioners had promised that, if peace were made, they would give the Indians ammunition for the fall hunt. The commissioners were unable to induce the suspicious chiefs to sign a treaty, but they were confident that a "full and perfect understanding was arrived at."[24] At this point, the commissioners planned to travel to Fort Laramie and talk with Red Cloud and other representatives of the northern Sioux. However, the Sioux, who were fighting the soldiers in the Powder River country, sent word that they would be unable to attend, and after notifying the chiefs that a council would be held at Fort Laramie on November 1, the commissioners returned to St. Louis. There, they prepared for a conference with the recalcitrant tribes of the southern Plains.[25]

That conference was much more successful. In October, the commissioners negotiated a treaty with the Kiowas, Arapahoes, Southern Cheyennes, Plains Apaches, and Comanches at Medicine Lodge

21. *Kansas State Record* (Topeka), October 23, 1867.
22. Samuel J. Crawford, *Kansas in the Sixties*, 263, 270–71.
23. *The Olathe* (Kansas) *Mirror*, November 7, 1867.
24. Indian Peace Commission, Report to the President, January 7, 1868, 489.
25. *Ibid.*

Creek in southwestern Kansas. By its terms, these southern Plains tribes were "localized" south of the Arkansas River, "a starting point for their gradual induction into a civilized condition." With this in mind, the commissioners included provisions for a program of education and training in agriculture and stock raising.[26] Samuel Tappan thought it "an honorable peace."[27]

With the Medicine Lodge treaty satisfactorily concluded, the commissioners journeyed to Fort Laramie with renewed confidence, eager to talk with Red Cloud, the "formidable chief of the Sioux," and halt the costly and fruitless Powder River War. The renowned Oglala leader again failed to appear, and the commissioners dispatched a message demanding that he cease hostilities pending a renewal of negotiations in the spring. Since his warriors needed to lay up a supply of buffalo meat for the winter months just ahead, Red Cloud agreed.[28]

Although many of the tribes had not exhibited any enthusiasm for the government's attempts to solve their difficulties—in fact, had been insulting and contemptuous at North Platte and Fort Laramie —the Peace Commission's efforts had not been completely wasted. If nothing else, the suspension of hostilities on the northern Plains, coupled with the successful negotiations with the tribes in the southern Plains, ended three years of savage warfare in those areas. In their report to President Johnson in January, 1868, the commissioners stated that "with anything like prudence and good conduct on the part of our own people in the future, we believe the Indian war east of the Rocky mountains is substantially closed."[29]

The year 1867 had seen the first cautious application of a peace policy to the frontier Indian problem. Even though born of desperation, this policy was the one advocated by the humanitarians, and it appeared to be working. It was a response not only to the warfare on the Plains but also to the growing awareness that, as Senator Lot M. Morrill (Republican, Maine) told his colleagues, "we have come to this point in the history of the country that there is no place beyond population to which you can remove the Indian. . . . and the precise question [now] is, will you exterminate him, or will you fix an abiding place for him?"[30] Few congressmen advocated deliberate ex-

26. Senator Edmund G. Ross, Report, *Kansas Daily Tribune* (Lawrence), in *Kansas State Record* (Topeka), November 6, 1867.
27. Tappan, "Autobiography."
28. Indian Peace Commission, Report to the President, January 7, 1868, 489.
29. *Ibid.*, 491.
30. *Congressional Globe*, 40th Cong., 1st sess., 1867, 672.

termination in 1867, but confining the tribes to reservations meant feeding them, for a time at least. In other words, it seemed to be a matter of either feeding them or fighting them, and most congressmen were convinced that feeding them was the less expensive solution. Senator Cornelius Cole (Republican, California) voiced a growing sentiment when he noted that an Indian war was not only expensive but, at best, inglorious for the nation. However, there was little sympathy for his conclusion that "peace is so desirable that it ought to be attained at almost any sacrifice."[31]

The report of the Peace Commission brought hope for those reformers who were already interested in the cause of Indian rights. Outside the halls of Congress, they were still too few to be clearly heard, but they were supporting the efforts of an increasing number of senators and representatives who were struggling to create a more humane policy.

31. *Ibid.*, 704.

3

The Humanitarians Turn
to Indian-Policy Reform

For many years, critics of Indian affairs had charged that Indian agents and traders were corrupt, but by 1868, they were claiming that thieving agents and traders were one of the primary causes of Indian wars and therefore a reason for drastic reform of the entire Indian Bureau. Frontier editors and politicians were just as likely to blame the agents as were their Eastern counterparts and the reformers. Kansas Governor Samuel Crawford held the agents responsible for the Plains Indian hostilities during 1867. "It was largely through their recommendations and misrepresentations," he recalled, "that the wicked policy then in vogue was adopted by the government and persisted in by the Interior Department." That department was furnishing the Indians with the arms and ammunition used against the frontier settlements while "back of the Interior Department was a gang of thieving Indian agents in the West, and a maudlin sentimentality in the East."[1]

The Daily Colorado Times noted that, although the government policy was to pay the tribes and grant them annuities for their lands, "these have not always been paid regularly or in the values agreed upon. . . . In many instances, the agents have cheated their savage and ignorant beneficiaries which has brought on ill-will and violence."[2] Not all the savage beneficiaries were ignorant, for a Seminole Indian told *The Louisville Journal* in 1867 that, although he had known one or two honest Indian agents, "the rest are all scoundrels, and invariably cheat the Indians out of seven-eights of their annuities."[3]

The report of the Peace Commission, published in January, 1868, seemed to indicate that these abuses had happened because few people were aware of the mistreatment of the Indians. The commissioners decried the fact that "nobody pays any attention to Indian matters" and criticized congressmen who "understand the Negro question, and talk learnedly of finance and other problems of political economy, but when the progress of settlement reaches

1. Samuel J. Crawford, *Kansas in the Sixties*, 263.
2. *The Daily Colorado Times* (Central City), June 21, 1867.
3. *The Louisville Journal*, in *The New York Times*, October 3, 1867.

the Indian's home the only question considered is 'how best to get his lands.' " Missionary societies and benevolent associations had "annually collected thousands of dollars from the charitable, to be sent to Asia and Africa for the purposes of civilization," while "scarcely a dollar is expended or a thought bestowed on the civilization of Indians at our very doors. Is it because the Indians are not worth the effort of civilization? Or is it because our people, who have grown rich in the occupation of their former lands—too often taken by force or procured by fraud—will not contribute?"[4]

Furthermore, the commissioners asserted, the civilization of the Indians and the protection of the Indians' rights to tribal land from encroachment by white people could abolish frontier warfare. "We have spent 200 years in creating the present state of things. If we can civilize [the Indians] in twenty-five years, it will be a vast improvement on the operations of the past." The commissioners were confident that teaching the Indian children the English language would remove differences and bring rapid civilization. This task should be the chief duty of the Indian Bureau, which should become a separate department of the government. The Army should handle only hostile or unmanageable tribes.[5]

The commissioners announced that they had inaugurated the "hitherto untried policy of endeavoring to conquer by kindness." They spurned the idea that a "handful of savages" should stop the advance of civilization; neither did they propose that those who were bringing civilization should, "with the ten commandments in one hand and the sword in the other," carry out a policy of extermination. They objected to the means by which civilization was advancing, not the end to be achieved—"the speedy settlement of all our territories. . . . We would only be understood as doubting the purity and genuineness of that civilization which reaches its ends by falsehood and violence, and dispenses blessings that spring from violated rights."[6]

Response to the Peace Commission's critical disclosure and its unabashed challenge to reformers came quickly. Shortly after the publication of the report, Lydia Maria Child penned an emotional attack on contemporary Indian policy. In *An Appeal for the Indians*, which first appeared on April 11, 1868, in *The National Anti-Slavery*

4. Indian Peace Commission, Report to the President, January 7, 1868, *Annual Report of the Commissioner of Indian Affairs*, 1868, *Annual Report of the Secretary of the Interior*, 40th Cong., 3d sess., 1868–1869, House Exec. Doc. No. 1 (Serial 1366), 502.
5. *Ibid.*, 503.
6. *Ibid.*, 492.

Standard and then in pamphlet form,[7] she praised the Peace Commission as "enlightened and liberal" and added, "at last we have an Official Document which manifests something like a right spirit toward the poor Indians!"

Even more liberal than the peace commissioners, Mrs. Child felt compelled to take issue with them in certain particulars. In the report's proposal that Indian children be instructed in English and "their barbarous dialects . . . blotted out," she saw "our haughty Anglo-Saxon ideas of force." Instead, she suggested in her pamphlet, "let their books, at first, be printed in Indian, with English translations, and let them contain selections from the best of their own traditionary stories." The commissioners stipulated that polygamy be punished, but Mrs. Child's *Appeal* proposed, "Let it be discountenanced, and reasoned against, and privileges conferred on those who live with one wife. . . . Indians, like other human beings, are more easily led by the Angel Attraction, than driven by the Demon Penalty." The Indians should be viewed "simply as younger members of the same great human family, who need to be protected, instructed and encouraged, till they are capable of appreciating and sharing all our advantages."

Mrs. Child, like other reformers of the time, was a believer in the doctrine of evolutionary progress. In the *Appeal*, she noted, "We Americans came upon the stage when the world had advanced so far in civilization that our record ought to be much cleaner than it is. . . . our relations with the red and black members of the human family have been one almost unvaried history of violence and fraud. . . . How can we blame the Indians for fighting, when we ourselves should have fought with half the provocation?" However, "the world has moved, and does now, though it is but slowly." Although in former ages the masses of people had been utterly ignored, "now the weakest cannot be outraged without finding powerful voices to proclaim their wrong." One of these powerful voices was that of John Beeson, whose earlier efforts to bring national attention to the urgency of the Indians' situation had strongly impressed her. The antislavery crusade and the war had intervened, but "the time has now come, when, without intermitting our vigilant watch over the rights of black men, it is our duty to arouse the nation to a sense of its guilt concerning the red men." She then called upon congressmen, ministers, missionaries, and Quakers to see that justice was done for that "much-abused race."

7. Lydia Maria Child, *An Appeal for the Indians*, 7, 8, 10, 13–15.

After the publication of Mrs. Child's *Appeal*, Peter Cooper became interested in the Indian problem. Cooper was a manufacturer, inventor, and founder of Cooper's Union for the education of the working class. He was nationally known and highly respected, and his beliefs that practical Christianity would eventually bring perfection to society and that all men should enjoy equal rights had prompted him at an early date to join the antislavery movement. In the spring of 1868, he initiated a movement for settling the problems raised by the angry Plains tribes, "who find themselves harassed by the inevitable progress of our people."[8] At his invitation, a number of clergymen and philanthropists held a public meeting at the Cooper Union on the evening of May 18 and resolved that an "association be formed for the protection and elevation of the Indians, and to cooperate with the United States government in its efforts to prevent desolation and wars on the frontiers of our country."[9]

The result of this meeting and Cooper's efforts was the formation of the United States Indian Commission, which, despite its name, was a completely private organization. The stated purpose of the commission was to protect and elevate the Indians and to cooperate with the United States government in its efforts to end frontier warfare.[10] Cooper, Henry Ward Beecher, and William Earl Dodge, a wealthy merchant from New York, were the most prominent members. Cooper became vice president of the organization, and his inspirational guidance and promotional work gave it the strength that contributed to its early influence on congressional legislation affecting Indian matters.

John Beeson enthusiastically supported the United States Indian Commission and became a friend and co-worker of Peter Cooper. In June, 1868, he addressed to Congress a memorial suggesting that five commissioners be appointed by the President to adjust all existing Indian difficulties and that these commissioners, as well as all persons officially employed in connection with Indian affairs, be nominated by the United States Indian Commission. The memorial also called for a separate department of Indian affairs and recommended that the Indians be given representation in Congress. Asking that a government policy of protection and perpetuation of the Indians be adopted, Beeson suggested that white counselors work with the chiefs "to develop their material resources and for general education and

8. *The New York Times*, May 22, 1868.
9. United States Indian Commission, Memorial, "The Indians," June 6, 1868, House of Representatives, Letters Received.
10. *Ibid.*

especially to promote honorable commercial relations."[11] Not to overlook any group that might be of help, he wrote an address to the women of America asking their sympathy and interest in behalf of the Indians.[12]

Cooper's Indian Commission promptly began a campaign to persuade the public that the Indians had been wronged. If the campaign were successful, Congress would be forced to apply "prompt and vigorous measures of redress and remedy" to the problems in the Indian policy.[13] On June 30, Henry Ward Beecher spoke at the Cooper Union on the corruption in the Indian Bureau. He described the Indian trader as a "Satanic fellow" whose method was to enervate the weak: "He has . . . a whiskey mill, and he uses it to grind the poor aboriginals off the face of the earth."[14] In a memorial sent to Congress on July 14, the commission declared that all Indian wars had been caused by white men's misdeeds. These misdeeds included making fraudulent treaties, ignoring treaty obligations, murdering the Indians, and illegally occupying Indian lands. The memorialists charged that only a small part of each congressional appropriation for the tribes ever reached them. They predicted that "when the true history of the Indian wrongs is laid before our countrymen, their united voice will demand that the honor and the interests of the nation shall no longer be sacrificed to the insatiable lust and avarice of unscrupulous men."[15]

The memorial was presented to Congress on July 20, 1868, just before the passage of the Indian appropriation act. The commission's charge that only a fraction of appropriated sums of money was reaching the tribes was instrumental in bringing the Senate to amend the act at the last moment. On Samuel Tappan's recommendation, the amended act directed that all appropriations for the Indians during the next two years be distributed by General Sherman, within whose jurisdiction a number of important Plains tribes lived.[16] Entrusting such a reputable man as Sherman with the distribution of the funds,

11. John Beeson, Memorial, June 16, 1868, Senate, Letters Received.
12. *The National Anti-Slavery Standard*, July 11, 1868.
13. United States Indian Commission, Memorial, July 14, 1868, *Annual Report of Commissioner of Indian Affairs*, 1869, *Annual Report of the Secretary of the Interior*, 41st Cong., 2d sess., 1869–1870, House Exec. Doc. No. 1 (Serial 1414), 538.
14. *The New York Times*, July 1, 1868. Because many agents were thought to be indirectly engaged in trade with the tribes to which they were assigned, the terms "agent" and "trader" had become generally synonymous.
15. United States Indian Commission, Memorial, July 14, 1868.
16. *The New York Times*, October 20, 1868.

the congressmen believed, would help to eliminate graft and thievery by the agents. Giving the task to a military man pointed to one of the most frequently proposed solutions to the Indian problem—transferring the Indian Bureau to the War Department.

In June, 1868, the humanitarians had been greatly encouraged by the official Peace Commission's successful settlement of Red Cloud's War. Red Cloud's demands for abandoning the Bozeman Trail and its military posts had been met, which the reformers thought was no more than just. However, they had little time for rejoicing. Two months later, the Cheyennes, discontented because the provisions of the Medicine Lodge treaty had not been fulfilled, began terrorizing settlers in the Solomon and Saline river valleys in western Kansas. Dispatches from Denver, Cheyenne, and Helena also reported murders, depredations, and horse stealing. General Sherman telegraphed the War Department, "This amounts to war. . . . I deem further forbearance with the Indians impossible."[17]

The widespread renewal of Indian warfare in the late summer and fall of 1868 involved tribes with which the Peace Commission had made treaties and brought a storm of abuse upon the congressional attempts to deal with the Indians by humane methods. In October, General Grant told the official Peace Commission, then meeting in Chicago, that the settlers must be protected, even if it meant the extermination of every Indian tribe. The commissioners, with the exception of Samuel Tappan and Commissioner of Indian Affairs Nathaniel G. Taylor, reversed their previous position of "endeavoring to conquer by kindness" and declared that the " 'burying of the hatchet' on our side, while it is full of activity on the part of the redskins" was not to be tolerated any longer. In a resolution, they recommended that military power be used to place all Indians on reservations.[18]

But the angry reaction on the part of the Peace Commission, General Grant, and other members of the Army to the renewal of Plains Indian warfare did not mean a reversal of the trend toward a program of peace and civilization. By the autumn of 1868, several factors had united to strengthen the movement to reform Indian policy. The interest in the problem had increased significantly. More humanitarians, individually and through organizations, were memorializing Congress, lecturing, and distributing propaganda. Also, the postwar reaction against war of any kind and even against the Army itself helped humanitarian efforts for a peaceful solution to

17. *Ibid.*, August 25, 1868.
18. *Ibid.*, October 16, 1868.

the Indian problem. This reaction prompted the Universal Peace Society's entry into the movement and stimulated more Quaker activity. Further, the prewar reform spirit was still alive, and the success of the antislavery crusade had given reformers increased confidence to tackle other social evils. The end of the "curse of slavery" meant the introduction of "a new order of things," Lydia Maria Child had predicted in 1865, and had made the United States "the pioneer of the nations in the path toward universal Justice, Freedom, and Humanity."[19]

Most reformers of this era unconditionally accepted the doctrine that all people were inherently entitled to equal rights and justice by virtue of a higher law that transcended that of man-made courts. This doctrine implied that everyone should be guaranteed citizenship and representation in the government. Any government, the reformers believed, was merely the protector of these immutable and universal principles, not a grantor that could withdraw or confer them at will. The advocates of Indian rights brought this doctrine and its implications down to earth by contending that since all Americans were entitled to equal rights before the laws of the United States, the Indians—the first Americans—could not be justly denied citizenship and representation in the Federal Government.

The Civil Rights Act and the Fourteenth Amendment applied to only those American Indians who were paying taxes. In excluding Indians who did not pay taxes, these pieces of legislation were merely repeating the decision embodied in Article I, Section 2, of the Constitution. Because only an insignificant minority of the Indians were taxed, most of them had no legal claims to citizenship. According to the reformers, this legal discrimination against the Indians was inexcusable. After a time, however, most reformers concluded that civilization should precede citizenship, and they then insisted that education and Christianization of the Indians should be the basis of government policy. Citizenship, with its rights, duties, and responsibilities, would come as a natural consequence.

Furthermore, most reformers became convinced that with the building of the transcontinental railroads and the rapid settlement of the frontier, the future of the tribes of the West rested in the hands of the Federal Government and with those who could influence its policies. Thus, the reformers directed their efforts toward Congress and the President as well as the public.

At a meeting of the United States Indian Commission on October 19, the members issued a public appeal asking for the formation

19. Lydia Maria Child, Personal Papers, Miscellaneous.

of mass meetings and auxiliary societies and for the help of the press in every town. The appeal stated, "There is no question so important before the nation as that of our Indian policy."[20] At Peter Cooper's request, Bishop Whipple, who was then widely known as the apostle to the Indians, read his report on the condition of the Western tribes. Although it was mostly a compilation of accumulated wrongs done to the Indians and the "blunders, frauds, and crimes" on the part of the government, it did include practical suggestions about what should be done to prevent disaster. Thoroughly convinced that the Indians were not at fault and that most of their troubles stemmed from mismanagement by the Indian Bureau, the Bishop advocated a complete reorganization of that body with a Cabinet member at its head. All agency employees should be married men of good moral character. Commissioners should be appointed to set up a positive program to civilize the Indians, and the congressional Peace Commission of July 20, 1867, should be expanded to include the best men in the country to carry out that objective. Immediate action was imperative because, Whipple warned, "The two waves of civilization between the Atlantic and Pacific will soon meet. The Indian question must now be settled on principles of justice which will bear the scrutiny of Almighty God."[21] Whipple's emotional account deeply moved the members of Cooper's Indian Commission and the large congregation at the Episcopal Board of Missions meeting, which Whipple addressed a short time later. "As I told the awful story, men and women wept," he later recalled.[22]

The official Peace Commission's reversion to a more severe policy had dismayed not only the humanitarians but also those senators and representatives who had supported the Peace Commission and the humane approach to the Indian problem. Warren Chase, editor of *The Banner of Light,* wrote in October, "We had hoped that a better policy would prevail with our government . . . but we see, by reports, that the same murderous and merciless policy is still adhered to."[23] Bishop Whipple pleaded with General Sherman to continue the commission's peaceful efforts, which "the Christian sentiment of this nation" would surely support, and he added, "You can under God save this poor people."[24] Sherman was becoming convinced, in view

20. *The New York Times,* October 20, 1868.
21. Henry Benjamin Whipple, *Lights and Shadows of a Long Episcopate,* 521.
22. *Ibid.,* 261.
23. *The National Anti-Slavery Standard,* October 24, 1868.
24. Robert G. Athearn, *William Tecumseh Sherman and the Settlement of the West,* 229.

of the increasing settlement of the West, that the forcible confinement of all the tribes to reservations was the only permanent solution
to the Indian problem. He believed that this plan, which the Peace
Commission had suggested in October, was the "only hope of saving
any part of these Indians from utter annihilation."[25]

During the ten years following the war, many humanitarians
participated in the movement for Indian rights in addition to such
other reform activities as protection of ex-slaves, temperance, wom-
en's rights, labor, and other current issues. One of these humanitarians was Wendell Phillips, president of the American Anti-Slavery
Society, an organization that was, at this time, championing the
rights of freedmen. He, like Mrs. Child, had been moved by the
January, 1868, report of the Indian Peace Commission, and he believed that the Indians were victims of a policy of extermination, however unofficial it might be. He also recognized the growing movement
for Indian rights as an integral part of the struggle for the rights of
all oppressed racial minorities. In his lectures and correspondence,
he repeatedly stated his belief that citizenship should be conferred
upon all Indians as a first step toward civilizing them. As citizens,
they should share in all duties pertaining to citizenship, be responsible to the civil law, and be protected by it. Phillips had great faith
in the ability and willingness of the Indians, as well as the freed
slaves, to assume these responsibilities. After they acquired this role
of equality with white Americans, the Indians would become civilized as a matter of course.

In 1868, Phillips' concepts were still strongly influenced by the
issues of the Civil War. His first postwar statement on Indian policy
indicated that he perceived the troubles with the Indians as the
diabolical plot of former Confederates. If the Federal Army were
forced to keep peace on the northwestern Plains, "the Ku-Klux,
Forrest [rumored to be the head of the Klan], Hampton and the rest
. . . [could] dip their hands in loyal blood with little chance of meeting their desserts."[26] Phillips also asserted that popular indifference,
the "selfish greed and bloodthirstiness" of white men on the frontier,
and political intrigue were obstructing reform, and he added, "We
shall never be able to be just to other races, or reap the full benefit
of their neighborhood till we 'unlearn contempt.' "[27] In January,
1868, at a celebration of the sixth anniversary of slave emancipation,
Phillips asked the people "to throw aside everything else and work
only for an amendment to the national Constitution. . . . In doing

25. *The New York Times*, November 21, 1868.
26. *The National Anti-Slavery Standard*, September 19, 1868.
27. *Ibid.*

this we must have such an amendment as would overlook the race and only see the man."[28] A year later, before the Massachusetts Anti-Slavery Society, he declared, "The great poison of the age is race hatred. All the great points of the epoch have arisen out of this hatred between races."[29] During his reform career, Phillips never compromised his conviction that all races of men should be equal in every respect before the law.

Not only individual humanitarians turned their attention to the problems of the Indians. Many reform organizations became involved in work for Indian rights in addition to their respective specialities. Most of these organizations, including the Radical Club of Boston, the Friends Social Union, the Union League Club, and the Equal Rights Association, did not devote much time to the Indians, but the Universal Peace Society did become fully involved.

The peace movement had been prominent on the American scene from 1828, when the American Peace Society was organized, until the 1850's, and it was one of the first of the prewar crusades to reactivate after 1865. Under the leadership of Charles Sumner, William Lloyd Garrison, and Elihu Burritt, the American Peace Society had opposed the Mexican War and had talked of a world congress of nations. But the antislavery movement and the Civil War had submerged the peace movement. Sumner and many other advocates of peace reasoned that peace with slavery was a greater evil than a war that would bring the eradication of slavery.

Alfred H. Love, like Charles Sumner, had been both an active antislavery and peace worker before the war, but unlike Sumner, he had refused to admit warfare as an acceptable means of abolishing slavery. In *An Appeal in Vindication of Peace Principles and Against Resistance by Force of Arms*, a pamphlet published in 1862, he had argued that all national problems, even that of slavery, could be solved by peaceful arbitration. After the war, Love had become the leader of the peace movement when he had founded the Universal Peace Society in the spring of 1866. Besides opposing militarism in all its forms, the society worked for reconciliation between the North and the South, acknowledgment of women's rights, abolition of capital punishment, and humanitarian treatment of the Indians.

The use of military force to keep the Indians subdued and to protect white men in their acquisition of tribal lands drew the Peace Society to the movement for Indian rights. In August, 1867, John Beeson wrote to Indian Commissioner Taylor that Love was thinking about making Indian rights a prime topic for the society and

28. *The New York Times,* January 2, 1869.
29. *The National Anti-Slavery Standard,* February 6, 1869.

advised Taylor that it would be "sound policy to accept and use its moral influence" to further the reform of Indian policy.[30]

In January, 1868, the Universal Peace Society held a two-day convention in Washington, D. C. Among those present were Beeson, who had made the long journey from Oregon to renew his reform work, and Lucretia Mott, vice president of the organization.[31] The society had just learned that the Alaskan Indians, who were being rapidly demoralized by soldiers and whisky, had no one outside the Army to protect their interests. This information prompted a lengthy discussion of the Indian problem and a petition to Congress "praying the appointment of Commissioners to go to Alaska to examine into the condition of the Indians."[32]

The following August, Love took the lead in bringing the Universal Peace Society and the European Union de la Paix under the name Universal Peace Union. Although the administrations of the two organizations remained distinct,[33] Love hoped that the affiliation would promote closer cooperation between the peace movement in the United States and the new, vigorous peace movement in Europe. At the second annual meeting of the Pennsylvania Peace Society, an ally of the Universal Peace Union, held in Philadelphia in November, 1868, Love presented the principles that would guide the Peace Union's work for reform of Indian policy. He proposed recognition of equal rights for all people, irrespective of color, sex, race, or condition. The Indian should be treated as "a child of the One Great Spirit" and should receive the rights of citizenship, "that he may give his consent as among the governed and have a fair representation." After demanding faithful observance of treaties, Love concluded with a fervent objection to the reservation system—a murderously "forcible colonization scheme."[34] His attack on the reservation system was his answer to the official Peace Commission's recent resolution that military power be used to force all Indians onto reservations.

The Peace Society sent to the United States Senate a long memorial embodying Love's views and several additional declarations. Although the memorial reminded the senators that it was "a mon-

30. John Beeson, letter to Nathaniel Taylor, August 20, 1867, Bureau of Indian Affairs, Letters Received.

31. *The National Anti-Slavery Standard*, February 29, 1868.

32. *The New York Times*, February 5, 1868; Vincent Colyer, *Bombardment of Wrangel, Alaska*, 6, 7.

33. *The National Anti-Slavery Standard*, September 5, 1868; Merle Curti, *Peace or War: The American Struggle, 1636–1936*, 80.

34. *The National Anti-Slavery Standard*, December 12, 1868.

strous usurpation of power in a government" to attempt to deprive the Indians of " 'life, liberty, and the pursuit of happiness,' " it said that the government itself was not guilty of intentionally making the Indians suffer. "Lawless white adventurors,—especially Government Contractors, Agents, and Speculators" were the guilty ones. Next, the memorial asked that the Constitution's "invidious" provision, "Indians not taxed," be removed in order to admit all Indians to the rights of citizenship. The tribes should be encouraged to appoint representatives to Washington to advise Congress about Indian affairs. Before anything could be accomplished, however, the Army and corrupt agents must be withdrawn and a delegation of "true friends" be allowed to "mingle among the Indians, and in a few months settle the existing troubles . . . without any material cost to the Government."[35] The memorial was signed by Love, Lucretia Mott, Gerrit Smith, Aaron M. Powell, and Cora Daniels.[36]

Besides signing the memorial, Cora Daniels, a member of the Pennsylvania Peace Society and vice president of the American Anti-Slavery Society, published an article in *The National Anti-Slavery Standard*. In it, she pleaded for humane treatment of the Indians and praised Whipple, Tappan, Phillips, and others for revealing the other side of a picture "which has all the time been presented with one face only, i.e., the terrible and barbarous depredations of the Indians—while the *criminal* and disgraceful course of the Indian agents and such 'Border Ruffians' as Chivington and Shoup, have been wholly concealed."[37]

A short time later, the Universal Peace Union met in association with the Longwood, Pennsylvania, Friends Meeting to discuss the reports of General Phil Sheridan's campaign against the Southern Cheyennes on the Washita River in Indian Territory—present Oklahoma—which were causing much concern about the "dark cloud of war . . . in the West." Sheridan had ordered the attack in reprisal for raids by the Southern Cheyennes in Kansas during the previous summer and fall. A few days before the meeting, Tappan had stopped in Philadelphia and called on Dr. Henry T. Child of the Peace Union. Bitterly condemning the Washita campaign, Tappan told Dr. Child that the Peace Union's members were right in their proposals for reform of the Indian policy and that they should promote them vigorously. The war, those who attended the meeting con-

35. Universal Peace Union, Memorial, November 19, 1868, Senate, Letters Received.
36. *The National Anti-Slavery Standard*, December 12, 1868.
37. *Ibid.*, November 28, 1868.

cluded, had no excuse save cupidity, and it was a violation of the Medicine Lodge treaty.[38]

After James M. Peebles, vice president of the Universal Peace Union, sent a firsthand report from Kansas about Sheridan's military preparations, the Peace Union's course of action was certain. Peebles had protested these preparations to Kansas Governor Samuel Crawford and to Army officers. The latter, he said, admitted the wisdom of his humanitarian position but said it was "Utopian and impracticable, and adapted to a hundred years hence." With his eyes "suffused with tears," Peebles asked, "Cannot there be something done to flank this Western war movement? It must start in the East. The extreme West is red for blood." If Congress withdrew the Army, insisted Love, and provided citizenship for the Indians, which would give them protection and security, the war would end.[39]

In 1868, one popular solution for the problem of dealing with the Indians was transferring Indian affairs to the War Department. As a Colorado editor analyzed it, treaties would be "far more likely to be kept with soldiers to deal with than with Indian agents . . . who all get rich in a year or two . . . by downright stealing."[40] Some Eastern newspapers and many congressmen from both East and West took a similar stand. Of those congressmen expressing a definite position on the transfer issue in 1867 and 1868, 15 favored the move—6 from west of the Mississippi—and 11 opposed it—5 of them Westerners. Most congressmen in 1868 favored some kind of change in the handling of Indian affairs, either reform or transfer.

When the efforts of the Peace Commission to bring an end to Indian wars apparently had failed, there were violent repercussions in Congress. The House blamed the difficulties on the Interior Department and in December, 1868, again proposed a bill authorizing the transfer of the Indian Bureau to the War Department. In the House debate on the transfer issue, Representative Sydney Clarke (Republican, Kansas) declared that the Indian question was not a question of either philanthropy or whether white people or the Indians were the aggressors, but it had become a question of practical administration.[41] The latter, he and most of his colleagues believed, could be more efficiently handled by the War Department.

In the Senate, the issue was viewed in a different light. Senator Thomas A. Hendricks (Democrat, Indiana) expressed the majority

38. "Report of the Executive Committee of the Universal Peace Union," *The Bond of Peace*, I, 12 (December, 1868), 3.
39. Alfred H. Love, "The Indians," *ibid.*
40. *The Daily Colorado Herald* (Central City), January 14, 1868.
41. *Congressional Globe*, 40th Cong., 3d sess., 1868–1869, Part 1, 18.

viewpoint when he pointed out that "it has cost this Government much more to fight the Indians than to feed them . . . and I think this is a question whether they shall be fed or shall be shot—fed or fought. I am in favor of that policy which I think is consistent with the sentiments of humanity and the high obligations of the American people toward the Indians."[42] Senator James A. Garfield (Republican, Ohio) said he approved of the War Department's controlling Indian matters because the cost of the entire Indian Bureau, including the agents' salaries, would be abolished. Military men, who were already on the government payroll, would be efficient agents "who are subject to a much stricter accountability than civilians can be. We shall thus remove one of the most tempting opportunities for corruption known to our Government."[43] When Senator William M. Stewart (Republican, Nevada) proposed that the Senate Committee on Indian Affairs, to which the measure had been referred, report in favor of transfer, protests from the other senators induced him to withdraw his motion.[44]

The Indian Affairs Committee's strong opposition to the War Department's control and the Senate's refusal to refer the bill to the Committee on Military Affairs, where it would have received favorable consideration, effectively killed all possibilities of transfer by special enactment. The proponents of the measure would attempt to add a transfer amendment to the Indian Appropriation Act of 1869 but would be unsuccessful, and hopes for success in 1869 were to be unexpectedly shattered a few months later by the inauguration of Grant's new Indian policy.[45]

The humanitarians agreed that reform was needed, but they could see little improvement in replacing a dishonest agent with a soldier—neither had the best interests of the Indians at heart. The solution, according to Mrs. Child, was to employ "none but honest, just and humane men" in the Indian Bureau.[46]

References to the existence of a shadowy but sinister "Indian Ring" were frequently expressed by critics of Indian policy in 1868. This "ring" was supposedly a clandestine group of unprincipled contractors, Indian agents, and politicians who made illegal profits from handling government transactions with the tribes. John Beeson, in a letter to *The National Anti-Slavery Standard*, had said that one

42. *Ibid.*, 41.
43. *Ibid.*, 17.
44. *Ibid.*, 41.
45. Loring Benson Priest, *Uncle Sam's Stepchildren: The Reformation of United States Indian Policy, 1865–1877*, 18–19.
46. Child, *An Appeal for the Indians*, 16.

purpose of Cooper's United States Indian Commission was "to bring
to light the secret crimes of unprincipled contractors and speculators."[47] For the next decade, the reformers would condemn this
activity in an effort to expose and destroy it.

On the other hand, the proponents of the War Department's
control of Indian affairs believed the "Indian Ring" to be so strongly
ensconced in the Senate that it was able to prevent passage of the
transfer bills. *The New York Times* saw in the House's passage of
a transfer bill in the late fall of 1868 the "doom of the Indian Ring"
but then recalled that the same bill had passed the House during the
preceding session and had been "strangled in the Senate, through
what influences we leave those of our readers who know the powerful
connections of the Indian Ring to imagine."[48]

More alarming to those who were working for Indian rights
was the attempt to associate Senate advocates of the peace policy with
the "ring." Some proponents of transfer adopted this approach and
further suggested that the Indian Bureau and agents had "alternately saddled on the country a futile war or an insecure peace, in
which we always paid tribute to the weaker power either in blood or
treasure." A portion of the treasure was siphoned into the pockets
of the members of the "ring."[49]

Many reformers favored the creation of a separate department
of Indian affairs. Such a proposal was suggested during debate on
the transfer bill, but it failed to gain any great support. Others felt
that a reformed version of the existing Indian Bureau was satisfactory if a positive humanitarian program was adopted and consistently followed. But there was no disagreement among the reformers
when the question of the War Department's control of Indian affairs
came up, as it did periodically. Military action was apparently necessary for subduing rebellious tribes, but by the end of 1868, the
humanitarians believed more strongly than ever that the War Department's treatment of the Indians would be characterized by
cruelty and brutality. Such incidents as the Sand Creek Massacre of
1864, General W. S. Hancock's destruction of a Cheyenne village on
the Pawnee Fork in Kansas in 1867, and General George A. Custer's
attack on Cheyenne Chief Black Kettle's camp—killing the chief and
more than one hundred warriors—during Sheridan's Washita campaign were, they insisted, unprovoked assaults on unoffending, helpless savages.

47. John Beeson, letter, July 27, 1868, *The National Anti-Slavery
Standard*, August 15, 1868.
48. *The New York Times*, December 12, 1868.
49. *Ibid.*, December 22, 1868.

Colonel Edward W. Wynkoop, who had recently resigned as agent of the Cheyennes and Arapahoes because he was opposed to troop operations against them, encouraged this view. Wynkoop had accompanied a party of adventurers to the Pikes Peak country in 1858. During the Civil War, he had joined the Colorado Volunteers and fought in the New Mexico campaign. He, as well as Samuel Tappan, had strongly opposed Chivington's attacks on the Indians. In 1866, President Johnson appointed Wynkoop Indian agent for the Upper Arkansas Agency. His resignation the following year received considerable publicity and aroused much interest among humanitarians.

In December, 1868, Wynkoop told a meeting of Cooper's Indian Commission that he had resigned because he believed he was being used to induce the Indians of his agency to gather in a locality where they were "liable to be fallen upon and at any moment and murdered" by Sheridan's troops. He blamed Congress and the Army for the Plains Indian wars. The military operations always brought hostile retaliation, and Congress had failed by not taking immediate action on the Medicine Lodge treaty. The congressional order to withhold arms and ammunition, which prevented the Indians from hunting buffalo, was especially harmful. His remedy for the Indian problem was "never fail to fulfill our contracts, and the cure will be complete." But a radical change of "incredible benefit" for the Indians' future would take place only if the sympathies of the people were "aroused for the Indian as they have been for the African."[50]

Wynkoop's fear of control by the War Department was shared by Commissioner of Indian Affairs Nathaniel G. Taylor. Taylor had been Chairman of the 1867 Peace Commission, and he completely agreed with the precepts of the humanitarian reformers. In his annual report for 1868, he pointed out that the civilization of the Indians, a task that "should enlist the sympathy of all lovers of humanity," must come first. The Indians were "worthy of the highest consideration of the philanthropist, and the government should invite the cooperation, in its great duty of protecting, educating and elevating the race . . . of all Christian societies or individuals who may be disposed to take part in the work."[51]

From January, 1868, when the Peace Commission's report was published, to November of that year, when Taylor's report appeared, most humanitarians had turned from an exclusive concern for the

50. Edward W. Wynkoop, *Address Before the Indian Peace Commission of Cooper Institute, New York, December 23, 1868*, 2–4, 5, 6.

51. *Annual Report of the Commissioner of Indian Affairs*, 1868, 461–62.

rights of the ex-slave to a broader concern that embraced the rights of mankind in general and those of the Indians in particular. The acceptance of the Peace Commission's challenge by the antislavery humanitarians and the founding of Peter Cooper's United States Indian Commission marked the real beginning of the postwar movement for Indian rights.

4

The Inauguration of the Peace Policy

By January, 1869, the publicity given the Indian problem had stimulated a new reform movement that closely resembled the prewar antislavery struggle in its determination to right the wrongs done to a racial minority. The new movement encountered the same problems that the abolition movement had faced—sectional antagonism, race prejudice, sometimes violent disagreement on methods to improve the situation, misunderstandings about reformers' intentions, and outbursts of opposition. Within a few months, the Philadelphia *Press* was observing, "To talk of the rights of the Indian today requires the same nerve and moral courage and conscientiousness it did twenty years ago to talk of the rights of the slave, and the man who asserts them is considered just as mad, foolish and visionary as were the Abolitionists of 1840 or 1850."[1]

Those people who participated in the new reform movement shared the same general assumptions upon which participants in other nineteenth-century reform movements had acted. They believed, first, in the doctrine of progress. According to historian George Bancroft, the Revolution had introduced the consensus that U.S. law codes and constitutions "should reflect ever more and more clearly the equality and brotherhood of man. . . . In a country which enjoyed freedom of conscience, of inquiry, of speech, of the press, and of government, the universal intuition of truth promised a never-ending career of reform and progress."[2] Wendell Phillips and Lydia Maria Child considered the nineteenth century a transitional age in which the nation was moving from the old era of equal rights for one race to a new era of full equality for all races. ("I am full of hope for the future of the world," wrote Mrs. Child in 1877.)[3] The editor of the Philadelphia *Press* apparently held the same belief, for he stated that "justice for the Indian will come just as surely as did the abolition of slavery, for both are founded on the eternal and immutable principles of right."[4]

1. *The National Anti-Slavery Standard,* May 1, 1869.
2. George Bancroft, *History of the United States of America,* V, 518.
3. Lydia Maria Child, letter to Sarah Shaw, December 19, 1877, Lydia Maria Child Papers, Houghton Library.
4. *The National Anti-Slavery Standard,* May 1, 1869.

The necessity of social progress was as basic a part of reform thought in the nineteenth century as it had been in the late eighteenth. In Bancroft's words, "The public conscience yearned for a nearer approach to ideal perfection."[5] This belief, combined with a "social gospel" form of Christianity and the deep-seated conviction that universal rights existed for all mankind, provided the same impetus for reforming the Indian policy that it had for abolishing slavery. The missionary spirit of a Christianity of equality and brotherhood was a powerful motivating force that did much to inspire both laymen and clergy to play an important role in the work for Indian rights. This concept of the equality and brotherhood of mankind, irrespective of race, consistently dominated humanitarian thought and action and made the reformers especially sensitive to any acts by government officials or military authorities that reflected race prejudice. The reformers' reliance on the principles of the Declaration of Independence and the New Testament led to their unequivocal demands for equality, justice, and the Indians' right to "life, liberty, and the pursuit of happiness." Wendell Phillips spoke for many reformers when he declared that the "great poison of the age is race hatred. . . . We must see the man, not the negro, the man and not the Indian, the man and not the Chinaman."[6] He championed a "working reform Christianity" that would bring about "the regeneration of the world," which he believed was then taking place.[7]

Other factors motivated the humanitarian spirit in postwar America. The desire for peace, order, and harmony, together with pacifism based on Christian tenets, generated rampant antimilitarism and soon brought the influential Universal Peace Union into the movement for Indian rights. Also, an uneasy feeling of guilt, both for themselves as individuals and for the nation as a whole, moved many people into reform work. Lydia Maria Child frequently spoke of the collective guilt of the people in their dealings with those weaker than themselves, and others pointed out that the continuation of the wrongs to the Indian race could not fail to bring upon the nation the severest form of retribution. John Beeson was convinced that injustice to the Indians was the source of the country's woes. This activity of conscience and the realization that an inexcusable wrong was waiting to be righted added urgency to the reformers'

5. *Ibid.*
6. *Ibid.*, February 6, 1869.
7. Wendell Phillips, *Christianity a Battle, Not a Dream*, 14–15. The view that the desire for reform of the Indian policy was largely a matter of Christian conscience is thoroughly analyzed in Henry E. Fritz, *The Movement for Indian Assimilation, 1860–1890.*

sense of moral responsibility, duty, and stewardship to the Indians. As a Quaker agent on the Omaha Indian reservation in Nebraska reported in 1870, he felt an obligation "which often raises up my heart, and fires me with devotion and renewed energy to spend and be spent in their cause."[8]

The specific reforms proposed by the people who worked to improve the Indians' situation were primarily means to justice, equality, civilization, and citizenship. If justice was to be served, treaties must be honored, fraud and corruption must be eliminated, and the protection of the law must be extended to all Indian tribes. To bring about equality, racial prejudice must give way to the concept of the brotherhood of man, and the Indians must be accorded the same treatment white people demanded for themselves. Discrimination in the courts and before the law must be abolished.

The election of U. S. Grant was viewed with apprehension by those reformers who could see only a cigar-smoking, whisky-drinking, military officer with no visible humanitarian instincts. There was little doubt that Wendell Phillips saw Grant in this mold. In January, 1869, when calling for an amendment to the Constitution to give equality to all races, he predicted opposition from the President-elect. The year before, he had charged Grant with drunkenness and had demanded an investigation.[9]

Most reformers, however, did not share Phillips' doubts. William Lloyd Garrison wrote to John Greenleaf Whittier in 1869 that he had "no distrust of Grant whatever" and was amazed at Phillips' "suspicion and censure."[10] Henry Ward Beecher predicted that Grant would be known "even more favorably for the wisdom of his civil administration" than for his military success.[11] Samuel Tappan was favorably disposed toward the new President because in 1864 Grant had told Governor Evans of Colorado that the Sand Creek affair was not a battle but a murder of Indians who were supposed to be under the protection of the Federal Government.[12]

Grant himself indicated that he had thought a great deal about the Indian question. According to *The Boston Daily Advertiser*,

8. Edward Painter, "Friends Among the Indians," *The Standard*, I, 1 (May, 1870), 17.

9. *The New York Times*, January 2, 1869; *The Daily Colorado Herald* (Central City), February 2, 1868.

10. William Lloyd Garrison, letter to John Greenleaf Whittier, January 26, 1869, "Antislavery Letters Written by William Lloyd Garrison, 1866–1870," Vol. 7, No. 95.

11. *The New York Times*, July 11, 1868, in Paxton Hibben, *Henry Ward Beecher: An American Portrait*, 221.

12. Samuel F. Tappan, "Autobiography," Samuel F. Tappan Papers.

Grant had stated, "Our present system is full of fraud. . . . It ought
to be reformed" and "Our dealings with the Indians properly lay us
open to charges of cruelty and swindling."[13] A week before his inauguration, Grant revealed that he planned to adopt a new Indian
policy. "All Indians disposed to peace will find the new policy a
peace-policy," he said. "Those who do not accept this policy will
find the new administration ready for a sharp and severe war policy."
His statement that he had "great faith in the humane Quaker plan"
was especially significant. The Washington reporter for the *Daily
Advertiser* concluded that "a pretty radical change is indicated."[14]

The correspondent's prediction proved to be correct, for Grant
did initiate a new and different Indian policy early in his Administration. It embodied many of the principles of the Quaker reformers,
and several Quakers worked closely with members of the new Administration to construct the policy. Although its official label was
the Peace Policy, it became popularly known as the Quaker Policy.

The Society of Friends had been active in Indian welfare work
since the seventeenth century, and in 1866 nearly all of the Quaker
yearly meetings in the United States had standing committees engaged in benevolent work among several tribes. The Quakers long
had been convinced that the Indian was open to persuasion "when
enforced by a constant Christian example; but resents coercion, harsh
and unjust treatment and upbraiding language." The lack of proper
appreciation of those facts, they had asserted, explained most, if not
all, the troubles that the government was having in dealing with the
Indians.[15]

The Society of Friends had endorsed a Senate bill introduced
by Doolittle in March, 1866, that provided for an annual inspection
of Indian affairs by boards selected from candidates suggested by the
various religious denominations. The boards would have the power
to supervise and inspect the whole administration of the government's
Indian operations—civil, military, and educational. William Welsh,
a prominent Philadelphia Episcopalian and collaborator with the
Quakers in Indian-policy reform, lobbied in Washington on behalf
of the measure. The bill passed the Senate on March 19, 1866, by a
vote of 19 to 16 and came before the House early in 1867.[16] This bill

13. *The Boston Daily Advertiser*, January 2, 1869.
14. *Ibid.*, February 25, 1869.
15. Philadelphia Yearly Meeting, *A Brief Sketch of the Efforts of The
Philadelphia Yearly Meeting of the Religious Society of Friends, to Promote
the Civilization and Improvement of the Indians; Also, of the Present Condition of the Tribes in the State of New York*, 2, 15.
16. *Congressional Globe*, 39th Cong., 1st sess., 1865–1866, Part 2,
485–86.

was one of the first attempts to reform Indian policy, and the few humanitarians concerned with these issues at that time were anxious for its passage. Both Samuel Tappan and Bishop Whipple wrote to the Chairman of the House Committee on Indian Affairs, William Windom, recommending passage, and a delegation from the Society of Friends met with Windom in Washington. But congressmen had not yet been sufficiently aroused to take any step beyond authorizing investigating committees. In the 1866–1867 session of the House, a transfer bill was substituted for the inspection-boards bill. Windom called it "a bill to massacre the Indians and deplete the treasury."[17] To the relief of the reformers, the transfer measure failed to pass the Senate.

The Quakers had stepped up their activities during the summer of 1867. The Friends of both Indiana and Pennsylvania had dispatched memorials to Congress pleading for a reformed Indian policy,[18] and their efforts had moved *The Washington Weekly Chronicle* to state:

> The treaties made by William Penn were always respected by both parties, and the peaceful sect of which he was a distinguished member have been traditional friends of the aborigines, and always kindly regarded by them. We have often thought that if the Society of Friends, who so successfully colonized and civilized the Senecas in western New York, and with such judgment and benevolence managed their affairs with the Government, could be induced to take charge of the subject of colonizing the Indian territory, and instructing the Indians, they might prepare them for the inevitable future.[19]

In the fall of 1867, a large delegation of Friends had gathered in Baltimore, Maryland, to discuss the Indian problem and to hear a report by Bishop Whipple on the Indians' plight and the need for immediate action. At this conference, they had heard that several "prominent statesmen connected with the government" had expressed the desire that the Society of Friends take over the care and civilization of the Indians. Acting on this information, the delegates had notified Congress that they were willing "to enter unselfishly and without compensation" into any service beneficial to the Indians.[20]

17. *Ibid.*, 2d sess., 1866–1867, Part 2, 879, 896; Fritz, *Indian Assimilation*, 48, 49.
18. *The National Anti-Slavery Standard*, June 29, 1867.
19. Rayner Wickersham Kelsey, *Friends and the Indians, 1655–1917*, 164–65.
20. *Ibid.*, 165–66.

Meanwhile, the Quakers of the Iowa, Indiana, Western, and Ohio yearly meetings had formed a joint committee on Indian concerns, which promptly memorialized Congress. The memorial urged "that in the appointment of officers and agents, to have charge of their [the Indians'] interests, care should be taken to select men of unquestioned integrity and purity of character."[21] In June, 1868, a delegation of Pennsylvania Friends, together with William Lloyd Garrison and Alfred H. Love, had drawn up a memorial to Congress on behalf of the Indians and a circular letter to be forwarded to the various Indian tribes.[22]

This activity was only a prelude to Quaker participation in reforming Indian policy. Prompted by a study of the congressional Joint Special Committee's 1867 report on the condition of the Indian tribes and the findings of the July 20, 1867, Peace Commission, delegates from seven yearly meetings, representing fifteen states, convened in Baltimore in January, 1869. Here, they drew up a memorial to Congress opposing control of Indian affairs by the War Department and calling for a policy that would promote education, industry, and morality. They also expressed their support for a House bill that proposed a department of Indian affairs and provided for the consolidation, civilization, and government of the tribes. The author of the bill, Representative Thomas D. Eliot (Republican, Massachusetts), presented it and the Friends memorial to the House on January 25. In his presentation of the memorial, Eliot stated, "This document presents in a clear and brief manner the condition of Indian affairs in this country."[23]

On the day that Eliot's bill and the memorial came before the House, the Quaker delegation met with President-elect Grant and introduced plans for an Indian policy based on peace and Christianity. The next day, a committee of Friends from Philadelphia also memorialized Congress and interviewed the President-elect. Both committees were impressed with Grant's "cordial, sympathetic attitude toward them, and his apparently earnest desire to inaugurate a more peaceful and humane" policy in dealing with the Indians.[24]

Grant's interest in the welfare of the Indians began when he was a young officer stationed at Fort Vancouver, Washington Territory. There, he had observed the operations of the government's

21. *Ibid.*, 166.
22. *The National Anti-Slavery Standard*, June 13, 1868.
23. *Congressional Globe*, 40th Cong., 3d sess., 1868–1869, Part 1, 581–82.
24. Kelsey, *Friends and the Indians*, 167.

Indian system, and like John Beeson, he had been shocked at the unjust and vicious treatment of tribes in the Northwest. "This poor remnant of a once powerful tribe," he wrote a fellow officer in 1852, "is fast wasting away before those blessings of 'civilization,' whisky and small pox." In a letter to his wife, he observed that "the whole Indian race would be harmless and peaceable if they were not put upon by the whites."[25] In March, 1869, Grant told George W. Childs, publisher of the Philadelphia *Public Ledger*, that during his experience in the Northwest, he had decided to use any influence or power he might acquire to improve the condition of the Indians.[26]

Grant apparently was favorably impressed by the Quakers, for less than three weeks after the interviews with the two committees, Ely S. Parker, aide to General Grant and a member of the Seneca tribe, wrote to the various Friends committees on Indian concerns asking for their participation in the new Administration's Indian program. Stating that General Grant was "desirous of inaugurating some policy to protect the Indians in their just rights and enforce integrity in the administration of their affairs, as well as to improve their general condition," Parker requested that the Friends send him a list of their members who would be suitable to serve as Indian agents. He added that, as President, Grant would give these agents and their Society all possible encouragement and protection in their efforts to improve, educate, and Christianize the Indians.[27]

Both Grant and the Quakers agreed that besides emphasizing education and Christianization, the new Peace Policy should be based upon fair and upright dealings. Above all, the government should faithfully observe treaties. The Quakers strongly opposed the transfer of Indian affairs to the War Department, but they did agree with the new Administration that the Army would be a necessary adjunct to the operation of the program, at least in its first stages.

Grant had decided that the Peace Policy would be carried out as a combined civil-military operation in which Army officers would fill all the positions in the Indian service except two superintendencies and seven agencies. These would go to the Quakers.[28] Otherwise, the Army was to become, in effect, a police force with the responsibility of curbing lawlessness and keeping the whites out of

25. Lloyd Lewis, *Captain Sam Grant*, 313–14.
26. George Hay Stuart, *The Life of George Hay Stuart*, 239; Charles Lewis Slattery, *Felix Reville Brunot, 1820–1898*, 141.
27. Kelsey, *Friends and the Indians*, 168; Samuel M. Janney, *Memoirs of Samuel M. Janney*, 251.
28. *The New York Times*, May 17, 1869.

Indian territory and the Indians within it. Keeping contact between the races to a minimum, it was hoped, would bring an end to the costly Indian wars.

Neither Grant nor the Quakers thought that civilization of the Indians could be accomplished quickly. "The transition from a barbarous to a civilized state is necessarily slow," a Friends committee on Indian concerns had stated three years earlier.[29] Shortly after the inauguration of the new policy, The Friends' Intelligencer stated, "We are not sanguine of results. . . . we must not be disappointed should difficulties and discouragement assail us."[30]

The Peace Commission of July 20, 1867, had recommended a nonvoluntary reservation system, and Grant concurred. The Quakers, too, agreed because they believed that restricting the tribes to a limited and permanent area was a necessary prerequisite to successfully civilizing them. On a reservation free from white intrusion, schools and churches could be established, lands could be allotted in severalty, and agriculture could be taught and practiced. Once the Indians had become adjusted to a settled, civilized life and to self-support in the manner of their white neighbors, then they could receive full rights of citizenship.

In his inaugural address, President Grant's statement on Indian policy was brief. "The proper treatment of . . . the Indians—is one deserving of careful study. I will favor any course toward them which tends to their civilization and ultimate citizenship."[31] As George Hay Stuart recalled later, "Nothing in General Grant's inaugural excited more attention or awakened more discussion than his strong expression of his desire and purpose to see full justice done to the Indian tribes."[32]

The first reaction of the reformers varied from cautious approval to enthusiastic praise. "With full heart and most earnestly, we thank him," wrote Wendell Phillips for The National Anti-Slavery Standard.[33] At a meeting of the Pennsylvania Peace Society in Philadelphia, Alfred H. Love exclaimed, "How grand it is. . . . President

29. Philadelphia Yearly Meeting, A Brief Sketch, 54.
30. The Friends' Intelligencer, April 22, 1869, in The National Anti-Slavery Standard, May 8, 1869.
31. James D. Richardson, ed., A Compilation of the Messages and Papers of the Presidents, 1789–1902, 1908 ed., VII, 8.
32. Stuart, Life, 239. A Scotch-Irish Presbyterian immigrant, Stuart had served in the U.S. Christian Commission during the Civil War. In 1868, he had endorsed Grant for the Presidency in a speech at Concert Hall, Philadelphia, and strongly supported him and his Indian policy after his election.
33. The New York Times, March 11, 1869.

Grant says amen to our wishes [for Indian rights]. . . . Let this work be stamped upon the nineteenth century."[34] The editor of *The National Anti-Slavery Standard*, Aaron M. Powell, lauded the "new just and humane Indian policy" and praised the Society of Friends for giving the nation a "timely precedent and example" with their humane experiment.[35]

The Eastern newspapers that had backed Grant for the Presidency were unstinting in their praise of the new approach. *The Boston Daily Advertiser* predicted that the Friends "will deserve the lasting gratitude of the country," while *The Boston Evening Transcript* stated that there was uprightness, common sense, and common honesty in the new policy.[36] The Philadelphia *Press* praised the Forty-first Congress for committing the Indian question to the discretion of President Grant and asserted that it was the one act that might "render it historic."[37] *The New York Times* announced, "We have never before had such a favorable state of things for maintenance of pacific relations with the Indians."[38]

On the other hand, most anti-Grant and Democratic journals, like *The New York Herald, The New York World*, and *The Boston Daily Globe*, either took no notice of the Peace Policy or were skeptical. As time went on, these papers became more openly hostile. Regardless of their political affiliation, most Western editors, particularly those of the Plains and Rocky Mountain regions, were sharply critical.

By the spring of 1869, the humanitarians generally agreed on the basic objectives that they wanted to see incorporated in the Peace Policy. The most important objectives were the reservation system, education, Christianization, the assimilation of the Indians into the social and economic system of the nation, and, finally, citizenship. These goals had to be accomplished without bloodshed. Nearly all of the reformers supported Indian citizenship and a reservation system in 1869. Writing in *The Bond of Peace*, Alfred Love recommended reservations where the Indians could take up agriculture and become attached to their homes. However, the Universal Peace Union did object to the removal of the tribes to reservations without the Indians' consent and without proper remuneration for the property they relinquished. The Peace Union also insisted that the Constitution should be amended to grant the Indians citizenship "and

34. *The Bond of Peace*, II, 4, 5 (April, May, 1869), 34.
35. *The National Anti-Slavery Standard*, April 10, 1869.
36. *The Boston Evening Transcript*, March 20, 1869.
37. *The National Anti-Slavery Standard*, May 1, 1869.
38. *The New York Times*, May 25, 1869.

thus encourage the appointment from their own midst of representatives to remain at the Capitol of the nation, and offer such advice and suggestions as may from time to time be demanded."[39] Love's recommendations were included in a memorial and forwarded to the Senate on November 19, 1868. Among the signers were Lucretia Mott and Gerrit Smith, both of whom had been abolitionists.

In full support of the Peace Union's position, Aaron M. Powell called for "permanent homesteads" with recognition and protection of the Indians as citizens.[40] Peter Cooper's United States Indian Commission proposed that the Indians be made "citizens of the republic" and settled on "suitable reservations" on each side of the Rocky Mountains.[41]

In March, 1869, the Universal Peace Union, the Pennsylvania Peace Society, and the Progressive Friends collaborated on a circular letter "to the Indians of America." The letter openly encouraged the Indians to prepare themselves for representation and participation in the Federal Government, "that you may enter the councils of the nation and set forth your grievances, your suffering, and your needs." It concluded with a plea for peace, for "in a kind and fraternal intercourse there will be found the true way to redress wrongs, vindicate rights, and establish the blessings of amity and peace."[42] The letter went to 150 Indian agencies with the hope that it would "meet with a warm response from the noble hearts of the children of 'The Great Spirit.'" The effect of such appeals is difficult to measure, but the writers of this letter were not entirely disappointed; eventually, they received appreciative replies from agencies in Wisconsin, Nebraska, Oregon, and California.[43] Also, within a year the first of many Indian delegations came to Washington, with government encouragement, to present their grievances.

Wendell Phillips enthusiastically responded to Grant's inaugural address. After saying that he was pleased that Grant's policy "looks to the 'citizenship' of the Indian," Phillips added, "Let him cover the Indian with this shield and give him . . . a Department in the Cabinet which shall watch his rights."[44] Phillips, Love, and

39. Universal Peace Union, Memorial, November 19, 1868, Senate, Letters Received.

40. Mrs. John T. Sargent, ed., *Sketches and Reminiscences of The Radical Club of Chestnut Street, Boston,* 175.

41. *The New York Times,* May 22, 1868.

42. *Ibid.,* July 10, 1869.

43. *The Bond of Peace,* II, 4, 5 (April, May, 1869), 34; *The National Anti-Slavery Standard,* July 17, 1869.

44. *The New York Times,* March 11, 1869.

the Peace Union proposed an amendment to the Constitution giving citizenship to the Indians. But, whereas the Peace Union suggested that Article I, Section 2, of the Constitution be revised to include all Indians, Phillips demanded equal rights before the law for all human beings.

A much more radical citizenship proposal had been presented by John Beeson in a letter to President Lincoln in 1862, wherein the Indians were to be citizens of a guaranteed "Domain and Sovereign Nationality" free and distinct from the rest of the nation.[45] Beeson gave a more detailed plan in a memorial to Congress and the President in 1864 when he suggested the formation of four Indian states to be governed by laws made and administered by their own authority and to be subject to the United States only as "dependent friendly allies." Residents of these states were to be represented in Congress by delegates of their own choice, "the same as the Territories, until such time as they are prepaired [sic] and disposed to become citizens."[46] By the mid-1870's, however, Beeson had replaced his dependent-states plan with the more realistic one of citizenship for the Indians.

Advocates of Indian rights did not debate the importance of educating the Indians. They were convinced that education, which included instruction in English, was a necessary prerequisite to civilization. If the Indians learned to speak English, they and the white people could achieve mutual understanding and cooperation more easily, and the acculturation of the Indians would proceed more smoothly. Education and Christianization, according to the humanitarians, would broaden the Indians' viewpoints and ambitions, help to destroy the old tribal organizations, and wipe out pagan practices. The educational program the humanitarians envisioned included vocational instruction in mechanics and agriculture in addition to the usual subjects. They hoped that this approach would make the Indians economically self-sufficient and would further weaken the communal tribal system.

Many reformers, particularly the Quakers, were not convinced that only the Secretary of the Interior or the Commissioner of Indian Affairs should administer the new program for civilizing the Indians. They favored the appointment of a board of commissioners—an idea that Bishop Whipple and the Episcopalians, among them William

45. John Beeson, letter to President Lincoln, November 18, 1862, Secretary of the Interior, Letters Received.

46. John Beeson, Memorial to Congress and the President, April 12, 1864, Senate, Letters Received.

Welsh, had suggested to President Lincoln in 1862.[47] and that John
Beeson and others had suggested to the Senate in June, 1868.[48] In
March, 1869, two separate delegations of church and civic leaders
called on President Grant, Secretary of the Interior J. D. Cox, and
members of the 1867 Peace Commission, including General Sherman,
with proposals for such a board. The first delegation was a committee of Philadelphia Friends and William Welsh, its chairman.
This delegation proposed that the President appoint a five-man
commission and empower it to act jointly with the Secretary of the
Interior in implementing the provisions of the treaties made by the
Peace Commission. According to Welsh, the proposal received the
"hearty approval" of government officials.[49]

The second delegation, led by George H. Stuart of Philadelphia
and Edward S. Tobey of Boston, met first with Grant and then with
Cox, who commended them to the Senate Committee on Indian Affairs. They received a full hearing in which they suggested that a
group of commissioners should control Indian matters and that
the Congress should give the commissioners complete control of
$3,000,000 to be used for civilizing and Christianizing the Indians.
The members of the Senate committee favored creating a commission, but they were reluctant to give it control of such a large sum
of money.[50]

The threat of continuing Indian hostilities in the West, however, made it imperative that the provisions of the many Peace
Commission treaties be carried out at once and convinced a majority
of congressmen that delegating the task to a board of honest philanthropists might be wise as well as expedient. With this in mind,
Congress enacted the Indian Appropriation Act of April 10, 1869.
The act authorized the President "to organize a board of Commissioners, to consist of not more than ten persons . . . eminent for
their intelligence and philanthropy" who were to serve without pay.
The commissioners were authorized to aid in the purchase and in-

47. Henry Benjamin Whipple, *Lights and Shadows of a Long Episcopate*, 140–41.
48. *The New York Times*, June 20, 1868.
49. William Welsh, letter to editor, *The Press* (Philadelphia), in *The
New York Times*, April 3, 1869; William Welsh, letter to Secretary of the
Interior Cox, March 26, 1869, Secretary of the Interior, Letters Received.
50. *The Boston Daily Advertiser*, March 26, 1869; *The National Anti-
Slavery Standard*, April 10, 1869. In the George Hay Stuart Papers is a
notation by Stuart, dated April 13, 1869, that he had been invited to Washington by Secretary Cox and that he had "helped to form the Indian Board
of Commissioners *nearly all* of whom were named by me." George Hay
Stuart Papers, Manuscript Division, Library of Congress.

spection of goods and to exercise joint control with the Secretary of the Interior over the disbursement of the appropriations made by the act, including a $2,000,000 civilization fund.[51] By mid-April, nine men who were noted for their religious, civic, and philanthropic leadership had agreed to serve on the new Board of Indian Commissioners. They were William Welsh, George H. Stuart, William E. Dodge, Nathan Bishop, Edward S. Tobey, Felix R. Brunot, John V. Farwell, Henry S. Lane, and Robert Campbell.

William Earl Dodge, one of the founders of Phelps, Dodge and Company, had become involved in the peace and temperance movements long before the Civil War, and he had actively opposed slavery. His conviction that war was an intolerable evil led to his becoming a Peace Congress commissioner in February, 1861. Lincoln had consulted him frequently during the war years. Dodge held only one elective office; he was a member of Congress for one year during 1866–1867. He was a loyal Republican moderate who backed Grant in 1868 and who would again in 1872.[52] The appointment to the Board of Indian Commissioners, Dodge believed, was an opportunity not only to reform the corrupt administration of Indian affairs, but also to inaugurate practical measures for civilization, education, and Christianization and thus to "rescue the poor Indians from the ruin which is now impending."[53] Combining the Peace Policy's tenets of humanitarian idealism, practicality, and a cautious optimism, Dodge exemplified the majority of the board members.

Some of the humanitarians who helped to administer the Peace Policy were not prominent businessmen, civic leaders, or well-known philanthropists. Such a one was Samuel M. Janney, a Quaker poet and historian who had become active in work for Indian rights when he joined a Friends committee on Indian concerns in 1864. In March, 1869, at the request of Ely S. Parker, who was then Commissioner of Indian Affairs, the Baltimore Yearly Meeting recommended Janney for the position of superintendent in the Indian service. When Parker offered the post, Janney accepted it with the hope that it would be an opportunity "for us to take some steps in the great work of civilizing the Western Indians."[54] Janney took charge of the Northern Superintendency when he arrived in Omaha on May 26. The Northern Superintendency was made up of agencies in Nebraska—the Great

51. Laurence F. Schmeckebier, *The Office of Indian Affairs: Its History, Activities, and Organization,* 55–57.
52. D. Stuart Dodge, *Memorials of William E. Dodge,* 73, 77, 82, 99.
53. William E. Dodge, letter to Felix R. Brunot, June 25, 1869, Bureau of Indian Affairs, Letters Received.
54. Samuel M. Janney, *Memoirs,* 251, 253.

Nemaha, Omaha, Winnebago, Pawnee, Otoe, and Santee Sioux. Janney and the six Quaker agents who were to serve under him were responsible for a total of 6,598 Indians.[55]

The arrival of this contingent of Quakers and those who worked under Enoch Hoag, Superintendent of the Central Superintendency, marked the beginning of the Grant Administration's Peace Policy. The Central Superintendency consisted of the Pottawatomie, Kaw, and Kickapoo agencies in Kansas and the Quapaw, Osage, Shawnee, Wichita, Kiowa, Upper Arkansas, and Sac and Fox agencies in the Indian Territory. Its agents were responsible for 17,724 Indians.[56] These agencies and those of the Northern Superintendency were only a small percentage of the existing agencies, the rest of which remained under the Army's jurisdiction for another year.[57] The Quakers had proposed starting on a modest scale and, if they were successful in those areas, assuming responsibility for other areas later.

The inauguration of the new Indian policy stimulated other actions by the reformers. In April, Peter Cooper's United States Indian Commission sent Vincent Colyer, secretary of the commission, to the Arizona Territory for his personal observations of the condition of the Navajo and Apache tribes. Two months later, the executive committee of the commission met at Cooper Union to hear Samuel F. Tappan demand the extension of civil law over the Indian country as proposed by the 1867 Peace Commission. The dangerous "ban of outlawry" under which the Indians existed, he declared, was the cause of all the past difficulties. Acting upon this assumption, the committee issued "An Address to the American People," which asked all citizens to help them create public sentiment so strong that it would "compel Congress to accept and act upon the humane report of its own Commission" and thereby completely settle the question "on the basis of law, equality, humanity and justice."[58]

In May, the annual convention of the Universal Peace Union in New York City expressed "much gratification" for Grant's management of Indian affairs, "though he had not gone to the full extent desired by the Society."[59] Alfred Love was particularly perturbed about President Grant's failure to appoint Indian commissioners who were "radical peace men." Love would have preferred commis-

55. Commissioner of Indian Affairs, *Annual Report of the Commissioner of Indian Affairs, 1872, Annual Report of the Secretary of the Interior*, 42d Cong., 3d sess., 1872–1873, House Exec. Doc. No. 1 (Serial 1560), 461.

56. *Ibid.*

57. *The Boston Daily Advertiser*, April 7, 1869.

58. *The National Anti-Slavery Standard*, June 26, 1869.

59. *Ibid.*, July 17, 1869.

sioners who were uncompromising opponents of the Army's participation in Indian affairs. Nonetheless, he was still convinced that a "thorough and patient trial" of the plan would be "eminently successful," and he offered a resolution in its support.[60]

Also at the May convention, Cora Daniels Tappan, who had become the wife of Samuel Tappan, charged that a crime of equal magnitude to that of slavery was about to be committed against the Indians. This crime would occur if the Army's "atrocious and infamous proposal to exterminate them"[61] were carried out. She submitted a substitute resolution stating that assigning military men as agents to the Indian tribes who were at peace and assigning Quakers and other friends of peace to those tribes who were justifiably warlike was not a fair trial for the Peace Policy. Because the peaceful Indians would remain at peace, the Army would appear to be successful. However, the agents had no power to carry out peaceful measures, and if the Indians for whom they were responsible did begin hostilities, the Peace Policy would appear to have failed. The failure would be a pretext for transferring Indian affairs to the War Department. Her resolution then called on the Peace Union to protest the use of the Army and to urge Congress to make a "full transfer of Indian affairs to the jurisdiction of a civil department, making them citizens, not outlaws."[62]

The fact that Army officers held all the positions in the Indian service—except the two superintendencies under Quaker jurisdiction—helped to inspire this attack. In addition, Mrs. Tappan and many other reformers considered such men as Sherman, Custer, and Sheridan bloodthirsty border ruffians who hungered for the extermination of the Western tribes. She correctly suspected that Sherman was not in sympathy with the Peace Policy, and his merciless suppression of the Indian rebellion during the previous fall and winter had served to bolster this belief.

This analysis of the role of the Army in Indian relations, however understandable from the viewpoint of those humanitarians who were thinking only in terms of a peaceful solution to the Indian problem, was biased and inaccurate. For example, in October, 1868, Sherman wrote to General Sheridan "that to accuse the military of wanting an Indian war was to accuse it of a want of common sense

60. *Ibid.*
61. *Ibid.*, May 29, 1869.
62. Mrs. Tappan's contention that the Army had been assigned to peaceful Indians, while the Quakers had been placed over only those tribes "who had just cause for war," was an exaggeration. Nearly all the Western tribes, according to most humanitarians, had just cause for war.

'and of that regard for order and peace which has ever characterized our regular army.' "[63] However, Sherman was quick to point out, there would be no kid-gloves policy for those Indians who wanted war. If such a war resulted in their annihilation, they had been frequently warned and thus should expect such a possibility.[64] In a letter to Senator Edmund G. Ross (Republican, Kansas), Sherman admitted that the Indians were in danger of extinction, and he conceded that in all fairness, they should be given a chance to survive and become affiliated with the dominant race.[65] The General advocated not extermination, but the order and peace that only an adequate and hard-hitting frontier military force could guarantee. Further, several high-ranking officers stationed in the West openly supported the Peace Policy in whole or in part. General W. S. Harney, who then was one of the Army's Indian agents, wasted no time in getting agricultural implements and instruction to the Sioux in his charge in the hope of civilizing them.[66] Also, Major General E. O. C. Ord of the Department of California maintained that the new views of Army officers were not to exterminate, but to civilize the Indians and give them some of the privileges and safeguards of citizenship.[67]

Most of the more radical reformers, however, could see the Army only as merciless annihilators. Wendell Phillips had no more respect for the Army than did Mrs. Tappan. Shortly after the Universal Peace Union's convention, he attacked Horace Greeley for praising "Custar's [sic] murders as 'brilliant victories' " in the columns of his Tribune. "He [Greeley] will cease to advocate 'extermination,' " Phillips declared, "merely because an ingrained Democrat and aristocratic West Pointer, General Sherman, dozes into that policy."[68] A few days later, Phillips announced that "the Indians have begun to tear up the rails, [and] to shoot passengers and conductors on the Pacific Road," and he concluded, "We see great good in this."[69] He then demanded that the government abandon the railroad and give the Great Plains back to the Indians. The Western reaction to Phillips' suggestion was as hostile as might be expected, and The New York Times, which seldom supported Phillips' views, con-

63. Robert G. Athearn, William Tecumseh Sherman and the Settlement of the West, 236.
64. Ibid.
65. Ibid., 237.
66. The New York Times, May 19, 1869.
67. Ibid., December 17, 1869.
68. The National Anti-Slavery Standard, May 29, 1869.
69. The New York Times, June 11, 1869.

demned Phillips' "sickly sentimentality" and accused him of gloating over the Indian "booty and butchery."[70]

At the same time, the Board of Indian Commissioners, which had been appointed on May 26, was finishing its preparations for an inspection tour of the Great Plains. Upon the advice of Ely Parker, the Indian country was divided into three sections, each to be examined by a subcommittee of the board. The northern section—Nebraska and the Dakota Territory—was assigned to William Welsh, John V. Farwell, and E. S. Tobey. Both Farwell and Tobey were prominent businessmen and leaders in their churches. Welsh, one of the founders of the board, had been appointed chairman, but in June, he resigned because he thought the board's powers were too restricted to accomplish its purported objective of civilizing the Indians.[71] The southern section—Kansas and the Indian Territory—was to be inspected by Felix R. Brunot, William E. Dodge, and Nathan Bishop, an educator from New York. Brunot, a Pittsburgh philanthropist, replaced Welsh as chairman in July, 1869.[72] The western section, consisting of all territory west of the other two divisions, was charged to Robert Campbell, a wealthy businessman from St. Louis; George H. Stuart of Philadelphia, a founder of the board who had suggested most of the appointees; and Henry S. Lane, an antislavery leader from Indiana and one of the founders of the Republican party. Lane was elected governor of Indiana in 1860. That same year, he became a United States senator and served for one term. Vincent Colyer, secretary of the United States Indian Commission, was appointed to the board in July and assigned to inspect the Alaskan tribes.

Colyer was an artist who had shown his sympathy with the antislavery movement through such paintings as his "Freedom's Martyr" and by raising a Negro regiment that he commanded during the Civil War. After the war, he was caught up in the movement for Indian rights and joined Peter Cooper's organization. Colyer was observing the condition of the Pacific Coast tribes for Cooper's commission when he was appointed to the Board of Indian Commissioners.

70. *Ibid.*, June 25, 1869. The *Times'* editors later explained that they had criticized Phillips because they could not "compromise with disorder, nor reason with murder and assassination. This was the error of Mr. Phillips when he applauded the Cheyenne warriors for pulling up the railroad track in Kansas." *Ibid.*, January 26, 1870.

71. Elsie Mitchell Rushmore, *The Indian Policy During Grant's Administrations*, 21.

72. Slattery, *Brunot*, 143.

William Dodge's letters to the board in Washington show that the agency inspection trips were strenuous. On August 8, he wrote that after leaving the railroad at Hays City, Kansas, the commissioners had spent eight days crossing the Plains to Camp Supply, Indian Territory. "We have found the road a hard one; the weather very hot and water very scarce. We have not seen a habitation of any kind for 250 miles, except Camp Dodge."[73]

At Camp Supply, the commissioners met with the Cheyenne and Arapaho chiefs, who, Dodge reported, "made excellent peace speeches."[74] After Brunot explained to them the principles of the Peace Policy, Dodge told them, "There are a great many people East who love the Indians and want to do them good. They wish to save the Indian from ruin. They remember that many moons ago the red man lived where the white man now lives, but they are gone." Following this admonition, he advised them to "begin to live like the white men. Cultivate your land, and we will send good men to teach your children to work, to read and write; and then they will grow up able to support themselves after the buffalo has gone."[75]

After a two-hour council, the results of which they considered "most favorable for our object," the commissioners moved on to the Kiowa and Comanche Agency near Fort Sill. There, they found less good will, especially on the part of Chief Satanta, a Kiowa. He told the commissioners, "We have tried the white man's road and found it hard; we find nothing on it but a little corn—which hurts our teeth. No sugar, no coffee. But we want to walk in the white man's road; yet you want us to make arrowheads." He then reminded the visitors that all the central Plains belonged to the Indians. "But," he said, "the whites have divided it up to suit themselves. I don't know that my heart feels good about this business." The commissioners reported that they placed little reliance on the promises of Satanta and the Kiowas but thought an issue of better rations would keep them quiet.[76] By mid-September, they had conferred with most of the principal chiefs in the southern section and had received solemn assurances from them that they would, hereafter, "walk the white man's road."[77]

73. *The New York Times*, August 14, 1869.
74. *Ibid.*, September 7, 1869.
75. Board of Indian Commissioners, Report, November 23, 1869, *Annual Report of the Commissioner of Indian Affairs, 1869, Annual Report of the Secretary of the Interior*, 41st Cong., 2d. sess., 1869–1870, House Exec. Doc. No. 1 (Serial 1414), 496; Dodge, *Memorials*, 173.
76. Slattery, *Brunot*, 159.
77. *The New York Times*, September 7, 1869.

When the commissioners returned to the East, they reported their great pleasure with the general results of the new policy. They had found the Quakers thus far quite successful.[78] Dodge emphasized his growing certainty that this "last remnant of the aborigines of our country" should be saved from extermination. "We are convinced," he told the American Board of Missions, "they may yet become a blessing to us and to the nation."[79]

There seemed to be little disagreement with the findings of the commissioners. General W. B. Hazen, who had been assigned to police the southern tribes, declared that the change in Indian policy was advantageous and worked well. He added that as soon as the Indians were placed on a reservation, "all that is wanted is an honest administration, and that the Quakers are giving them."[80] An editorial in *The New York Times* praised the "good effect" of the new policy and concluded that Congress would have "a clearer field than ever before for settling a broad Indian policy."[81] The Pennsylvania Peace Society observed that "the whole world is looking on to see the results of the Peace Policy" and stated that its success was already certain because the "wrongs toward the aborigines were being done away with."[82] Late in 1869, Alfred Love further encouraged reformers when he assured them that a more progressive spirit prevailed among the masses.[83]

In his first annual message to Congress, President Grant cautiously appraised the initial accomplishments of the new policy but expressed his hope of its being "attended ultimately with great success." The building of railroads was rapidly bringing the settlements into contact with all Indian tribes, and he noted that "they do not harmonize well, and one or the other has to give way in the end. A system which looks to the extinction of a race is too horrible for a nation to adopt." Grant could see no alternative, for the time being, to a reservation system in which the Indians would be given absolute protection.[84]

After visiting thirty-one Western tribes for Peter Cooper's United States Indian Commission, Vincent Colyer had predicted that

78. *Ibid.*, November 18, 1869.
79. Dodge, *Memorials*, 175.
80. *Republican* (St. Louis), September 22, 1869, in *The New York Times*, September 26, 1869.
81. *The New York Times*, September 30, 1869.
82. *The Bond of Peace*, II, 12 (December, 1869), 99; *ibid.*, III, 1 (January, 1870), 8.
83. *The National Anti-Slavery Standard*, December 11, 1869.
84. James D. Richardson, ed., *A Compilation of the Messages and Papers of the Presidents*, 1897–1917 ed., VIII, 3993.

"in less than two years we shall have heard the last of 'Indian outrages.' "[85] By the end of 1869, many humanitarians were convinced that a utopian age in Government-Indian relations was near and that a final solution was in sight.

85. *The New York Times*, July 15, 1869. See Vincent Coyler, "Report of Vincent Colyer of His Inspection Trip During 1869," *Annual Report of the Commissioner of Indian Affairs*, 1869, 530.

5

Humanitarian Idealism in Action

The new year had hardly begun when the optimism of late 1869 received a rude jolt. In the latter part of January, 1870, the Eastern press began receiving reports of an Army massacre of a Montana Indian band in which men, women, and children were slaughtered indiscriminately.[1] At first, slight regard was given this unofficial story, which an Indian had apparently told to officials at Fort Benton, Montana. As more details of the alleged slaughter filtered into the East, the Indian Bureau and advocates of Indian rights began to take notice. From newspaper correspondents in Helena, they learned that on the morning of January 23, 1870, a battalion of cavalry under the command of Colonel E. M. Baker had staged a surprise attack on a camp of Piegans, a band of the Blackfeet tribe, and had killed 173 Indians. Militarily, it appeared, the Baker expedition had been a huge success because considerable stolen property was reported to have been recovered.[2]

In 1870, such a severe military chastisement of any band of Indians, even known troublemakers, was not likely to be praised in the East, but in this case, the reaction in the Eastern press, in Congress, and among the humanitarian supporters of the Indian Peace Policy brought long-lasting repercussions. The reaction began with the reading of a letter from Vincent Colyer, secretary of the Board of Indian Commissioners, before the House of Representatives on February 25. A revelation of the "sickening details of Colonel Baker's attack," Colyer's letter declared that of the 173 Indians killed, all but 15 were women, children, and old men. It pointed out that 50 of the casualties were children under twelve years of age and that many of these "were in their parents' arms." Furthermore, the whole village had been suffering for two months from an epidemic of smallpox, from which approximately six victims were dying each day. To make the allegations even more serious, Colyer revealed that the Blackfeet agent, Lieutenant W. B. Pease, had given him this information and

1. *The New York Times,* January 28, 1870.
2. Major General Winfield S. Hancock, Report, November 1, 1870, *Annual Report of the Secretary of War,* 1870, 41st Cong., 3d sess., 1870–1871, House Exec. Doc. No. 1 (Serial 1446), 29.

that General Alfred Sully, Indian Superintendent of the Montana Territory, had endorsed it.[3]

Immediately following the reading of the Colyer report before the House of Representatives, Daniel Voorhees (Democrat, Indiana) denounced the Baker attack. This system of warfare, he exclaimed, "cannot be justified before the civilization of the age, or in the sight of God or man." To Voorhees, it was a paradox for the President to welcome his Quaker Indian agents to tell him of their progress as missionaries of a gospel of peace and a beneficent government while he extended the other hand to "the man, General Sheridan, stained with the blood of innocent women and children!"[4]

Voorhees, a Democrat, might be expected to use the occasion to attack a policy of the Grant Administration, but some Republicans were just as critical. Job Stevenson (Republican, Ohio), who had no sympathy for the Peace Policy, praised the Army and declared that he "would not give Phil Sheridan, 'Glorious Cavalry Phil,' for all the wild Indians between the Mississippi and the Pacific."[5] On the other hand, Aaron Sargent (Republican, California), a strong proponent of a humane policy and an admirer of the Quakers, expressed disappointment in the present Peace Policy because it was "too warlike" toward the Indians. He added that the place to strike such a system was the military appropriation bill, and he proposed that it be amended so that Army funds would be cut off at any time such actions were repeated.[6] The rebellious mood in Congress brought from Grant a plea for sufficient appropriations to carry out the treaties made by the Peace Commission of 1867. "I earnestly desire," he said, "that if an Indian war becomes inevitable the Government of the United States at least should not be responsible for it."[7]

The New York Times asked if the killing of 173 people, of whom 140 were women and children, could be called anything but a "sickening slaughter" and demanded an immediate congressional investigation. *The New York Semi-Weekly Tribune* described the affair as a "national disgrace."[8] Among the humanitarian journals, *The National Anti-Slavery Standard* and Alfred Love's *Bond of Peace* vigor-

3. *Congressional Globe*, 41st Cong., 2d sess., 1869–1870, Part 2, 1576.
4. *Ibid.*, Part 2, 1581.
5. *The New York Times*, March 1, 1870.
6. *Congressional Globe*, 41st Cong., 2d sess., 1869–1870, Part 2, 1576–77.
7. James D. Richardson, ed., *A Compilation of the Messages and Papers of the Presidents, 1789–1902*, 1908 ed., VII, 52.
8. *The New York Times*, February 24, 1870; *The New York Semi-Weekly Tribune*, March 15, 1870.

ously condemned the Army attack and particularly General Sheridan. William E. Dodge, a member of the Board of Indian Commissioners, insisted that those responsible "for this late outrageous murder of women and children should be held, at least by the public, to a strict reckoning."[9] The Pennsylvania Peace Society met in Philadelphia, adopted a resolution calling for a thorough government investigation of the Piegan Massacre, and sent copies of it to the House and Senate.[10] In response to an invitation by members of Congress and Indian sympathizers, Mrs. Cora Tappan lectured in the Masonic temple in Washington, D. C., on the subject "Moke-ta-va-ta; or, The Nation and its Wards." Her moving rendition of the poem "The Massacre of the Piegans" was the highlight of her program. One verse colorfully described Colonel Baker's attack:

> Women and babes shrieking awoke
> To perish 'mid the battle smoke,
> Murdered, or turned out there to die
> Beneath the stern, gray, wintry sky;
> Here, a great Christian warrior's plan
> There, Pity, and the poor Piegan.[11]

In the trans-Missouri West, the Army could find more defenders. According to *The New York Times*, Westerners in the Rocky Mountains and Great Plains praised Baker and Sheridan and demanded more of such courageous military leaders who did not fear "bloodthirsty savages," the Indian Bureau, or the Eastern "Indian lovers." Several hundred residents of Wyoming Territory sent a petition to General Sheridan heartily approving his Indian policy and endorsing the "so-called 'massacre' of the Piegans by Colonel Baker."[12] Governor James M. Harvey of Kansas begged for more troops and urged that the Plains Indians be dismounted and disarmed, forced upon their reservations, and held there by military power.[13] Montana Territory's Democratic delegate to Congress, James Cavanaugh, one of the frontier's most virulent critics of the Peace Policy, singled out Samuel Tappan as an example of the "notorious" peace commissioners "who seem to have 'Indian on the brain.' " He added, "There

9. D. Stuart Dodge, *Memorials of William E. Dodge*, 175.
10. *The National Anti-Slavery Standard*, March 26, 1870.
11. *Ibid.*, April 9, 1870; Shenandoah, "The Massacre of the Piegans," *The Standard*, I, 2 (June, 1870), 90–91.
12. *The New York Times*, April 10, 1870.
13. James M. Harvey, letter to General J. M. Schofield, February 8, 1870, James M. Harvey, Correspondence Received, Subject File: Indians, 1869–1872.

never was a grosser fraud perpetrated upon the American Government than that peace commission."[14]

General Sheridan expressed his opinion that Vincent Colyer was "trying to deceive a kind-hearted public" and that he was undoubtedly working in the interest of the old Indian agents. The real problem to be solved, he pointed out, was, Who shall be killed, the whites or the Indians?[15] Colyer publicly repudiated Sheridan's charges and declared that the General

> strikes out at me almost wildly as he did at the poor Piegans, and with about as much justice. . . . Of the outrages against the poor settlers of the border he says that I 'want it to go on.' No General, you know you are not justified in any such an inference as this. Because I pull aside the curtain and let the American people see what you call a 'great victory over the Indians,' it don't follow that we do not want the *men* who perpetrate the horrid crimes you portray with so much zest justly punished. Strike, if you must strike, the guilty—not the innocent.[16]

To counteract the critical uproar, General Winfield Hancock, Commander of the Department of Dakota, ordered the publication of Baker's official Army report in order to give the public a true account of the attack. However, its admission that 53 of the dead were women and children and that over 100 women and children prisoners had been released when the temperature was forty degrees below zero because the Army lacked sufficient stores to feed them added to the controversy. *The New York Times* declared that the Baker report only confirmed the butchery and that Hancock's excusatory remarks added further condemnation to the affair.[17] In a passionate *Bond of Peace* editorial, Alfred H. Love asserted that "all the dispatches of Sheridan, Sherman and Baker on the late murderous and diabolical raid upon the Small Pox Camp of Pigeon [*sic*] Indians . . . in no measure excuse the disgraceful and wicked act."[18] Meanwhile, the Army conducted its own investigation and reported that the expedition against the Piegans was fully justified.[19] A few days later, General Sully denied that he had censured the actions of Colonel Baker and the military authorities and declared that the telegraphic reports

14. *Congressional Globe,* 41st Cong., 2d sess., 1869–1870, Part 2, 1643–44.

15. *The New York Times,* March 8, 1870.

16. *The Bond of Peace,* III, 4 (April, 1870), 42.

17. *The New York Times,* March 12, 1870.

18. *The Bond of Peace,* III, 4 (April, 1870), 41.

19. Secretary of War, *Letter transmitting the report of Brevet Colonel Baker, upon the late expedition against the Piegan Indians, in Montana,* 41st Cong., 2d sess., 1869–1870, House Exec. Doc. No. 197 (Serial 1418), 1–3.

of the Associated Press had thrown a "false light" on his analysis of the affair.[20]

The Army's defense of its case failed to gain the sympathy of either Congress or the Eastern public and certainly not of the humanitarians. At stake was a clause in the Army appropriation bill transferring Indian affairs to the War Department—a bill that had been very near passage. Congressional investigation of the matter only served to solidify the majority conviction that the Army's policy of force and punishment and the Interior Department's policy of "peace, protection, and civilization" were at opposite poles. Thus, if the Grant Administration's Indian policy was to be continued as a true policy of peace, Indian affairs must not be transferred to the War Department.

The Piegan Massacre not only destroyed any possibility of transfer for several years to come, but it also aggravated a deep-seated and rather widespread spirit of antimilitarism among the Eastern public in general and the humanitarians in particular. On the other hand, Grant's Peace Policy escaped much criticism and generally received praise as the only real solution for the Indian problem. Furthermore, during the spring of 1870, there was a rising chorus of demands that church control be extended to all Indian agencies and that greater restrictions be imposed on the use of the Army. More than ever, the Army became the scapegoat for the humanitarians, not only because it had carried out the Piegan Massacre, but also because it symbolized what appeared to be a completely incongruous factor in the government's peace and civilization program.

The more extreme antimilitaristic sentiment was expressed in Lydia Maria Child's attack on "our model military heroes." She wrote:

> Men thought . . . the whip was more efficient than wages to get work out of the black man; and now the approved method of teaching red men not to commit murder is to slaughter their wives and children! . . . indiscriminate slaughter of helpless women and innocent babies is not war—it is butchery; it is murder. . . . Shame on General Sheridan for perpetrating such outrages on a people because they were poor, and weak, and despised![21]

Wendell Phillips, at the first meeting of the Reform League, scornfully denounced Army-Indian relations. His remarks appeared in *The National Anti-Slavery Standard*. "I only know the names of

20. *The New York Times*, March 21, 1870.
21. Lydia Maria Child, "The Indians," *The Standard*, I, 1 (May, 1870), 1–2.

three savages upon the Plains," Phillips exclaimed, "—Colonel Baker, General Custer, and at the head of all, General Sheridan (applause) . . . . Thank God for a President in the White House whose first word was for the negro, and the second for the Indian; (applause). Who saw protection for the Indian, not in the rude and blood-thirsty policy of Sheridan and Sherman, but in the ballot, in citizenship, the great panacea that has always protected the rights of Saxon individuals."[22]

The Reform League was organized April 9, 1870, to replace the dissolved American Anti-Slavery Society. Its purpose was to promote eradication of caste spirit and to advance the cause of Indian civilization, enfranchisement of women, temperance, labor, and prison reform. At the Reform League's first meeting, Frederick Douglass pointed out that the spirit that had animated the Anti-Slavery Society "is to continue its activity through new instrumentalities, first for the Indian, whose condition today is the saddest chapter of our history. The most terrible reproach that can be hurled at this moment at the head of American Christianity and civilization is the fact that there is a general consent all over this country that the aboriginal inhabitants . . . should die out in the presence of that Christianity and civilization."[23]

At its fourth anniversary meeting in May, Alfred Love's Universal Peace Union condemned the "wretched policy of the Military Department in the brutal massacre of the Piegans, and the threatened extermination of the red man" and advocated repeal of all military and war powers that Congress and the Chief Executive had been granted in the Constitution.[24]

The most influential criticisms were issued by a nationwide convention of humanitarians gathered at Cooper Union in New York under the auspices of the United States Indian Commission. Delegates included representatives of the Board of Indian Commissioners, the Cherokee and Creek tribes, the Methodist Episcopal Church, the Land Reform Society, and the Universal Peace Union. The meeting opened with a message of somber warning from Secretary of the Interior J. D. Cox. Unless the government could have the organized help of the "good people of the land" on a scale entirely beyond anything heretofore attempted, he said, the doom of the Indians would be sealed.[25] A discordant note was interjected into the proceedings

22. *The National Anti-Slavery Standard,* April 16, 1870.
23. *Ibid.*
24. *The New York Times,* May 27, 1870.
25. Samuel F. Tappan, "Our Indian Relations," *The Standard,* I, 3 (July, 1870), 165.

when a letter from General Sherman was read to the assembled delegates. Sherman's blunt declaration that such meetings "accomplish little or no good" and his comment that the "wild Indians are rather damaged than benefitted by the conflict of extreme opinions which these public meetings engender" did little to endear the General, or the Army, to the audience.[26]

William Lloyd Garrison replied to Sherman's letter with a stinging condemnation of the Piegan Massacre and the officers responsible for it and asserted that the spirit of General Sheridan was one of "terrible vindictiveness." Quaker Indian agent Benjamin Tatham also severely criticized the tone and tenor of the General's remarks. These denunciations were followed by the reading of a letter from Wendell Phillips to Samuel Tappan describing the hands of Sheridan as "foul with Indian blood, shed by assassins who acted under his orders and received his approval."[27]

In a resolution addressed to President Grant, Secretary Cox, and both Houses of Congress, the assembled delegates voiced their earnest support of the President's "humane and just policy," denounced the Piegan Massacre and "other similar horrors," and stated that the "present military policy is unwise, unjust, oppressive, extravagant, and incompatible with Christian civilization."[28] Although criticism of the Army seemed to dominate the activities of the meeting, its real purposes were twofold. One was to help prevent the Indian war that would soon break out if Congress failed to vote sufficient appropriations to effect the treaties of 1867. The other was to determine how to enlist on behalf of the Indian "that philanthropic and Christian effort which has been so valuable an aid in the elevation of the freedman." In an open letter to the American people, the delegates asked for an all-out effort to increase the number and strength of those members of Congress and government officials "who fearlessly advocate the right."[29]

These views provided welcome support for those congressmen who backed a humanitarian solution to the Indian problem and who were exerting considerable control over Indian policy. The many resolutions and memorials that the Congress received after the Piegan Massacre helped the congressmen to push through legislation for

26. *The New York Times*, May 19, 1870; "Report of the Convention of the Indian Commission in New York," *The Nation*, X (May 26, 1870), 329.

27. *The New York Times*, May 19, 1870.

28. Tappan, "Our Indian Relations," 164; *The New York Times*, May 19, 1870.

29. *Ibid.*, May 20, 1870.

Indian rights and to expand the operations of the Peace Policy. Aaron Powell, in *The National Anti-Slavery Standard*, joyfully wrote that the "Indian question is of late receiving a large measure of public and Congressional attention."[30]

In early February, the House brought attention to four Indian treaties, then in the Senate, that had granted large areas of Kansas and Nebraska Indian reservations to railroad companies at ridiculously low prices. This information prompted President Grant immediately to withdraw the treaties from further consideration.[31] Furthermore, as a result of Colyer's reports of smallpox among the Piegans, the government began the shipment of large quantities of vaccine to the Western Indian agencies in an attempt to halt the spread of the disease.[32] Congress also discussed the merits of eliminating the Indian-treaty system, favorably considered granting self-government to the tribes of Indian Territory, and explored the possibilities of conferring citizenship on them. Even more significant was the passage of a provision prohibiting any Army officer on the active list from holding any civil office whether by election or appointment.[33] By forcing Army officers to resign as Indian agents, this ruling opened the way for the extension of church control over all agencies.

The crowning event of the year for the advocates of the humanitarian Indian policy was the visit to Washington, D. C., and New York City by Red Cloud and other Sioux chiefs. In April, Red Cloud had informed the commander of Fort Fetterman, Wyoming Territory, that he and some of his principal chiefs wished to go to Washington to see the "Great Father."[34] General Sherman, with little enthusiasm, decided to relay the request to the President and the Indian Bureau because, he thought, "we might as well commence to deal with these people now as to wait longer."[35]

Secretary of the Interior Cox had informed Peter Cooper's Indian Commission, which was then meeting, of the Sioux chiefs' intended visit and added that "if while they are here they can receive practical evidence of the nation's determination to keep faith instead of repudiating solemn treaties, we may reasonably expect good results from the impression made on them by the power and greatness

30. *The National Anti-Slavery Standard*, March 19, 1870.
31. *Ibid.*, February 19, 1870; George W. Julian, "The Land Question," *The Standard*, I, 1 (May, 1870), 33.
32. *The New York Times*, April 17, 1870.
33. *Congressional Globe*, 41st Cong., 2d sess., 1869–1870, Part 6, 5402.
34. *The New York Times*, April 29, 1870.
35. *Ibid.*, April 30, 1870.

of the nation."[36] The official suggestion of the importance of the visit to further peaceful Indian-Government relations and the inclusion of the New York organization was not lost upon its members. Nearly two years before, John Beeson, representing Peter Cooper's Indian Commission, had written Secretary of the Interior O. H. Browning requesting that an Indian delegation then in Washington be allowed to attend a meeting of the commission. Browning had not objected but had refused to pay the costs of the enterprise, and the plan fell through.[37] Now, the humanitarians agreed that the Sioux delegation should receive a royal welcome.

The Indian delegates' arrival in Washington initiated a carefully planned program of official interviews and social receptions. On June 2, Chief Spotted Tail conferred with President Grant and said he was for peace but his fidelity to the government had not been reciprocated. He added that he hoped white men would, hereafter, treat the Indians as brothers.[38] Government reaction was swift. On June 4, the War Department published an order that stated, "When lands are secured to the Indians by treaty against occupation by the whites, the military commander shall keep intruders off by military force if necessary."[39] Two days later, the chiefs were feted at a White House reception and banquet. The guests were duly impressed, but awe of the white man's civilization failed to suppress their convictions that they were the victims of white perfidy. The day following the reception, Red Cloud spoke at the Indian Office to Secretary of the Interior Cox, Indian Commissioner Parker, Vincent Colyer and Felix Brunot of the Board of Indian Commissioners, and other officials. "The Great Father," he told them, "may be good and kind but I can't see it. . . . [He] has sent his people out there and left me nothing but an island. Our nation is melting away like the snow on the sides of the hills where the sun is warm; while your people are like the blades of grass in the Spring when summer is coming."[40] During the next three days, Red Cloud became more and more critical of the government's past dealings with his tribe. On June 10, he complained to Secretary Cox that most of the promises contained in the Fort Laramie Treaty of 1868 had never been fulfilled. "The object of the whites was to crush the Indian down to nothing," the Sioux leader charged, and then he added unhappily, "All the words I sent

36. *Ibid.*, May 19, 1870.
37. O. H. Browning, letter to N. G. Taylor, June 25, 1868, Bureau of Indian Affairs, Letters Received.
38. *The New York Times*, June 3, 1870.
39. *Ibid.*, June 8, 1870.
40. *Ibid.*

never reached the Great Father. They are lost before they get here.
. . . I will not take the paper [Fort Laramie treaty] with me. It is
all lies."[41]

The Sioux had apparently won Red Cloud's War of 1866–1868
and had been guaranteed permanent possession of their choice hunting grounds, a vast area embracing the northeast quarter of Wyoming
Territory, but the Indians were deeply concerned. They had come to
Washington to protest the presence of Fort Fetterman in Sioux Territory (a violation of the Fort Laramie treaty), the government's
failure to deliver promised annuity goods, and the survey for the
Northern Pacific Railroad across land claimed by the Sioux. Now
that they had seen the immense population and resources of the
white men, they were for the first time really convinced that the
Western Indians and their way of life were doomed to extinction
unless the government would honor its treaty obligations to the
letter.

The annuities had not been delivered because congressmen were
wrangling over the Indian appropriation bill—the supporters of the
Peace Policy on one side and the opponents, consisting of frontier
representatives and delegates and skeptical Easterners, on the other.
Reformers impatiently demanded legislative action. Samuel Tappan
denounced Congress for embarrassing the Indian Bureau by refusing
the necessary appropriations and warned that it was thereby tacitly,
if not expressly, repudiating all Indian treaties, "which is sure to
provoke war."[42] President Grant had refused to agree to the removal
of Fort Fetterman, but the uncompromising attitude of the Sioux
delegation had convinced him that Indian hostilities were inevitable
unless the appropriation bill was passed soon. His message to Congress, in which he emphasized his fear of renewed warfare on the
Plains, together with the pressure from the reformers, brought support for the act.[43] Finally, a determined group of Republican Peace-
Policy congressmen were able to push the Indian Appropriations Act
for 1870–1871 through the House shortly before its adjournment for
the summer.

After the interview with Cox, Red Cloud said he wanted to return to his people at once, but government officials, who were certain
that the visiting chiefs held the key to peace on the Plains, were
uneasy over the angry mood of the delegates. Thus, on the evening
of June 12, Senator Morrill, Chairman of the Senate Appropriation

41. *Ibid.*, June 11, 1870.
42. Tappan, "Our Indian Relations," 163.
43. *The National Standard*, July 30, 1870; Richardson, *Messages and Papers*, 1908 ed., VII, 79.

Committee, called on Red Cloud at his hotel and told him that if he were to go to New York, he "would find multitudes of friends who would be glad to take his hand and stand by him and his people."[44] Red Cloud made it clear that he did not wish to return home by such a roundabout route, but the worried government officials were not easily dissuaded. After his train was well under way, Red Cloud discovered that the white men had once again beguiled him and that he was bound for New York after all.

Early on the morning of June 15, several members of the United States Indian Commission, among them Peter Cooper, Vincent Colyer, Benjamin Tatham, and its new president, Howard Crosby, interviewed the Sioux delegates at their suite in the St. Nicholas Hotel. Red Cloud, obviously piqued about the government officials' duplicity, complained to his visitors that, in Washington, he had asked for seventeen horses but had been refused them by President Grant. Cooper quickly declared that if the government would not furnish the horses, he would. His quick thinking saved the day for the local humanitarians. Red Cloud replied that if the horses were offered to him as gifts, he would take them because he wished to be friendly. The visiting chiefs then agreed to tour the city with the Indian Commission members and promised to speak at the Cooper Union.

The commissioners, thinking to save the chiefs from the "more trivial and seductive amusements of the city," planned an evening of elevated and intellectual entertainment at the Jubilee. However, New York financier James Fisk, Jr., induced Red Cloud and his warriors to visit the Grand Opera House, where they "appeared to take especial delight in the fantastic gambols of the semi-nude coryphees and the gorgeous display of parti-colored fustian, glittering tinsel and red fire."[45]

The following morning, the Sioux delegation appeared as scheduled before a huge crowd at Cooper Union. There, Peter Cooper introduced them as the "very men of whom but yesterday we were assured that nothing could be expected but merciless war!" Dignified and eloquent, Red Cloud said he was a representative of the original American race, the first people of this continent. "We are good, and not bad," he told his audience. "The reports which you get about us are all on one side. You hear of us only as murderers and thieves. We are not so." Stabbing at uneasy consciences, he declared that if the Indians had more lands to give the whites, they would give them, but they had no more. "We are driven into a very little island," he added,

44. Katherine C. Turner, *Red Men Calling on the Great White Father*, 124.
45. *The New York Times*, June 16, 1870.

"and we want you, our dear friends, to help us with the Government.
. . . I have tried to get from the Great Father what is right and just. I
have not altogether succeeded. I want you to help me to get what is
right and just. . . . We do not want riches, we want peace and love."
After this emotional plea, Red Cloud struck once more at the government. "The riches that we have in this world, Secretary Cox said
truly, we cannot take with us to the next world. Then I wish to know
why Commissioners are sent out to us who do nothing but rob us
and get the riches of this world away from us?"[46]

With this simple, irrefutable logic and quick penetration to the
heart of the matter, Red Cloud's description of the wrongs suffered
by the Indians and his dignified appeal for help deeply moved his
listeners. Almost every sentence received enthusiastic applause, re-
minding a reporter for *The Nation* that the emotional effect upon
the assembly "was comparable to nothing so much as the public recital of a fugitive slave in former years." He added that it would be a
"peculiar disgrace" if Congress alone should show itself deaf to the
Indians' just complaints.[47]

The sympathy for the Indians generated by the Piegan Massacre
and further stimulated by the visit of Red Cloud and the Sioux delegation greatly increased public interest in the plight of the Indians.
The widespread concern was particularly rewarding to Peter Cooper's Indian Commission, for its expressed aim was to "array on the
side of justice and humanity the influence and support of an enlightened public opinion."[48] Furthermore, a new Indian-rights organization was founded in June. Called the Massachusetts Indian
Commission, it was organized in Boston's Old South Church and had
such important people on its executive committee as Massachusetts
Governor William Claflin, its president; Edward S. Tobey, a member
of the Board of Indian Commissioners; James Freeman Clarke, Harvard Professor of Religion; William Lloyd Garrison; and Reverend
John T. Sargent, a veteran abolitionist and a founder of the new
National Reform League. At its first meeting, Wendell Phillips and
Samuel Tappan spoke on the Indian question, and the members
adopted resolutions supporting a humane Indian policy.[49]

All of this activity was to the good, but government officials

46. *Ibid.*, June 17, 1870.
47. *The Nation*, X (June 23, 1870), 396.
48. Commissioner of Indian Affairs, *Annual Report of the Commissioner of Indian Affairs*, 1869, *Annual Report of the Secretary of the Interior*, 41st Cong., 2d sess., 1869–1870, House Exec. Doc. No. 1 (Serial 1414),
538.
49. *The Standard*, I, 3 (July, 1870), 182.

knew that if visits from discontented or hostile tribes were to improve understanding between the races, as well as to promote the Peace Policy, a positive Federal program must follow. On July 22, the Board of Indian Commissioners, at the request of Indian Commissioner Parker, dispatched Robert Campbell and Felix Brunot to Fort Laramie to visit Red Cloud and other Oglala Sioux leaders. The object of their mission was to inspire confidence in the just intentions of the government and to urge the Indians' cooperation in the government's "benevolent plans for their civilization." In addition, the commissioners were to select a location for Red Cloud's agency and superintend the delivery of the Sioux annuity goods.[50] Fortunately, Congress, under the prodding of Grant and the humanitarians, had passed the Indian Appropriation Act the preceding week.

On the way to Fort Laramie, Campbell and Brunot stopped at Omaha to examine the accounts and investigate the general management of Samuel Janney's Northern Superintendency. The commissioners reported that Janney was "a judicious and efficient officer" who was faithfully and successfully carrying out the designs of the Administration for the improvement of the Indians.[51] Janney was now well into his second year as head of the Northern Superintendency, and he firmly believed that the Indians "can be civilized here, and prepared for citizenship in a reasonable time, if treated with kindness and justice."[52] Janney thought that improving the condition and the civilization of the Indians could best be accomplished by educating the rising generation.[53] To support this program, the Society of Friends memorialized Congress in March, 1870, asking for an appropriation of $140,000 to supply the Indians of the Northern Superintendency with agricultural implements and livestock, to establish schools, and to pay teachers.[54]

Congress responded by approving the first general appropriation for Indian education. For the fiscal year 1871, the House authorized $100,000 for the "support of industrial and other schools among the

50. Commissioner of Indian Affairs, *Annual Report of the Commissioner of Indian Affairs, 1870, Annual Report of the Secretary of the Interior*, 41st Cong., 3d sess., 1870–1871, House Exec. Doc. No. 1 (Serial 1449), 848.

51. *Ibid.*

52. Samuel M. Janney, letter to Vincent Colyer, July 23, 1870, Bureau of Indian Affairs, Letters Received.

53. Samuel M. Janney, letter to Ely S. Parker, February 2, 1870, *ibid.*

54. Superintendent and Agents of the Northern Superintendency, Memorial to the President, Secretary of the Interior, and Commissioner of Indian Affairs, February 28, 1870, *ibid.*

Indian tribes not otherwise provided for."[55] However, only $30,000 was allocated to the Northern Superintendency, and this was to be used for purchasing teams, tools, agricultural implements, and other items. The money for educational purposes was to come from the general fund. Although the sum was completely inadequate for carrying Janney's plans to fruition, it did enable him and his agents to "begin their great work."[56]

Janney believed that civilization of the wild tribes could be accomplished in a single generation by proper education of the young. In a letter to the Commissioner of Indian Affairs, he recommended that all Indian children who were between six and twelve years of age should be "carefully taught to speak, read and write the English language" and then transferred to a boarding school. In these schools, the boys would learn farming, gardening, and mechanical arts; the girls would be instructed in housekeeping and sewing. He also believed that all members of the tribes should receive some religious instruction "adapted to their condition" and that they should see practical Christianity "illustrated by example." In addition to education, Janney proposed that each family should be allotted a piece of land, that they should be given seeds, livestock, and agricultural implements, and that they should have assistance in building cottages. "By these means," he concluded, "I believe the enlightened and humane policy of President Grant may be successfully established, and the aborigines of our country saved from extinction."[57]

As the Peace Policy entered its second year, the humanitarians turned from criticism of the Army and the Piegan Massacre to more concrete proposals for civilizing the Plains tribes. In May, Mrs. Child declared that strict and impartial laws must be enacted in order to bring the "demoralized tribes of the West" to the status attained by the Cherokees. The whisky dealers must be barred from the reservations, and the Indians must be guaranteed security in the possession of their land. Like Janney, she was convinced that the Indians must be taught agricultural and mechanical skills as well as the English language, and she suggested an incentive plan in which the pupils would be rewarded with "premiums" and "certain benefits" for cooperation and success.[58] "Human nature is essentially the same in all races and classes of man," she told Aaron Powell. "Its

55. U.S. *Statutes at Large*, XVI, 359.
56. Superintendent and Agents of the Northern Superintendency, Memorial to the President, Secretary of the Interior, and Commissioner of Indian Affairs, August 20, 1870, Bureau of Indian Affairs, Letters Received.
57. Samuel M. Janney, *Memoirs of Samuel M. Janney*, 279–81.
58. Child, "The Indians," 5–6.

modifications for good or evil" could be attributed to the "education of circumstances." Therefore, if Grant's Indian policy did not succeed, faithlessness and dishonesty on the part of the government and its agents would be the cause. "My faith never wavers," she concluded, "that men can be made just by being treated justly, honest by being dealt with honestly, and kindly by becoming objects of kindly sympathy."⁵⁹

During the summer of 1870, both the Connecticut and Pennsylvania branches of the Universal Peace Union congratulated the President on the success of the Peace Policy. The Connecticut branch asked that the program be expanded by increasing the number of teachers and urged that the Indians be given citizenship and representation in the government. But they reminded Grant that "while Sheridan and [the] other Generals go to Europe to see a fight, there is more peace in the Indian country, and Red Cloud and [the] friendly chiefs are more successful in establishing peace."⁶⁰

Wendell Phillips wrote to the United States Indian Commission in May that he was for an "immediate, entire, and permanent change" of Indian policy. He advocated making the Indians citizens, holding them responsible to civil law, and giving them its protection. "Call home the cheats and cutthroats who exasperate and abuse them," he advised the government. "Do justice if you expect to receive it. Show them civilization before you expect them to enjoy it."⁶¹

Before an audience in Boston, Phillips lauded the ratification of the Fifteenth Amendment, but he pointed out that its "truth, that all men are created equal" applied to only Negroes and white people. He warned that "this generation and the next must make it true of the Indian and Chinese."⁶² Phillips thought that the truly great guarantee for individual rights was citizenship and the ballot. In this contention he was enthusiastically supported by Aaron Powell, who in July issued a clarion call for a "revival of the pure gospel of human rights, applied to the Indians in support of the claims for civilization and citizenship."⁶³ To ensure the rights of the Indians, as well as those of the freedmen and the immigrants, Phillips urged the creation of a special bureau or a Cabinet department to watch over these

59. *The National Standard*, August 27, 1870.
60. *Ibid.*, September 10, 1870. In the summer of 1870, General Sheridan and several other Army officers were sent to Europe to observe the operations of the German army in the Franco-Prussian War.
61. Wendell Phillips, "Wendell Phillips to the United States Indian Commission, May 17, 1870," *The Standard*, I, 2 (June, 1870), 114–15.
62. Moncure D. Conway, "Wendell Phillips," *The Fortnightly Review*, XIV, 43 (July 1, 1870), 73.
63. "The Indian Delegation," *The Standard*, I, 3 (July, 1870), 178.

"*wards* of the nation."[64] John Beeson and Senator John B. Henderson had suggested a similar plan earlier, and in 1870, Congress did
consider a bill based on the idea, but it went no further.

In March, 1870, Secretary Cox had asked the United States Indian Commission to submit a plan for a more effective application
of the Peace Policy. During the spring of 1870, Cooper's commission
prepared a twenty-six-article proposal for submission to Congress.
The first step proposed for Congress was the passage of laws to enforce the fulfillment of all existing treaties. All tribes west of the
Mississippi should be concentrated on no less than four nor more
than seven reservations from which all white men—except those sent
"to benefit the Indians"—would be excluded. The agents must be
married, of "well attested philanthropic proclivities," and of Christian character—a proposal suggested to the commission by Samuel
Janney. Furthermore, the civilization program was to be based upon
industries operated by Indians and well-staffed educational institutions. In addition, all rights and titles were to be guaranteed to the
reservations and their occupants.[65]

Meanwhile, the congressional prohibition on Army officers serving in any civil capacity permitted the extension of church control
over all the superintendencies. This ruling, plus the initial success
of the Peace Policy, prompted Grant to order Commissioner Parker
to explain the objectives of the policy to the other religious denominations, both Protestant and Catholic. Those that concurred in the
plan were asked, as were the Quakers the previous year, to choose
those persons "possessing good Christian character" who would be
willing to work as Indian agents. Those chosen were not only required to carry out the agency duties, but also were expected to "lend
their personal and official influence to such educational and missionary or religious enterprises" as their denominations might
undertake.[66]

With this step, the Peace Policy ceased to be a doubtful experiment, and the government became fully committed to its policy of
peace and civilization under church and humanitarian guidance. By
1872, 13 separate denominations had been placed in charge of 73
agencies where nearly 239,000 Indians lived.[67] In his second annual

64. Wendell Phillips, "The New Powers of Congress," *The Standard*,
I, 2 (June, 1870), 101.
65. *The New York Times*, June 17, 1870; June 20, 1870.
66. *Annual Report of the Commissioner of Indian Affairs*, 1869, 474.
67. Laurence F. Schmeckebier, *The Office of Indian Affairs: Its History, Activities, and Organization*, 55.

message, Grant referred to the Peace Policy with much more optimism than he had the year before and confidently predicted that in a few years, all the Indians would be pursuing "peaceful and self-sustaining avocations" on reservations that were complete with houses, schools, and churches.[68]

By the end of 1870, many humanitarian organizations were praising the President and the new Indian policy. In November, the Friends' Social Union of New York City passed resolutions expressing its appreciation to the President for the "humane spirit, the wisdom, and executive ability" shown in the new Indian policy.[69] A month later, the Reform League met at Cooper Union, heard Samuel Tappan describe the civilization policy, and passed similar resolutions.[70] The *St. Paul Press* commented, "Had the Republican party done nothing more than rescue our Indian affairs from the errors and rascality that have heretofore characterized their management, it would deserve the gratitude of the country."[71]

The favorable reaction of such influential journals as *The Nation* to Red Cloud's visit to New York encouraged the reformers. Not only was the trip "well advised," said *The Nation's* editors, but public opinion "was perhaps affected by it more widely and more favorably than we can estimate."[72] Even more reassuring were reports from Wyoming and Dakota territories that Red Cloud and the other chiefs who had made the Eastern tour were exercising a good influence and had prevented war parties from leaving the Whetstone Agency in Dakota Territory.[73] Further evidence of the impact of awakened public opinion was the founding of the Indian Aid Society in New York City. Its objective was to provide the tribes with the material items necessary to carry out the Peace Policy's civilization program.[74]

Although the year 1870 had been one of steady progress in the program of civilization, there were some distressing events. The Senate had officially ruled that the Fourteenth Amendment had "no effect whatever" upon the status of the Indian tribes, and the Senate Committee on Indian Affairs had reported adversely on a bill to

68. Richardson, *Messages and Papers*, 1908 ed., VII, 110.
69. *The National Standard*, November 12, 1870.
70. *Ibid.*, December 10, 1870; December 24, 1870.
71. *St. Paul Press*, December 6, 1870, in *The National Standard*, December 17, 1870.
72. *The Nation*, X (June 23, 1870), 396.
73. *Daily Colorado Tribune* (Denver), July 15, 1870; *The National Standard*, August 6, 1870.
74. *The National Standard*, December 3, 1870.

create a separate department of Indian affairs,[75] but the most om-
inous information came from Indian Commissioner Parker. In his
annual report, he warned that the rapid construction of railroads,
some of which were receiving grants of Indian reservation land,
might well cause trouble. Any attempt to build railroads through the
territory of the "powerful and warlike" Sioux, he stated, "must produce a collision."[76] Time would soon prove that Parker's fear of an
impending conflict with this northern Plains tribe was far from
groundless.

75. Senate, Committee on the Judiciary, *The Effect of the Fourteenth
Amendment on the Indian Tribes,* 41st Cong., 3d sess., 1870–1871, Senate
Report No. 268 (Serial 1443), 115.
76. *Annual Report of the Commissioner of Indian Affairs,* 1870, 475.

6

Civilization or Extermination?

Indian sympathizers shared a conviction during the early postwar years that the chief perpetrators of injustice toward the Indians were dishonest agents, border settlers who were greedy for land, and Army officers who supported a policy of extermination. The United States Indian Commission referred to each of these groups in its memorial to Congress in July, 1868. It had charged that the honor and interests of the nation were being sacrificed to "the insatiable lust and avarice of unscrupulous men."[1] The 1865 Joint Special Committee's report, *The Condition of the Indian Tribes*, indicated that many congressmen had reached the same conclusion. This account charged that most Indian wars could be traced to the aggression of lawless white people, "always to be found on the frontier."[2]

Although white people on the frontier had been blamed for Indian troubles before, now they had replaced the Indians as the archvillains. The line of settlement, in moving well beyond the Missouri River into the Great Plains, had come into conflict with an Eastern image of the Plains region as permanent Indian country. Invasion of that region by white people was wrong. This viewpoint, plus the aroused humanitarian conscience of the antislavery crusade and a popular desire for a return to peace and order, served to recast the role of the pioneers. They were no longer heroes impelled by manifest destiny to conquer the wilderness for civilization. They had become "unprincipled, reckless, devoid of shame, looking upon an Indian as a fair object of plunder,"[3] according to Indian Commissioner D. N. Cooley in 1866, and the humanitarians who were working for Indian rights agreed with him.

When the congressional peace commissioners and the humani-

1. Commissioner of Indian Affairs, *Annual Report of the Commissioner of Indian Affairs*, 1869, *Annual Report of the Secretary of the Interior*, 41st Cong., 2d sess., 1869–1870, House Exec. Doc. No. 1 (Serial 1414), 538.

2. Congress, Joint Special Committee, *Condition of the Indian Tribes*, 39th Cong., 2d sess., 1866–1867, Senate Report No. 156, 3–10.

3. Commissioner of Indian Affairs, *Annual Report of the Commissioner of Indian Affairs*, 1866, *Annual Report of the Secretary of the Interior*, 39th Cong., 2d sess., 1866–1867, House Exec. Doc. No. 1 (Serial 1284), 20.

tarian reformers blamed the frontier populace for most of the Indian troubles, an acrimonious war of words broke out. Spokesmen for the frontier region usually saw this verbal conflict as East against West, with the Mississippi River an approximate dividing line. Such a generalization was traditional and convenient, even though there were many exceptions to the majority opinion in each section.

The formation of sectional and congressional Indian-policy battle lines, during the years 1865 through 1868, set the pattern for the disagreement and conflict that would emerge during the next ten years. The resulting lack of national unity, complicated by the Interior and War departments' disagreement about which could best manage Indian affairs, often seriously weakened the effectiveness of reform. The East-West dissension on Indian policy was further agitated by sharply opposing views on the nature of the Indians. During the nineteenth century, many people believed that race determined the character of peoples.[4] Therefore, almost any discussion of Indian policy—by congressmen, the reformers, members of the Army, or the border settlers—usually included an analysis of racial characteristics.

Newspaper editors on the Plains were especially uninhibited on this subject. The editor of the Kearney *Herald* in July, 1866, declared:

> Nothing is more absurd to the man who has studied the habits of the Indian savage than to talk of making permanent treaty negotiations with these heartless creatures. They are destitute of all the promptings of human nature, having no respect for word or honor. Their only creed is that which gives them an unrestricted license to use and abuse beings, brutes and things, as though earth and its contents were inanimate wooden heaps, made purposely to gratify a heathenish pleasure. To the Indian, destruction is gain; it is a generative instinct and one which goes from infancy to the grave. Educated to look upon the white man with inveterate enmity, he ignores peace and civil associations. Now and then you will hear a chicken-hearted historian, who knows nothing of the red savage, extolling his noble characteristics and praising his natural knightly endowments. The earnest defenders of this barbarian monster would turn away in disgust could they see him in all of his original desperation. The best and only way to reconcile the blood-washed animal will be to impose upon him a worse schooling than has ever befallen the inferior races.[5]

4. Thomas F. Gossett, *Race: The History of an Idea in America*, 244.
5. *Kearney* (Nebraska) *Herald* in *The Marysville* (Kansas) *Enterprise*, July 14, 1866.

If such editors were expressing the views of their local readers accurately, the "worse schooling" that most frontier people seemed to favor was extermination of the Indians. Another indicator of this view was the frontier expression "The only good Indian is a dead Indian." It was not always meant literally, but it was no wonder that Plains people were categorized in the East as inhumane when congressional delegates, like James Cavanaugh of Montana, declared before the House, "I have never in my life seen a good Indian (and I have seen thousands) except when I have seen a dead Indian." He then reproved advocates of the Peace Policy for their ignorance of Indian character, pointing out that they had never been chased, as he had been, by the "red devils—who seem to be the pets of eastern philanthropists."[6]

Frontier people did not necessarily consider military control of the Indians tantamount to extermination. They strongly supported the transfer measure because the Army, they believed, would be less expensive and more effective in handling the problem. "The idea of transferring the Indian Bureau to the War Department is a good one," wrote the editor of *The Daily Colorado Herald* in 1868. "We hope that Congress will make the change, and we believe this is the opinion of western people generally. We also believe that the western people are the best judges in this matter."[7] They were convinced that the fault lay with the Indian Bureau and its agents, in league with the corrupt "Indian Ring," and with the treaty-breaking savages whose behavior was only worsened by the methods of the Peace Policy.

Most frontier newspaper editors had backed Grant for the Presidency in 1868 because they believed he would place the Army in charge of the Indians and make short work of the hostiles. They were keenly disappointed when they heard about the adoption of the Peace Policy, and it was to be expected that neither political loyalties nor such acceptable features as the restricted reservation system brought much praise for the Grant program in the frontier press, especially in the Plains and Rocky Mountain regions, where Indian hostilities were current.

The closest approach to praise came from the editor of the *Kansas State Record*. He was a Republican who thought that the Quaker plan had "elements of honesty and humanity" that entitled it to a fair trial, providing just enough "Sheridanism" was used to keep the hostile Indians on their good behavior.[8] However, the Leav-

6. *Congressional Globe*, 40th Cong., 2d sess., 1867–1868, Part 3, 2638.
7. *The Daily Colorado Herald* (Central City), January 14, 1868.
8. *Kansas State Record* (Topeka), November 3, 1869.

enworth *Bulletin* reflected popular feeling when it bluntly informed its readers, "If more men are to be scalped and their hearts boiled, we hope to God that it may be some of our Quaker Indian Agents, and not our frontiersmen who want and are trying to do something for the improvement of the country."[9] And *The Junction City Weekly Union* observed that "even William Penn could not palliate the cruel deeds of hostile Indians of today. Many plans have been tried to produce peace on the border; but one alternative remains— EXTERMINATION."[10]

Before 1880, most congressmen from the Plains and Rocky Mountain states and territories agreed with such editorial attacks on the Peace Policy. Among the minority was Senator Samuel Pomeroy, who advocated a peace and civilization program under both Johnson and Grant. Influenced by his antislavery work, he saw the frontier conflict as a "war of races," drew parallels between the Negro and Indian problems, and sympathized with both.[11] His Senate colleague, Edmund G. Ross, described Indians as degraded, debauched, and treacherous, but he did oppose extermination as too inhuman and too costly. He preferred the congressional peace-policy rationale that it was "cheaper to feed them than to fight them."[12]

Kansas Republican Representative Sydney Clarke opposed the peace-policy position until 1870, when he became a proponent of Grant's Peace Policy and Chairman of the House Committee on Indian Affairs. Clarke was one of the few congressmen from the West who changed positions on Indian policy before the Custer tragedy of 1876. His political loyalty probably helped him decide, although political affiliation was usually subordinate to voter sentiment where Indian policy was concerned.

Throughout this period, Nebraska's Republican congressmen refused to support the Grant Administration's Peace Policy. Montana's Democratic delegates, as might be expected, were among the most vehement critics, while its lone Republican did support a civilization program that emphasized education. Most Texans of both parties condemned the Peace Policy. The one exception was Representative John Hancock, a Democrat who had faith in the work of

9. *Bulletin* (Leavenworth, Kansas), June 4, 1869, in *Western Observer* (Washington, Kansas), June 17, 1869.
10. *The Junction City* (Kansas) *Weekly Union*, June 19, 1869.
11. *Congressional Globe*, 38th Cong., 2d sess., 1864–1865, Part 2, 709.
12. *Ibid.*, 40th Cong., 1st sess., 1867, 705–6; *Kansas State Record* (Topeka), November 6, 1867. There was little opposition to the Peace Policy during its formative years from congressmen representing the states immediately west of the Mississippi. Some of the strongest support came from Republicans James Harlan of Iowa and William Windom of Minnesota.

the Quakers and in the prediction that the Indians would soon become self-sustaining and no longer a cost to the government. Like most frontier people, he advocated military control of the hostiles. Another exception was a Democratic delegate from Wyoming, William Steele, who tended to support the Peace Policy for a time because he thought that civilizing the Indians would end conflict on the frontier.[13]

The great number of hostile tribesmen in the Dakota and New Mexico territories stimulated a different reaction than it had in Montana and Texas. Delegates from the Dakota Territory, regardless of party, favored the Peace Policy, particularly the reservation system, as a way to encourage settlement and bring federal funds into the territory.[14] A Republican delegate from New Mexico, Jose F. Chavez, gave strong support to a civilization program for his territory, where "we are entirely surrounded by Indians. . . . It is nearly impossible to move about or get out of the Territory without coming across some hostile band of Indians."[15] In New Mexico, it was a matter of feeding or fighting a foe that had the advantage.

Of those congressmen who represented areas west of the Rocky Mountains and who, before 1876, took a stand on the Peace Policy, Republicans were evenly divided, but Democrats stood 3 to 1 in opposition. Their sentiments were strongly influenced by the temper of the prevailing relations with the local Indian tribes and by politics. Representative Samuel Axtell (Democrat, California) argued in June, 1870, that because the Indians in his state, where they worked as farm laborers, were peaceful and harmless, there was no need for the new Indian policy and its reservation system. His colleague from California, Republican Aaron Sargent, favored church participation, praised the work of the Quakers, and advocated complete assimilation of the Indians.[16]

The Indians in Nevada were no longer a serious problem, but Nevada congressmen apparently saw a threat in the Apaches close by in the Arizona Territory. Representative Thomas Fitch (Republican, Nevada) said the Apaches were the kind of Indians that he believed should be exterminated. He maintained that Indian affairs should be under Army jurisdiction to protect the settlers and to promote honest dealings with the Indians. Senator William A. Stewart, an antislavery Republican from Nevada, agreed with Fitch about

13. *Congressional Record*, 43d Cong., 1st sess., 1873–1874, Part 4, 3526.
14. Howard Roberts Lamar, *Dakota Territory, 1861–1889*, 105, 122.
15. *Congressional Globe*, 39th Cong., 2d sess., 1866–1867, Part 2, 1344.
16. *Ibid.*, 41st Cong., 2d sess., 1869–1870, Part 6, 4971–73, 5009.

the need for military control, but Stewart saw the need for reform and thought the Peace Policy might work if the Army were in charge.[17] Delegate Richard McCormick (Republican, Arizona Territory) doubted that the Peace Policy's methods would accomplish anything.[18]

By 1870, the fact that most congressmen from the West and the East favored the reservation system made it the nearest approach to a national consensus on the Peace Policy, but there were a few objections to reservations like that voiced by Representative Axtell of California. Senator James W. Nye (Republican, Nevada) opposed reservations because they isolated the Indians from civilization and prevented their learning by example.[19] He was perpetuating the theory of Senator Pomeroy who, like Senator Nye, had been an abolitionist and saw the Negroes and Indians in much the same context. In 1867, Pomeroy had pointed out that since Negroes had not been placed on reservations, neither should the Indians. "The policy of isolating a race on this American continent, where everybody should be an American citizen and a voter, is the ruinous policy in this whole Indian arrangement. . . . The policy of civilizing and evangelizing the Indians by making them citizens, by associating them with white men, by educating their children with our children, is the solution of this question." However, in 1870, Pomeroy abandoned this plan because he was convinced that the Indians would make the best progress when they were isolated from the demoralizing influence of white people.[20]

The East-West sectional disagreement on nearly all matters concerning the Indians was most easily observed in congressional debates. In the debate on the Indian appropriation bill for 1870–1871, attacks on the Indians, the Peace Policy, and the humanitarians were as heated and uncompromising as those of the previous four years. In defending extermination, Republican Representative Edward Degener of San Antonio, Texas, described civilization as the manifest destiny of mankind and stated, "He who resists gets crushed. That is the history of the wild Indian." As law-abiding citizens, Texans were ready to "bury the hatchet," but, he said, "Let the advocates of the Peace Policy show their readiness to defend us."[21] Representative

17. *Ibid.*, 3d sess., 1870–1871, Part 1, 731, 733; *ibid.*, 2d sess., 1870, Part 5, 4005–6.

18. *Ibid.*, 3d sess., 1870–1871, Part 1, 735.

19. *Ibid.*, Part 2, 1500.

20. *Ibid.*, 40th Cong., 2d sess., 1867–1868, Part 2, 709; *ibid.*, 41st Cong., 2d sess., 1869–1870, Part 2, 4160.

21. *Ibid.*, 41st Cong., 3d sess., 1870–1871, Part 1, 656.

Fitch was less conciliatory. After emphasizing that he did not entirely disagree with the idea that the only good Indians were the dead Indians, he proposed a policy of "effective warfare" against the Apaches of Arizona.[22] Henry L. Dawes (Republican, Massachusetts) accused Fitch of wanting to "butcher the Indians," and James A. Garfield of Ohio added that the "ballot, rather than the bullet of our friend from Nevada," would be the ultimate settlement of the Indian question.[23] To the Westerners, the ballot promised no immediate solution. John C. Conner (Democrat, Texas) claimed that people were leaving Texas frontier counties because of the President's Peace Policy, which prompted Fitch to suggest that the best Indian policy would be "to place in the hands of the settlers of the frontier the means of settling the Indian problem in their own way."[24]

After Degener denounced the Peace Policy and described horrible outrages committed by the Indians in Texas, Dawes complained, "We hear from every quarter this outcry and this attempt to put down by sneers and by ridicule the policy of peace and reason and humanity." The treatment that the Indians had received at the hands of those "who plunder him one day and then murder him the next"[25] was a disgrace to civilization. The allusion failed to squelch Degener, but he did qualify his proposal and explained that he meant to apply coercive measures to only those "savage fiends that cannot be cultivated by schools and teachers and the New Testament." He concluded by saying to Dawes, "The curse under which our frontier is now groaning was planted into our system years ago by the peaceful men of Massachusetts. You were the cause, we suffer the effect."[26]

In these congressional wrangles about the proper Indian policy to be pursued, the question of the opponent's intelligence and integrity often seemed more important than the welfare of the Indians. For example, in the House debates on the Indian appropriation bill for 1869–1870, Delegate Edward D. Holbrook (Democrat, Idaho) was censured by the House for accusing Benjamin Butler (Republican, Massachusetts) of making assertions "which he knew at the time he made them to be unqualifiedly false."[27]

The agitation for humane treatment of the Indians and the propaganda of the reformers did not cause the Indian troubles, nor

22. *Ibid.*, 731, 733.
23. *Ibid.*, 733–34.
24. *Ibid.*, 736.
25. *Ibid.*, 737.
26. *Ibid.*, 738.
27. *Ibid.*, 40th Cong., 3d sess., 1868–1869, Part 2, 882–83.

did it necessarily increase frontier opposition to the Indians, but blaming white people for the outbreaks of violence did tend to accentuate racial antagonism and to arouse emotional expressions of existing sentiment created by the situation itself. In this sense, Western reaction was similar to that of the Southern slaveholders toward the abolitionists. With the exception of the racial antipathy, however, the basic conditions were not at all similar.

The Indian problem was a direct product of the westward movement. The resulting contact between Indians and white people on the frontier became, finally, a struggle for possession of the land. It mattered little whether land meant hunting grounds and buffalo herds or mineral wealth, pasture, and farms. In either case, undisputed control of the land was basic.[28] Survival itself was often at stake—the contest contained all the elements needed to make it desperate and uncompromising. Where material aspirations, or even life itself, seemed to hinge upon government regulations and protection, the average Westerners were deeply suspicious of any change of policy that threatened their interests. They condemned the humanitarian theories of Indian management and feared what they considered the ignorant and misdirected efforts of the reformers almost as much as they feared the Indians. Most of them considered Army control, or even extermination, of the Indians the only realistic approach to the problem.

Most Plains newspaper editors, politicians, and average citizens were genuinely concerned about anything that might jeopardize the growth and prosperity of the region, and Eastern accusations that Indian wars served to benefit the settlers were, therefore, even more infuriating. A Montana settler wrote that he wished the accusers

> could be compelled to travel across the plains without escort, and have an opportunity of seeing the numerous graves, the burned buildings and devastated fields of the frontiersmen, and realize the terrible crimes which the red fiends have committed, and see the alarm and dread which prevails wherever an Indian outbreak is apprehended, then we should hear no more of their cruel falsehoods.[29]

During the debate on the formation of the 1867 Peace Commission, Senator John M. Thayer (Republican, Nebraska) asserted that "the people of . . . Kansas and Nebraska, and the Territories beyond . . .

28. Robert W. Mardock, "Irresolvable Enigma? Strange Concepts of the American Indian Since the Civil War," *Montana Magazine*, VII, 1 (Winter, 1957), 38.
29. *Kansas State Record* (Topeka), October 23, 1867.

dread an Indian war, because it is like an incubus upon them and their prosperity."[30] In the same vein, Senator Edmund G. Ross wrote to the Lawrence *Tribune*, "What we all most ardently desire is the immunity of our frontiers from the disturbances and devastations which have so effectually retarded the settlement and development of the West."[31]

The frontier image of the Indians as fierce and brutal "red fiends" was frequently accepted by newcomers to the region, even those who had strongly sympathized with the Indians. Mark Twain expressed such a change of heart during his journey to the Far West in the 1860's. Shocked and disillusioned by the sight of the Gosiute Indians of Nevada in their wild state, Twain, a confessed "Indian worshipper," concluded that he had been overestimating the Indian "while viewing him through the mellow moonshine of romance."[32] A. J. Grover, who traveled from Earlville, Illinois, to Santa Fe in 1869, experienced an even more pronounced transformation. After observing the frontier Indian problem, he wrote to the editor of *The National Anti-Slavery Standard* that the result was "as it would be with yourself and Wendell Phillips, my sympathies have changed sides, and are now decidedly with the settlers and against the Indians," who were "prowling, stealing and murdering continually." Describing the Peace Policy as "sickly sentimentalism" that was doing immense mischief, Grover asked, "How would you and Wendell Phillips denounce such a policy as against the Ku-Klux of the South? And yet the Indians are ten times as savage and bloodthirsty."[33]

More unexpected, perhaps, was the conversion of James M. Ashley of Ohio. As a young man, he had become so violently opposed to slavery while traveling in the South that in 1848 he had left the Democratic party to become a Free Soiler. Motivated by the same convictions, he had helped to found the Republican party in Ohio in 1854. He was elected to Congress in 1858 as an abolitionist and soon became a leader in antislavery legislation. After Ashley failed to be re-elected in 1868, President Grant appointed him Territorial Governor of Montana the following spring. Ashley was a courageous man who hated oppression and loved liberty but who permitted irreversible personal reactions to conditions as he saw them to shape his political principles. His travels in the South had led him to espouse the cause of the enslaved Negro, and his life in Montana,

30. *Congressional Globe*, 40th Cong., 1st sess., 1867, Part 1, 689.
31. *Kansas State Record* (Topeka), November 6, 1867.
32. Mark Twain, *Roughing It*, I, 132.
33. *The National Anti-Slavery Standard*, November 27, 1869.

where the Indians were actively hostile, convinced him that white settlers were the real victims of oppression on the frontier. They were not only the victims of Indian attacks but also the innocent targets of Eastern reform criticism. James Ashley and John Beeson were motivated by the same underlying convictions: Both reacted swiftly to the urgent need of groups they considered underdogs in an unequal struggle.

By the fall of 1869, Ashley had become especially sensitive to Wendell Phillips' frequent assaults on frontier people and to his declarations on equal rights for all races—Negroes, Indians, and Chinese. In answer to the reformer's theories of equality, Governor Ashley wrote to the editor of *The National Standard*:

> The Indian race on this continent has never been anything but an unmitigated curse to civilization, while the intercourse between the Indian and the white man has been only evil, and that continually, to both races, and must so remain until the last savage is translated to that celestial hunting ground for which they all believe themselves so well fitted, and to which every settler on our frontier wishes them individually and collectively a safe and speedy transit. . . . In Montana we want no more Chinamen or Indians or barbarians of any race;—we already have enough and to spare.[34]

Remembering Ashley's antislavery service, editor Aaron Powell was shocked by his condemnation of the Indians. In a sharp rebuttal to these "violent and illiberal sentiments," Powell expressed his fear that the "western atmosphere" was unfavorably affecting Ashley's political views and added that perhaps he was unfit for the governorship of the Montana Territory.[35] Shortly thereafter, Ashley was removed from his office and replaced by Benjamin Potts, whose devotion to the principles of the Peace Policy were less questionable.

The belief that the Indians were an "unmitigated curse" to civilization grew from practical frontier experiences, not imagined grievances.[36] The only way to remove this threat, from the settlers' standpoint, was to remove the Indians themselves, either by extermination or by their complete subjugation through ruthless military action and permanent confinement to distant reservations. In 1868, the *Kansas State Record* of Topeka had reminded Easterners that the frontier settlers "are not thieves, constantly striving for an Indian war, for the purpose of speculation; but . . . are . . . ever in the pres-

34. *The National Standard*, October 1, 1870.
35. *Ibid.*
36. Loring Benson Priest, *Uncle Sam's Stepchildren: The Reformation of United States Indian Policy, 1865–1887*, 88.

ence of an overshadowing and terrible danger" as long as there were Indians in the state.[37] Three years later, Governor James M. Harvey wrote Grant that Indians hunting buffalo south of the Platte had always committed horrible atrocities on frontier citizens. Therefore, he declared, he would regard such hunting, even if it had the permission of the Indian Bureau, as a hostile invasion of his state. He warned the President that if such an incursion did occur, he would work not only expel the invaders immediately, but also to punish the Indian agents who had been instrumental in bringing the Indians there.[38]

In April, 1870, a dispatch from South Pass, Wyoming Territory, reported that Indians had killed and "shockingly mutilated" six white men near Atlantic City and added, "Our people are loudly calling for General Sheridan or Colonel Baker."[39] A few days later, in direct opposition to the humanitarian stand on the Piegan Massacre, citizens of Georgetown, Colorado, prepared a resolution declaring:

> That war to the knife is the only way of avenging the many depredations that are daily being committed on the border.
> That we of the West, who live in an Indian country, are the best judges of what is slaughter and useless bloodshed, and that in our opinion the punishment of Piegans by Colonel Baker was well merited.[40]

A newspaper editor in Forth Worth, Texas, expressed his complete approval of General Sherman's policy of forcing the wild Indians to make peace and to respect treaties. "And he should be permitted to execute it," the editor added, "for it is in the interest of civilization and humanity, the only true interest of the white and red man—the antipode, however, of the impotent Quaker policy of President Grant, Cooper and Company, which has and continues to work so disastrously with the wild Indians."[41]

In spite of the possibilities of Indian attack, buffalo hunters, cattlemen, gold seekers, railroad builders, and homesteaders continued to move into the trans-Missouri West. The consequent need

37. *Kansas State Record*, in *The Manhattan* (Kansas) *Independent*, August 22, 1868.
38. *The New York Times*, May 4, 1871; James M. Harvey, Correspondence Received, 1869–1873.
39. *The New York Times*, April 4, 1870.
40. *The Weekly Colorado Herald* (Central City), April 13, 1870.
41. Clipping dated July 1, 1871, sent by Z. J. Dehiel of New Albany, Indiana, to Felix R. Brunot, member of the Board of Indian Commissioners, Bureau of Indian Affairs, Letters Received.

for more and more land for settlement and exploitation of mineral resources brought the new settlers against boundary barriers embodied in the stipulations of Indian treaties. The results were increasing demands for reduction of Indian territory or even for outright violation of the treaties. In February, 1870, Governor Campbell of Wyoming Territory went before the Senate Committee on Indian Affairs in an attempt to secure a modification of the Fort Laramie Treaty of 1868. He wanted the Sioux removed from lands assigned to them in Wyoming.[42] At the same time, the Kansas House of Representatives passed a resolution asking Kansas senators and representatives in Congress to use their influence to bring the "speedy removal of all Indians" from the state. The Kansans wanted the Osage Indians' huge reservation to use for railroad grants and to sell to settlers.[43]

Despite the repeated protests, petitions, and memorials against violation of treaties from the humanitarians and their organizations, the Sioux eventually were forced onto reservations in the Dakota Territory. In Kansas, the Osage tribe was removed to Indian Territory, and the vacated lands were opened to homesteaders in 1873. Besides outright appropriation, many ingenious schemes to acquire Indian property appeared. For example, in January, 1871, the Humanitarian Pioneers Association asked Secretary of the Interior Columbus Delano for permission to occupy and acquire title to land in the Indian Territory sufficient for the purposes of the members. The alleged objective of this association was to bring civilization to the Indians.[44] The Secretary quickly rejected the proposition, but the pressures from citzens and officials of Western territories, as well as land-hungry Easterners and railroad builders, continued to increase.

Agitation for the opening of the Indian Territory to white settlers had reached alarming proportions by 1871. In March, the Society of Friends reminded the government that it had accepted the invitation of President Grant to participate in the Peace Policy upon the condition that the government would guarantee "sufficient territory in which these people could be thus instructed and shielded from adverse influences." The Quakers added, "If the condition is to be disregarded and the floodgates of iniquity are to be opened upon

42. *The New York Times*, February 4, 1870.
43. Kansas House of Representatives, House Concurrent Resolution No. 26, Archives, Kansas State Historical Society.
44. P. Papin, letter to Columbus Delano, January 19, 1871, Secretary of the Interior, Letters Received; E. S. Parker, letter to Columbus Delano, February 3, 1871, *ibid.*

them it will be worse than useless to expect success" in civilizing the Indians.[45]

The humanitarians' opposition did help to stave off wholesale confiscation of Indian lands for several years, but as the government implemented the nonvoluntary reservation program, it gradually released to settlers territories that treaties had guaranteed to the Indians. Reservations were invariably much smaller than the huge areas granted in perpetuity to tribes through earlier treaties. Even the Board of Indian Commissioners and most reformers who accepted the reservation system eventually gave in to demands to trim down some reservations. They did see such transactions as practical moves wherein the tribes would benefit through the use of the money paid for the land by the government. When Quaker Superintendent Samuel Janney recommended that, if the Indians consented, portions of those reservations containing more land than the Indians needed should be sold at fair market value, he stipulated that the proceeds be applied to improvements.[46] For a similar reason, Felix Brunot, Chairman of the Board of Indian Commissioners and a conscientious advocate of Indian rights, found it expedient to talk the Utes of Colorado into ceding some 3,500,000 acres of land to the government. *The Denver Weekly Times* approved his action as a practical measure, and it pointed out that the ceded land included the San Juan mines, which were of "no great value to the Utes, but out of their bowels the miners will take fortunes."[47] These actions did bring about limited agreement, at least about the ends achieved, between frontier residents and reformers.

Frontier settlers' hostility toward the Indians, especially the hostility among those who had suffered loss of loved ones and property at their hands, frequently exceeded all reason. Blind hatred often led otherwise honorable men to abandon moral scruples, and to take revenge on the most convenient encampment of Indians, guilty or not.[48] A soldier in Chivington's command explained the reason for the ferocity of their attack on the Cheyennes at Sand Creek. The attack was retaliation for the Indians' slaughter of a ranch family who were particular favorites of the regiment. As he

45. Executive Committee of the Society of Friends on Indian Affairs, letter to the Board of Indian Commissioners, March 2, 1871, Secretary of the Interior, Letters Received.

46. Samuel M. Janney, *Report to the Convention on Indian Affairs of Friends, October 29, 1871*, 15.

47. *The Denver Weekly Times*, September 24, 1873.

48. Priest, *Uncle Sam's Stepchildren*, 88–90.

related it, a squad of the First Colorado Cavalry stopped at the house and "discovered the children laying around the floor scalped and their throats cut. Their mother laid there also, scalped, throat cut, body ripped open, and her entrils [sic] covering her face." Was it any wonder, asked *The Junction City Weekly Union* editor, that when that regiment came upon the Indians at Sand Creek a few weeks afterward, some five or six hundred of them were killed?[49]

The killing of eighty-five Apaches near Camp Grant, Arizona Territory, in April, 1871, by a party of white citizens and Papago Indian allies was typical of the extreme frontier reaction to Indian outrages. A shock wave swept through humanitarian ranks when Camp Grant's commanding officer reported that the details of the "late Indian massacre . . . are more horrible than at first supposed" for "more than 100 are dead or missing. All save 8 are women and children."[50]

The editor of *The Tucson Citizen* voiced the frontier viewpoint when he wrote, "The suffering and exasperated people have commenced the work of retaliation on the Indians. Their patience has been remarkable, but the killing of four good citizens . . . by Indians who had been fed and otherwise provided for at Camp Grant, exhausted it. . . . It is certain that the citizens of Arizona will no longer witness the murder of their fellows and the stealing of their property and tamely endure it."[51]

On the other side of the controversy, Wendell Phillips voiced humanitarian extremism when he declared before a Boston audience that "these ruffians of Arizona and these murderers of the Apaches shall be hung just as certainly as if they committed murder in the yard of the State House, or upon the very steps of the capitol."[52] Such peremptory condemnation of wrongdoing recalled Phillips' uncompromising attacks on slaveholders a decade past, and the reaction to him was much the same. On the frontier, as well as in the South, he had become a symbol of militant reformism. To frontier people, Phillips personified the maudlin sentimentalism of the Eastern humanitarians who loved the red race more than their own.

Influential Eastern journals often were not far behind Phillips

49. *The Junction City* (Kansas) *Weekly Union*, June 5, 1869.
50. Lt. Royal S. Whitman, letter to Capt. Thomas Duma, Camp Lowell, Arizona Terr., May 1, 1871, in *The New York Times*, May 31, 1871.
51. *The Tucson Citizen*, May 3, 1871, in *The New York Times*, May 12, 1871; Vincent Colyer, "Report on the Apache Indians of Arizona and New Mexico," *Annual Report of the Commissioner of Indian Affairs*, 1871, *Annual Report of the Secretary of the Interior*, 42d Cong., 2d sess., 1871–1872, House Exec. Doc. No. 1 (Serial 1505), 41–94.
52. *Annual Report of the Commissioner of Indian Affairs*, 1871, 40.

in critical judgment of the frontier population. *The Boston Daily Advertiser* blamed the Indian traders and the "hostility of the border people" for the Indian wars that made it necessary to keep the nation's elaborate military machinery in operation.[53] An editorial in *The New York Times* concluded that, in order to secure peace and protection for the Indian, while leaving him his liberty, it would be necessary to reform the whole frontier society, which was composed of "ruffians, who fear neither God nor man."[54] *The Nation* stated that the frontier population, "in spite of its many virtues," was "perhaps, the most ruffianly population in the world."[55]

When incidents like the Sand Creek and Camp Grant massacres occurred, military officers many times singled out the frontier people for blame. Here, the Army and the humanitarians were able to find one area of agreement. For instance, General Sherman emphasized the settlers' culpability in a letter to the United States Indian Commission in May, 1870. In it, he described the manners and morals of the white frontiersmen as the most important part of the Indian problem. The solution, he believed, was either to evangelize the whites or to remove the Indians.[56]

It was an exceptional reformer who could see both sides of the Indian-policy controversy. Shortly after the Piegan Massacre, Lydia Maria Child pleaded that white settlers "must be protected! . . . It is more than can be expected of human nature that the white frontier settlers, living as they do in the midst of deadly peril, should think dispassionately of the Indians, or treat them fairly."[57] When Francis A. Walker, Commissioner of Indian Affairs from 1871 to 1873, analyzed the problems obstructing the Peace Policy, he made an appraisal of the Western viewpoint that was unusual for one associated with the Indian Bureau. Using Arizona as an example, he admitted that the expressions used by the press and people alike created the impression that they "hated an Indian as an Indian, and have no humane sentiments whatever towards the race," but when the Arizona newspapers

> cry out against the Indian policy of the government, and denounce Eastern philanthropy, they have in mind the warlike and depredating bands, and they are exasperated by . . . the weakness and indecision of the executive in failing to properly

53. *The Boston Daily Advertiser*, February 15, 1869.
54. *The New York Times*, May 22, 1870.
55. *The Nation*, X (June 16, 1870), 375.
56. *Ibid.*, May 26, 1870, 329.
57. Lydia Maria Child, "The Indians," *The Standard*, I, 1 (May, 1870), 2.

protect the frontier. Indians to them mean Apaches, and their violence on the Indian question arises from the belief that the administration of Indian affairs has been committed to sentimentalists, who have no appreciation of the terrible stress which these Indian outrages bring upon the remote settlements.[58]

Walker believed that each side was seeing only the more extreme position of the other and that the natural result was disagreement about government policy and mutual contempt. If the existing records of contemporary opinions are any criteria, such objectivity was rare.

Other observers at the time, in analyzing the extreme positions of both Eastern humanitarians and frontier settlers, concluded that neither side was right and that the truth was somewhere in between. Samuel Bowles, editor of the Springfield (Mass.) *Republican*, came to believe, after a trip through the West in the late 1860's, that the "wild clamor of the border population for the indiscriminate extermination of the savages . . . is as unintelligent and barbarous, as the long dominant thought of the East against the use of force, and its incident policy of treating the Indians as of equal responsibility and intelligence with the whites, are unphilosophical and impracticable." Bowles, at the same time, was convinced that the Indians were destined to die, for they could not continue their barbarian life and could not be civilized. In view of such a certain fate, the editor concluded that "all we can do is to smooth and make decent the pathway to his grave."[59] Samuel Bowles, as far as the Indian was concerned, might be classified as a "humanitarian exterminator."

Colonel Richard I. Dodge, who participated in several Indian campaigns in the 1870's, thought that people who "believe the Indian is a supernatural hero, with a thousand excellent qualities" were victims of "sentimental prejudice, without foundation in knowledge or reason." However, those who did "firmly believe it is impossible to civilize the Indian, and argue that humanity and policy alike point to his extermination as the most prompt and effectual" way of solving the Indian problem were also wrong. Dodge, writing more than ten years after Samuel Bowles had, held out more hope for the Indians, but only if they were placed under the jurisdiction of the War Department, granted citizenship, and assimilated into the white culture.[60]

In 1871, the reformers, who were aware of the increasing crit-

58. Francis A. Walker, "The Indian Question," *The North American Review*, CXVI, 239 (April, 1873), 337–40.
59. Samuel Bowles, *Our New West*, 155, 158.
60. Richard I. Dodge, *Our Wild Indians*, 66–67, 651–53.

icism from the frontier and stirred by reports of the Camp Grant Massacre, became more deeply convinced that their labors were needed. Because the news of the massacre was late reaching the East, the various reform organizations that held their annual meetings in May did not know about it. In June, however, Vincent Colyer described the affair at a gathering of humanitarians in Boston, said that it equaled in horror the Sand Creek Massacre of seven years before, and denounced it as the crowning outrage against the Indians. Earlier, at the Cooper Union in New York, B. N. Martin, a professor at New York City University and a member of Cooper's United States Indian Commission, had called for prompt punishment of the guilty parties, and Phillips expressed similar sentiments in the Boston meeting.[61]

Since the perpetrators of the crime were civilians, the Army escaped the humanitarians' wrath. Colyer, Martin, and Phillips attacked the desperate frontier "ruffians," but Samuel F. Tappan, in a letter to President Grant, denounced the land speculators and the railroad monopolists in Congress. These self-seeking men, he charged, had not only repudiated the Indian treaties but also rushed "blindly and madly on, evidently intent upon robbing the Indian of every inch of his land" and killing the last of the Indians by the "cowardly and bloody hand of betrayal and massacre." Tappan warned the President that his "wise and humane" Indian policy must be made permanent and powerful by incorporating it into the laws of the land in order to prevent the "recent fate of the Apaches at Camp Grant, Arizona from falling on the remnants of the race,"[62] and he asked that a simple form of government for the tribes be instituted.

Meanwhile, prompt action by President Grant's special Indian Commission prevented, for a time, the eruption of a full-scale Indian war in the Southwest. After several weeks of ticklish negotiations with the suspicious and angry Indians, Vincent Colyer, Chairman of the commission, triumphantly telegraphed Secretary Delano in October that the President's Peace Policy was "most successfully inaugurated" among the Apaches of Arizona.[63]

While the special commission was pacifying the Apaches, the Board of Indian Commissioners, with the backing of the humanitarian associations, was putting pressure on the President and Con-

61. *Annual Report of the Commissioner of Indian Affairs*, 1871, 38, 40.
62. Samuel F. Tappan, letter to President Grant, May 25, 1870, Bureau of Indian Affairs, Letters Received.
63. Vincent Colyer, telegram to Columbus Delano, October 19, 1871, Secretary of the Interior, Letters Received; Woodworth Clum, *Apache Agent: The Story of John P. Clum*, 78–80.

gress to recognize the government established by the Indians of the Indian Territory at Okmulgee.[64] Self-government for the Indians had long been the dream of such Indian-rights advocates as John Beeson, Samuel Tappan, and Alfred Love. Grant, too, saw the value of allowing the Indians to operate their own territorial government as a step toward self-support and civilization. He expressed his approval and recommendation of the project to Congress on January 30, 1871, and again in his annual message in December.[65]

In the spring of 1871, the reformers learned of another alleged crime against the Indians. At Fort Sill, General Sherman had arrested three Kiowa Indians—Satanta, Big Tree, and Satank—for admittedly leading an assault on a wagon train and killing seven of the teamsters. Convinced that an example should be set, Sherman ordered the culprits sent to Texas for trial in a civil court. En route, Satank attacked his guards and was mortally wounded, but his accomplices were tried by a frontier jury and promptly sentenced to death. To the humanitarians, this sentence was a flagrant abuse of justice. The Universal Peace Union petitioned the President to set aside the death penalty so that no act committed by the government would counteract the successful operation of the peace movement. Upon learning that Grant had referred the matter with a recommendation for commutation to Governor Edmund Davis of Texas, the Peace Union dispatched an appeal for executive clemency directly to the Texas governor. In September, Davis wrote to Alfred Love that the sentence against the Indian chiefs had been commuted to life imprisonment and that "this was done in the hope that it would have the effect anticipated" by the Peace Union.[66] Because Governor Davis was a Texas Unionist and radical Republican who championed civil rights for Negroes, his concern for the success of Grant's Peace Policy was not entirely unexpected. It was particularly encouraging in view of Montana Governor Ashley's defection, the border Texans' antipathy toward Indians and humanitarians in general, and the attitudes of governors of other border states.

A dramatic and colorful tour of the East by a party of six Wichita, Cheyenne, and Arapaho chiefs soon overshadowed the humanitarians' success in the West. Encouraged by the success of the Sioux

64. Board of Indian Commissioners, Report on the Indian Territory Council, January 16, 1871, *Congressional Globe*, 41st Cong., 3d sess., 1870–1871, Part 1, 708.
65. James D. Richardson, ed., *A Compilation of Messages and Papers of the Presidents*, 1897–1917 ed., IX, 4073, 4106.
66. *The National Standard*, September 23, 1871; *Annual Report of the Commissioner of Indian Affairs*, 1871, 169.

visit the year before, government officials, the Quaker Indian agents, and the Indian-rights organizations all welcomed the delegation. In Washington, the Indians conferred with Department of the Interior officials about settlement of reservation boundaries. To their dismay, Secretary Delano told them, "We cannot stop this clearing of land and building of cities and railroads all over the country. The Great Spirit has decreed it and it must go on."[67] The disheartened delegation then traveled to New York City for a reception at Cooper Union. Peter Cooper introduced the visiting speakers and emphasized that the Indians' presence at his Institute was a practical illustration of President Grant's Peace Policy.

Little Raven, a stern-faced, stoutly built Arapaho, responded gravely that he had been waiting many years for the government to give the Indians their rights but that it had only sent agents and soldiers who had driven them from their lands. "The white man has taken away everything," he added. "I want to tell you of this, because I believe if you know it you will correct the evil. . . . I want my people to live like white people and have the same chance." Little Raven received cheers from the overflow crowd. The next speaker was Buffalo Good, a Wichita. Presenting a clerical appearance from the cut of his white man's clothing, Buffalo Good, with his fluent speech and graceful gestures, was the acknowledged orator of the group. He received a burst of applause when he described Peter Cooper as "the old gentleman who loves everybody," and he then told the audience that they should all be brothers. "The white people have done a great deal of wrong to our people," he said, "and we want to have it stopped. If you are going to do anything for us we want you to do it quick." He had often heard that the Indians had a great many white friends in the East, and now he believed that to be true. As friends, they should "stop the white men from killing the Indians after this. The Indian loves to live as well as the white man. They are there, and they can't help being there."[68]

The only way to save the Indians, answered William E. Dodge, was to place them on reservations and spend "a little of the money that had been spent in butchering them, to educate, elevate and Christianize them." The friends of the Indians, he pointed out, should "manufacture public opinion" that would support the program to civilize the Indians. Describing the "great crime" committed by the "depraved frontier population" at Camp Grant, Professor B. N. Martin called for the government to punish this "atrocious outrage on its good name and on its helpless prisoners." A resolution to

67. *The New York Times*, May 23, 1871.
68. *Annual Report of the Commissioner of Indian Affairs*, 1871, 32.

that effect was later drawn up and passed by the commission.[69] The audience cheered when Benjamin Tatham urged them not to cast a ballot for a President who "felt less for the Indian than did General Grant."[70]

In 1870, the itinerary of the Indian chiefs had been limited to Washington and New York City, but in 1871, Boston was included at the request of the Massachusetts Indian Commission. Therefore, the next stop for the delegation was Tremont Temple, where a large crowd gave the chiefs an enthusiastic ovation. Following addresses by William Claflin, Governor of Massachusetts and president of the Massachusetts Indian Commission, and Mayor Gaston of Boston, Little Raven, duly impressed, briefly remarked, "There are a great many chiefs listening to what I say tonight, and I want to say that I only ask for justice." Stone Calf, a Cheyenne who was colorfully garbed in his native costume, complained of nonfulfillment of treaties and asked why his tribe was "confined to this small strip of country that is left to us in return for the whole Territory of Colorado that belonged to us?" He warned the Bostonians that "you can't build railroads through our territory without white men being left among us on each side of the railroad, and they will come in conflict with us." He then implored the "white chiefs" present to "stop at once the progress of any railroads through our country, so that we may live in peace for a long time with the American people."[71]

In response to impatient calls from the audience, Wendell Phillips took the stage and launched into a defense of the Indians' right to resist the overwhelming pressure of the white settlers. No matter how ruthless be the weapon or method employed, he declared, the Indians were asserting a fundamental right in defending "sacred justice" and "sweet liberty." Phillips severely criticized the violation of treaties with Indian chiefs who never broke their word and fiercely denounced such atrocious massacres as the one at Camp Grant. He then implored his audience, and every editor in Massachusetts, to assure the President that the "justice of the American people . . . overrides the lines of party, and will not only save but lift higher the man who, risking office, trampling under foot party lines, forgetting all the greed of Indian rings, shall carry out the most perfect protection . . . to every atom of property and the most trifling right of the smallest Indian tribe."[72]

69. *Ibid.*, 32, 34; *The New York Times*, June 2, 1871.
70. *Annual Report of the Commissioner of Indian Affairs*, 1871, 34.
71. *Ibid.*, 36, 37.
72. *Ibid.*, 39–40.

The Indians returned to the western Plains loaded with gifts
and pleased with the kind treatment they had received from the
Easterners. In fact, they had been so favorably impressed, reported
the Board of Indian Commissioners, that they later refused to support the angry Kiowas who wanted to avenge the arrest of Satanta,
Big Tree, and Satank. Without Cheyenne and Arapaho support, the
Kiowas could not carry out their plans, and an Indian war was
averted.[73] With this accomplishment, 1871 proved to be a year of
positive achievement from the humanitarians' point of view.

In addition to saving the Kiowa chiefs from a Texas gibbet,
promoting a territorial government for the Indians, establishing the
Peace Policy in Arizona, and convincing the Indian delegates to the
East that peace would accomplish more than war, the reformers
worked to terminate the treaty system. They had long insisted on
the discontinuance of the treaty-making policy as a first step toward
bringing the Indians into the nation as equals and responsible citizens. Their efforts were rewarded by the Indian Appropriations Act
for 1871–1872, which was enacted on March 3, 1871. The act contained a clause stipulating that "hereafter no Indian nation or tribe
within the territory of the United States may contract by treaty."[74]
After 1871, the results of all Government-Indian negotiations became
part of the general statute law, after ratification by both Houses of
Congress, and were usually embodied in the annual appropriation
act.[75] The reformers were pleased, but most of them saw the change
as only one step in the direction of Indian citizenship. At a meeting
of the Reform League in May, Phillips, Lucretia Mott, Cora Tappan, Julia Ward Howe, and others endorsed a resolution demanding
immediate citizenship for all Indians.[76]

During 1871, the increasing power of the humanitarian Board
of Indian Commissioners led to the angry resignation of Ely Parker,
the Commissioner of Indian Affairs. He complained that the board's
supervision and control had reduced his office to a mere clerkship.
William Welsh had previously charged that Parker had defrauded
the government and the Indians. Parker was cleared by a House
committee, but persistent rumors that he was in league with the

73. *Ibid.*, 13.
74. U.S. *Statutes at Large*, XVI, 566. Also during 1871 the Board of
Indian Commissioners had supervised $2,000,000 in purchases by the In-
dian Bureau and had saved the government $457,816. Charles Lewis Slat-
tery, *Felix Reville Brunot, 1820–1898*, 186–87.
75. Laurence F. Schmeckebier, *The Office of Indian Affairs: Its History, Activities, and Organization*, 64–65.
76. *The National Standard*, May 13, 1871.

"Indian Ring," plus the expansion of the board's supervision of his office, led him to resign.[77]

Immediately upon receiving word of Parker's resignation, Grant wrote to Commissioner George H. Stuart, "I will be careful that no one is appointed who is not fully in sympathy with a humane policy towards the Indians. I will see too that he has the full confidence of the Peace Commissioners."[78] The reformers had achieved unprecedented influence over the conduct of Federal Indian policy.

By December, 1871, the success and permanence of the Peace Policy appeared more certain than ever. The Board of Indian Commissioners reported that it was confidently anticipating the day when the bitterness assailing the policy in those areas where it was least understood "will fill a page in history as unnatural and curious as that which records the old hatred against freedom and the friends of the slave."[79]

77. Arthur C. Parker, *The Life of General Ely S. Parker*, 155–59; *The Nation*, XIII (August 17, 1871), 100–101.
78. Ulysses S. Grant, letter to George H. Stuart, July 22, 1871, in Ulysses S. Grant Letters, George Hay Stuart Papers.
79. *Annual Report of the Commissioner of Indian Affairs*, 1871, 21.

7

Politics and Peace Parleys

The new year began on a positive note for the Indian-rights reformers. In January, 1872, the Board of Indian Commissioners called for a mass meeting of representatives of nearly all religious denominations engaged in the Indian service and other friends of the Indian. Among the latter were the secretaries of the United States Indian Commission of New York and the Massachusetts Indian Commission of Boston. Those who attended the meeting, which was held in Washington, D. C., heard encouraging reports on the progress that had been made in civilizing the Indians in spite of inadequate funds. The representatives unanimously protested the removal of tribes from their present reservations to those in the Indian Territory—an action that would virtually defeat the humane policy. Secretary Delano and Indian Commissioner Walker attended the meeting, expressed their sympathy for the civilization program, and promised to give it their "hearty cooperation."[1]

Aaron Powell described the affair as an illustration of the "true catholicity and good will on the part of the representatives of nearly all religious denominations cordially united in harmonious cooperation for a common end and a truly good work" and called on all humane men and women to help "checkmate the removal scheme."[2] Powell's wishes were soon fulfilled, for Indian-rights workers, who had joined together in an informal association, held several such gatherings in New York City during the following months. In February, the workers reported that the "demoralizing influence" of the soldiers, who were inclined to "strong drink and social vice," and the "absence of the restraints and protection of law," which permitted treating the Indians like outlaws, were among the greatest obstacles to Christian civilization of the Indians. Aaron Powell, Benjamin Tatham, and others prepared a memorial to Congress asking for

1. Commissioner of Indian Affairs, *Annual Report of the Commissioner of Indian Affairs*, 1871, *Annual Report of the Secretary of the Interior*, 42d Cong., 2d sess., 1871–1872, House Exec. Doc. No. 1 (Serial 1505), 185–86; *The National Standard*, February 6, 1872; Vincent Colyer, letter to Francis A. Walker, January 5, 1872, Bureau of Indian Affairs, Letters Received.

2. *The National Standard*, February 6, 1872.

passage of an act granting civil government and protection of law over all Indians who were willing to carry out and enforce the same within their respective reservations. This legislation did not touch on the more controversial issue of citizenship, but most reformers agreed that law and government were necessary if the Indians were to be civilized. In a bid for congressional support, the memorialists noted that their plan would reduce the need for troops and "save millions in annual taxation caused by Indian wars."[3]

The success of the Indian delegations' visits in 1870 and 1871 had shown skeptical government officials that the advantages of bringing potentially hostile tribes to Washington more than offset the expense. The Indians' impression of the "strength of the government, and the wealth and power of the whites," was a more effective peacemaker than many soldiers, declared the new Indian Commissioner Francis A. Walker. He explained that "it is at once cheaper and more humane to bring the savages to a realizing sense of their own weakness and the impossibility of long contending with the government, by giving a few chiefs and braves free rides on our railroads and Broadway omnibuses, than by surprising their camps on winter nights and shooting down men, women, and children together in the snow."[4]

Upon the invitation of the government, Red Cloud again visited Washington in the spring of 1872. He and twenty-nine members of his tribe met with government officials, who wanted to persuade the Indians to accept the removal of the Red Cloud Agency from its location on the North Platte River in Wyoming Territory to the Sioux reservation in Dakota Territory. Although the officials wanted the Indians to agree to the change, they were even more interested in impressing the visitors with the power of the government, because the Northern Pacific Railroad was approaching the buffalo hunting-grounds of these Indians in the Powder River country.[5] Military surveying parties on the Yellowstone River already had suffered several minor attacks, and the officials knew that the Red Cloud Sioux were the nearest reinforcement for the hostile camps in the upper Missouri region. These hostiles were mainly Uncpapa Sioux, one of

3. *Ibid.*, April 14, 1872. Representatives of the Methodists, Presbyterians, Episcopalians, Baptists, and the Orthodox and Hicksite Friends attended the meetings. The memorial committee included a Quaker agent, Benjamin Tatham, and Aaron Powell, editor of *The National Standard*.

4. Commissioner of Indian Affairs, *Annual Report of the Commissioner of Indian Affairs*, 1872, *Annual Report of the Secretary of the Interior*, 42d Cong., 3d sess., 1872–1873, House Exec. Doc. No. 1 (Serial 1560), 98.

5. *Ibid.*, 97.

whose leaders—Sitting Bull—was soon to be a byword for Indian resistance to white invasion. Their villages on the Yellowstone were a haven for the "bad characters" at the agencies and further encouraged a spirit of resistance among all the Sioux, especially the discontented young men.[6]

As in 1870, the Oglala delegation visited New York City and Peter Cooper's Union, where the leading chiefs addressed curious but sympathetic spectators. This time, Red Cloud was noticeably more conciliatory than he had been during his previous appearance. Instead of defiantly recounting the wrongs suffered by his people, he said that he would return to teach them "to imitate the whites," although he did wish the "Great Father" would withdraw the soldiers.[7] The other Indian speakers were just as congenial, but if the crowd had come to hear a dramatic and fiery recital of Indian woes, it did not show its disappointment. All in all, observed John Beeson, the public's reception of Red Cloud and the others at the Cooper Union was a "grand affair . . . the house was packed full and hundreds went away for want of room."[8]

The success of the meeting prompted the Indian Commission members to write to Walker suggesting the "desirableness of further employing the same means of reaching the public." They pointed out that a series of similar meetings held in the large cities would greatly help to spread the true state of the Indians, would interest the people in the efforts to save and civilize them, and would vindicate and support the Peace Policy of the Administration.[9]

Government officials needed no further encouragement. They firmly believed that personal conferences with dissatisfied chiefs, awed by the strange and impressive wonders of the white people's civilization, were working miracles that the old system of treaty negotiations in the Indian country could never have achieved. During the summer of 1872, six more delegations from Western tribes visited Washington and other Eastern cities. To discourage resistance to the building of the Northern Pacific, the government invited a party of nineteen Sioux from the vicinity of Fort Peck, Montana, and the hunting grounds of the Yellowstone River. Although those who agreed to come were described as "implacables" from the hostile

6. J. W. Daniels, Agent, Red Cloud Agency, report, September 15, 1872, *ibid.*, 269.

7. *The New York Times*, June 8, 1872.

8. John Beeson, letter to B. R. Cowen, Assistant Secretary of the Interior, June 11, 1872, Secretary of the Interior, Letters Received.

9. Benjamin N. Martin, U.S. Indian Commission, letter to the Commissioner of Indian Affairs, June 10, 1872, Bureau of Indian Affairs, Letters Received.

camps, the failure of Sitting Bull and other influential leaders to respond prevented the complete success that had been hoped for.[10]

Many reformers thought that the Grant Administration would be the most likely to continue the humanitarian Indian policy, and their views were an important new factor in the presidential campaign of 1872. The situation was complicated by the formation of the Liberal Republican party, the result of a reform movement to purify the government and make it one that the "best people would be proud of." Led by reform-minded liberals like Carl Schurz, Gideon Welles, and Charles Francis Adams, who had broken with the Grant Republicans over radical Reconstruction and Administration corruption, the new party secured the support of Samuel Bowles of *The Springfield* (Mass.) *Republican* and Senator Lyman Trumbull (Republican, Illinois), who had played a major part in securing passage of the Fourteenth Amendment. With the support of these well-known figures and with Horace Greeley as its candidate for President, the Liberal Republican party became a strong attraction to some humanitarians.

However, others saw defects in the party's platform and its presidential candidate. The Liberal party platform said nothing specific about Indian policy, and no definite commitments on the subject came from any of the party leaders. The sweeping plank that called for "equality of all men before the law . . . and equal and exact justice to all, of whatever nativity, race, color, or persuasion, religious or political" appeared to have no loopholes. Nevertheless, because the Indians had been excluded from the Fourteenth and the Fifteenth Amendment, many reformers were skeptical of such broad proposals embracing "all men." Although Greeley's long record of antislavery and reform activity had made him a leader among the humanitarians, his proposal of general amnesty for ex-Confederates and his securing the bail bond for Jefferson Davis had cost him the support of many of his antislavery followers. Many advocates of Indian rights also remembered Greeley's writing in his *Tribune* that Custer's Indian campaigns were "brilliant victories" and Phillips' condemnation of Greeley's advocacy of "extermination."[11] Further, Greeley's nomination in July by the Democrats, still the party of copperheadism to many Northerners, lowered his status even more. Finally, not one of the new party leaders had been actively involved in Indian-policy reform.

Even though a few prominent ex-abolitionists like Sumner and

10. *Annual Report of the Commissioner of Indian Affairs*, 1872, 98.
11. *The National Anti-Slavery Standard*, May 29, 1869.

Schurz joined the Liberals, most of them remained with the regular Republican party because of its antislavery record. Among these were Gerrit Smith and William Lloyd Garrison. More important, those humanitarian reformers who had a particular interest in Indian rights had, by 1872, accepted the Grant Administration's Indian policy as their own. Accordingly, the Peace Policy proved to be a politically binding tie, despite the lure of a liberal party whose avowed objective was liberty and reform. Lydia Maria Child wrote as early as January, 1872, that she thought Grant the best man for the Presidency. "His policy," she explained, "has been all for peace; and his wise and humane course toward the Indians has gained my heart."[12]

In subsequent correspondence, she reiterated her support for Grant. She objected to his cigar smoking and his military profession, but she admired his sincere love of peace, his "spirit of justice . . . on the colored people," and above all, his Indian policy. Her political stand brought her into heated disagreement with Charles Sumner. His campaign speeches, she believed, were "obviously unjust and I have, very respectfully, told him so. For instance, he refuses to give Grant the slightest credit for his humane policy toward the Indians, but curtly dismisses it as one of his 'failures,' because the 'massacres on the frontier still continue.'" To Sumner, she wrote that such warfare was a direct result of the manipulations of the "Indian Ring" and the "ruffianly Sheridan." She concluded that Sumner was "as unjust in charging this state of things upon President Grant as those were who charged the blame of the Civil War upon the *abolitionists*, when it resulted from the *slaveholders'* determined efforts to frustrate their exertions to bring about peaceful emancipation."[13]

As a labor-reform and temperance candidate for the office of Massachusetts governor in 1870, Wendell Phillips would appear to have been well suited for Liberal party ranks. Like Garrison, however, he believed that Greeley's election would mean the surrender of the Negroes to mistreatment in the Southern states, as well as the neutralization by Congress of the Fourteenth and the Fifteenth Amendment. When a group of Boston Negroes asked his advice on whom to support in the forthcoming election, after Sumner had endorsed Greeley, Phillips told them to remain with Grant. Phillips' reasons for this conclusion were not only his fear of the loss of Negro rights, but also Grant's "truly original, statesmanlike, and Christian

12. Lydia Maria Child, letter to George W. Julian, January 31, 1872, in Lydia Maria Child Letters, Giddings-Julian Papers, 1863–1899.
13. Lydia Maria Child, letters to Sarah Shaw, May 20, 1872, July 13, 1872, August 15, 1872, Lydia Maria Child Papers, Houghton Library.

policy toward the Indians."[14] Thus, he remained with the regular Republicans and helped to draw up the party's labor plank.[15]

Convinced of the inseparableness of the Grant Administration and the humane Indian policy, some humanitarians combined the promotion of Indian rights with political activity. Before a Republican mass meeting in Brooklyn, Henry Ward Beecher pointed to the progress made in the reform of Indian affairs. The Republican party, he said, had been one "signally characterized by progressiveness and a reformatory spirit. So it has been, and will, under the administration of General Grant, be the party of progress and reformation." To make these views official, the Brooklyn Republicans adopted a resolution praising the extension of justice and humanity to the Indians.[16]

A few days later, William E. Dodge spoke at the Cooper Union to a mass demonstration for Grant. He, too, praised the Administration's efforts in organizing and carrying out measures for the civilization of the tribes, the establishment of permanent reservations, and the "securing to them in perpetuity, as families, sufficient lands for agricultural purposes." These efforts, he said, were a marked feature in Grant's program and had "attracted the attention and sympathy of the whole Christian and philanthropic world."[17]

The political significance of the Peace Policy was even more apparent to John Beeson. In a letter to Assistant Secretary of the Interior B. R. Cowen, he suggested that "in order that the Republican Party may maintain its past prestige," a plank for the Indians should be prominent in its platform. He had earlier asked the Secretary of the Interior for money and permission to carry out a lecture tour, upon which he would be accompanied by a group of philanthropic ladies and a choir of Indian singers. The tour would introduce the public to the needs of the Indians and make it aware of the credit due the President for his "humane and wise policy." If he preached on Sundays and held mass meetings on weekdays in the "most 'Greely' [sic] affected states," Beeson assured the Secretary, he would be able to "get the sympathy of all parties and seem to be neutral in politicks [sic] and yet being [sic] doing the best work direct for the administration."[18]

In October, Beeson wrote Indian Commissioner E. P. Smith that although he was not a member of any political party, he wanted to

14. Ralph Korngold, *Two Friends of Man*, 375–76; George L. Austin, *The Life and Times of Wendell Phillips*, 282.

15. *The Nation*, XIV (June 13, 1872), 381.

16. *The New York Times*, April 11, 1872.

17. *Ibid.*, April 18, 1872.

18. John Beeson, letters to B. R. Cowen, June 1, 1872, June 11, 1872, Secretary of the Interior, Letters Received.

help the President "stem the torrent against the Peace Policy" because Grant should have full credit for doing his best under the circumstances. His plan, this time, was to visit the tribes in Indian Territory in order to spread the gospel of the Peace Policy. He asked Commissioner Smith for permission to extend the government's invitation to such "representative Indians as we may deem worthy" to accompany his party on a lecture tour of the various states. Even with Peter Cooper's signed statement approving the project, he did not receive either "pecuniary aid" or official authority to carry out his project.[19] Failure to receive the authority and financial aid necessary to carry out his numerous proposals to aid the Indians did not deter the aging crusader from his self-appointed task. To the contrary, his activities and his zeal tended to increase in the face of personal disappointment and hardship, and government officials and Indian-rights advocates came to regard "Father" Beeson with increasing respect during the 1870's.

Beeson was especially sensitive to attacks on the Administration's Indian policy. In two public lectures, Theodore Tilton, the editor of the *Independent* and a Greeley supporter, had charged Grant with full responsibility for the massacres and frauds recently suffered by the Indians. If Beeson succeeded in getting any political party to adopt resolutions approving Grant's Indian policy, Tilton warned, he would "tear it in pieces." Beeson advised his opponent to read the annual reports of the Indian Commission, and then he wrote to Assistant Secretary Cowen suggesting that he prepare a tract to "show up these false accusations."[20] A month earlier, at Cooper Union, Senator Henry Wilson, a founder of the Republican party who was soon to be its vice-presidential candidate, answered the Liberal Republican party's criticism of Grant. "They forget," he said, "that he has adopted a humane and Christian Indian policy, enough to immortalize any administration."[21]

The Universal Peace Union's leaders emphasized their support of the Peace Policy but judiciously refrained from entering the political battle on either side. Instead, they took all the candidates to task for concentrating on "personal venom" and for showing a disposition to "censure and condemn" the opposition regardless of the issues.[22]

Worried by political charges that Grant was contemplating a re-

19. John Beeson, letter to E. P. Smith, October 7, 1872, Bureau of Indian Affairs, Letters Received.
20. Beeson, letter to Cowen, June 1, 1872.
21. *The New York Times*, April 18, 1872.
22. Resolutions of the Connecticut Peace Society, August 16, 1872, Bureau of Indian Affairs, Letters Received.

gression to a more warlike Indian policy, George H. Stuart, a member of the Board of Indian Commissioners and a representative of the Universal Peace Union, wrote Grant for a clarification of future policy. The President denied the charges and told Stuart that "if any change is made it must be on the side of the Civilization and Christianization of the Indian." He added, "I do not believe our Creator ever placed different races of men on this earth with the view of having the stronger exert all his energies in exterminating the weaker.—If any change takes place in the Indian Policy of the Government, while I hold my present office, it will be on the humanitarian side of the question."[23]

This forthright statement completely relieved any concern among advocates of Indian rights. Alfred Love read Grant's letter to a gathering of 2000 Philadelphia citizens, and he reported to the President that they applauded every sentence.[24] From Iowa, an Indian missionary, L. S. Williams, wrote Grant that his letter had "called forth fervent thanksgivings from multitudes who believe that 'God has made of one blood all the nations of [the] earth.' "[25]

The presidential campaign of 1872 aroused widespread interest in Government-Indian relations, while the criticism of the Peace Policy by political opponents created considerable confusion in the minds of the voters. To clear up a growing misunderstanding about the use of force to establish a policy of peace, Indian Commissioner Walker explained that implementing the reservation system and repressing depredations required occasional use of the Army. He emphasized that this approach was consistent with the Peace Policy because the policy had two distinct parts: one regulating the treatment of hostile tribes and the other regulating the treatment of those tribes that were friendly or incapable of resistance. In defense of Grant's policy, Walker repeatedly stated that the "vigorous application of the scourge to refractory Indians" in no way violated the Peace Policy itself.[26] Despite the Commissioner's explanation, this part of the policy continued to disturb those humanitarians who took the word "peace" literally. Significantly though, even the most radical peace proponents gave complete support to the Administration's Indian program in 1872. Grant won the 1872 presidential

23. Ulysses S. Grant, letter to George H. Stuart, October 26, 1872, in Ulysses S. Grant Letters, George Hay Stuart Papers.
24. Alfred H. Love, letter to President Grant, November 2, 1872, Bureau of Indian Affairs, Letters Received.
25. L. S. Williams, letter to President Grant, November 14, 1872, Bureau of Indian Affairs, Letters Received.
26. *Annual Report of the Commissioner of Indian Affairs*, 1872, 4–6.

election by a substantial popular majority, and the Indian-policy reformers saw the victory as a vote of confidence for the Peace Policy. In his annual message in December, the President threw off his usual cautious reserve, proudly cited the accomplishments of his Indian policy, and declared that it had been as successful "as its most ardent friends anticipated within so short a time."[27] Commissioner Walker noted that prospects of success were "never more bright and hopeful than today."[28] Even a British publication, the *Pall Mall Gazette*, asserted that the U.S. government could be justly proud of the success of its new Indian policy.[29] At no other time had the future of Government-Indian relations appeared so indisputably favorable.

The tragic Modoc Massacre, however, seriously marred the favorable record of the Peace Policy in 1873. It had been several years in the making. In October, 1864, a treaty had been negotiated with the Modoc Indian tribe of southern Oregon, but unfortunately Congress had not ratified it until December, 1869. The five-year delay justifiably aroused the Modocs' suspicion, and when the treaty was read to them, their leader, Kintpuash—better known as Captain Jack—protested that it was not their original agreement. Captain Jack was particularly angry because the Modocs were to share a reservation with their old enemies, the Klamaths. With many misgivings, he did finally agree to abide by the terms of the treaty, and the tribe of 300 Indians settled on the Klamath Reservation. They had begun to build cabins and enclose fields for cultivation when the Klamaths began harassing them. Captain Jack complained to the agent, who promptly moved the Modoc tribe to another location, but the Klamaths continued their aggression. The agent's proposal that the Modocs make a third move was too much for their injured pride. In the summer of 1871, they angrily left the reservation and returned to their old home near Tule Lake, charging that the third location selected was a trap to place them in the power of the Klamaths.[30] Throughout the following year, settlers in Oregon increasingly complained of depredations and demanded that Captain Jack and his redskin "blackmailers" be apprehended. During the fall of 1872, reports of clashes were so frequent that the government issued orders for the

27. James D. Richardson, ed., *A Compilation of the Messages and Papers of the Presidents,* 1897–1917 ed., IX, 4154.
28. *Annual Report of the Commissioner of Indian Affairs,* 1872, 6.
29. *Littell's Living Age,* I, 5 (January 4, 1873), 145.
30. House of Representatives, *Official Modoc War Correspondence,* 43d Cong., 1st sess., 1873–1874, House Exec. Doc. No. 122 (Serial 1607), 5. Hereafter cited as *Modoc War.*

arrest of the Modoc leaders. At the same time, four companies of cavalry and three of infantry were sent to the area to protect the frontier and force the Indians to return to the reservation.[31]

When the Modocs defiantly refused to negotiate, the Army immediately began operations to bring them to submission. The result was full-scale warfare. After two months of fighting in the mountains and lava fields of northern California, the Army had nothing to show but a long casualty list. In fact, the troopers had seldom even seen the Indian snipers. During the last major assault upon the Modoc stronghold, 400 men, supported by howitzers, were unable to dislodge the defenders after a day's fighting and a loss of 40 killed and wounded. Colonel Frank Wheaton reported that the Indians were "scarcely exposed at all to our persistent attack. . . . One of our men was wounded twice during the day, but he did not see an Indian at all, though we were under fire from 8 A.M. until dark."[32]

Meanwhile, Secretary of the Interior Columbus Delano, Secretary of War William Belknap, and the President conferred and agreed that the war must be stopped. General Edward Canby was immediately notified by telegraph to use his troops to protect the inhabitants but, if possible, to avoid war. Delano appointed three commissioners and at once sent them to the scene of the hostilities. There, under the direction of General Canby, they were to take the "most effective and judicious" measures for preventing continued hostilities and to make "amicable arrangements" for locating the Indians on a new reservation.[33]

After weeks of delicate negotiations, the Modocs reluctantly agreed to confer with the commissioners. The tragedy that followed shocked and angered the entire country and touched off the first nationwide attack on Grant's Indian policy. On April 12, the Adjutant General in Washington, D. C., received a telegram reporting that the Modoc representatives had murdered Canby and Commissioner Reverend E. Thomas and severely wounded Commissioner A. B. Meacham. The Army ordered an immediate attack upon the Indians, and Sherman telegraphed the commander of the Pacific Division that the President "now sanctions the most severe punishment of the Modocs, and I hope to hear that they have met the doom they so richly have earned."[34]

As the details of the treacherous attack upon the commissioners unfolded, the public's anger grew. They learned that the victims,

31. *Ibid.*, 28–29.
32. *Ibid.*, 50–51.
33. *Ibid.*, 64, 65–66.
34. *Ibid.*, 77.

except Meacham, had been unarmed—the Indians had insisted upon this condition and had also agreed to bring no weapons. Also, the attack was premeditated and carefully planned, even to a diversionary assault under cover of a flag of truce upon the pickets of the Army encampment. The public's sympathy and inclination to mercy vanished.

The frontier population took full advantage of the tragedy to express intense opposition to Indians, humanitarians, and the Peace Policy. In Jacksonville, Oregon, the populace claimed that Secretary Delano was responsible for the massacre and hanged him in effigy. At Yreka, California, citizens demanded prompt extermination of the Modocs, and at San Francisco, the press strongly denounced the policy of dallying with treacherous savages.[35] In Denver, the *Weekly Times* exclaimed that when General Gillem "shakes the gory scalps of the Modocs at us we will give him three or four good cheers."[36] The Georgetown *Daily Colorado Miner* blamed the Administration's "experiments with the noble red man" for the tragedy and reminded readers that "western experience, in this and adjoining Territories, is decidedly against General Grant and the preachers."[37] Governor Horace Austin of Minnesota telegraphed the President that the people in the West "favor the decided policy in dealing with the Indians, the present missionary policy having no advocates on the frontier."[38]

While Western editors called for blood and blamed the Peace Policy, most Eastern journalists upheld the policy, although political sentiments strongly colored their editorial opinions. The anti-Peace Policy papers like the New York *Herald* and *World* and the Boston *Daily Globe* reiterated frontier demands for merciless extermination of the guilty Modocs and denounced the Indian policy and the humanitarians. The *Herald* suggested a new policy, "one that could be summed up in few words: 'Keep the peace or we shall kill you.' "[39]

On the pro-Peace Policy side, *The New York Times* opposed extermination but said the Modoc murderers should be hanged for the crime. The *Times* expressed fear that a severe blow had been dealt to Grant's policy, which he had "pursued . . . generally with such success."[40] *The Boston Evening Transcript* also stated the belief that punishment should be swift and severe, but it asked the nation to adopt "the calm judicial attitude which a civilized people should

35. *The New York Times*, April 13, 1873.
36. *The Denver Weekly Times*, April 23, 1873.
37. *Daily Colorado Miner* (Georgetown), April 22, 1873.
38. *The Boston Evening Transcript*, April 15, 1873.
39. *Ibid.*, April 14, 1873.
40. *The New York Times*, April 13, 1873.

maintain" and urged that the people "not hastily abandon" the Peace Policy.[41]

A Boston correspondent reported that in New York City, the news of the massacre seemed to shock the public "as no event has done since the death of President Lincoln," while in Washington, people had a "profound feeling of grief and indignation."[42] Government officials appeared to agree about the course to be pursued. Grant had immediately supported Sherman's policy of killing the offenders, not as an act of "passionate revenge . . . but as an act of justice as well as protection to the peaceful settlers." In an interview with reporters, Vice President Wilson said that the Modocs would be exterminated but contended that the Peace Policy itself should not be abandoned.[43] Secretary Delano also said that he would ask no mercy for the Modocs because the Peace Policy protected only the friendly Indians but punished those who were hostile. The massacre was an exceptional case, and in view of the past success of the policy, he did not despair of good results in the future.[44] These official views accorded with those held by the seriously wounded peace commissioner, A. B. Meacham. He had recovered enough by April 16 to write that "complete subjugation by the military is the only method by which to deal with these Indians."[45]

Many of the Peace-Policy advocates tended, at first, to accept without qualification the government's official viewpoint. In Washington, at a public meeting called by the Board of Indian Commissioners, General Oliver O. Howard upheld the Peace Policy but made no apology for the Modocs. He observed that although the President and the commissioners preferred peace to war, they believed in punishing both Indians and white men who broke the law. The new Commissioner of Indian Affairs, Edward P. Smith, told the gathering that he had overheard remarks on the street, in church, and in Sunday school execrating the Modocs and that even pious persons were demanding "kill the Indians who committed the crime." Smith then reminded his audience, "This act of atrocity should not turn aside the friends of Christian civilization from their beneficent purposes."[46] Ex-slave Frederick Douglass added that because of the Peace Policy, he now had hope for the Indians, but even if the In-

41. *The Boston Evening Transcript*, April 16, 1873.
42. *Ibid.*, April 14, 1873.
43. *Ibid.*, April 15, 1873; *The Boston Daily Globe*, April 17, 1873.
44. *The New York Times*, April 15, 1873.
45. Alfred B. Meacham, letter to Columbus Delano, Secretary of the Interior, April 16, 1873, Bureau of Indian Affairs, Letters Received.
46. *The Boston Daily Globe*, April 14, 1873; *The New York Times*, April 14, 1873.

dians became Christianized, he feared for their safety outside the protection of the government. Both General Howard and Douglass concluded that citizenship for the Indian would be a solution.[47]

Board member George H. Stuart agreed that the murderers should be properly punished but emphasized that the "act on the part of Captain Jack will not alter the policy of the Board."[48] Chairman of the board Felix Brunot, stung by the growing criticism, declared that the Peace Policy was in no way responsible for the Modoc troubles. "President Grant knows he is right in his Indian policy," Brunot asserted, "and those who seem to think they can move him from the right by personal denunciation, sneers at 'Quakers' and 'peace commissioners,' or flings at 'poor Lo,' the 'red devils,' and 'humanitarians,' may as well give it up."[49]

To support the Peace Policy, the commissioners quickly published a documented account describing the causes of the Modoc War. The Modocs had not received fair treatment from the beginning, and they had not been the aggressors. The Army and the frontier settlers, the commissioners implied, were mostly responsible for the situation. Finally, they saw behind the renewed attacks on the Peace Policy the "Indian Ring" and its speculators.[50] Although the board's analysis cited no new culprits, it provided important official evidence for the reformers.

Prior to the board report, some of the reform organizations had castigated the purported enemies of a truly peaceful method. Only a week after the massacre, the Philadelphia Radical Club, a human-rights organization led by Lucretia Mott, charged that the weakness of the Peace Policy was a "natural result of the war system." A general of the Army, Canby, with the Army at his back was not a suitable representative of the Peace Policy. In a remonstrance to the President, the club charged that Sherman's telegram expressing his hope that the Modocs "have met the doom they so richly have earned" was revengeful and unjust in its tone. The innocent members of the Modoc tribe, they asserted, were not responsible for the acts of their leaders. Therefore, the President should order a "merciful delay" before the Army carried out Sherman's summary punishment.[51]

In New York City, Peter Cooper's Indian Commission arranged for a special public meeting to be held at Cooper Union on April 30.

47. Ibid.
48. Ibid., April 15, 1873.
49. Ibid., May 4, 1873.
50. George Hay Stuart, The Life of George Hay Stuart, 245.
51. Philadelphia Radical Club, Memorial to President Grant, April 19, 1873, Bureau of Indian Affairs, Letters Received.

The purpose of the meeting was to protest the slaughter of Indians by "lawless" men.[52] The new American Indian Aid Association, also of New York, issued an appeal describing the wrongs done the Indians by both the Army and settlers on the frontier. To these advocates of Indian rights, the mishandling of the Modoc problem was "illustrative of the general mode of dealing with the Indians." They contended that Captain Jack and his band had not broken any treaties and had never killed white people except in self-defense or retaliation. They did not deny that murdering the peace commissioners was a treacherous act, but they quickly added that these killings were no worse than the government's treatment of the Seminoles.[53]

Lydia Maria Child supported these critical evaluations of the Indian policy. "General Grant has disappointed me," she confessed. "His Indian policy looked candid and just on paper; but he does not seem to have taken adequate care that it should be carried out." She, too, condemned the use of the Army and added ruefully that politicians seemed impossible to convince that it was not visionary to be guided by correct principles in the administration of affairs. The Modocs, she was certain, were the helpless victims of accumulated wrongs. It was "no wonder they turn at bay, in their desperation and despair."[54]

John Beeson also believed that the Modocs had been driven to violence by the white people's dishonesty and greed. On June 30, in a second meeting of the American Indian Aid Association at Cooper Union, Beeson said that most Indian wars were the result of the cupidity of agents and wholesale swindling by contractors.[55] The day before, he had written Indian Commissioner Smith that if the astounding reports of robbery and fraud in the agencies uncovered by President Lincoln's commission during the Civil War had been acted upon, there would have been "no Modoc or aney [sic] other Indian war."[56]

52. *The Denver Weekly Times,* July 2, 1873.

53. *The New York Times,* May 22, 1873. The refusal of the Seminole tribe to cede their Florida lands and submit to removal to Indian Territory in 1835 led to the second Seminole War, one of the most bloody and fiercely contested of all the Indian wars. Osceola, their leader, was seized by the Army while conferring with an officer under a flag of truce. He died in prison a few months after the betrayal. The Seminoles were subjugated by 1842, and the majority were removed to Indian Territory the following year. A few fled to the Florida Everglades, where their descendants still live. John R. Swanton, *The Indian Tribes of North America,* 140.

54. Lydia Maria Child, letter to Sarah Shaw, June 22, 1873, Lydia Maria Child Papers, Houghton Library.

55. *The Boston Daily Advertiser,* July 1, 1873.

56. John Beeson, letter to E. P. Smith, July 29, 1873, Bureau of Indian Affairs, Letters Received.

On June 4, Alfred Love offered the services of the Universal Peace Union to work with the captured Modocs. "We have among us some who would perhaps go out and live among them and would control and civilize them," he told Secretary Delano. Some of the members were confident that they could "manage this vexed question with entire ease." Now that the Modocs were helpless and completely within the power of the government, Love saw an opportunity for the nation to prove itself truly great by sparing their lives. He pleaded with Delano not to surrender any of them to the Oregon authorities, who would act "hastily and harshly."[57]

Love's fears of frontier summary justice were justified more quickly than expected, but it was not through legal channels. On June 6, seventeen Modoc prisoners, who were in government custody and en route to a nearby military encampment, were fired upon by men presumed to be Oregon volunteers. Other horsemen blocked the wagon road in both directions during the assault, in which three warriors died and a squaw was seriously wounded. Only the arrival of ten troopers prevented an even greater slaughter.

The news of this deed confirmed the humanitarians' charges that the "ruffians" of the frontier were largely to blame for the Indian troubles. As the Philadelphia *Evening Bulletin* observed, those persons "who have refused to believe that the Modocs were the victims of ill treatment from the government and the people of Oregon, may perhaps find in this wanton butchery an inducement to accept the truth."[58] Both the *Bulletin* and *The New York Times* demanded that the "white savages" be apprehended and then executed upon the same scaffold with Captain Jack and his accomplices.[59] The Philadelphia *Press* also denounced the perpetrators of the massacre and added that their "outrages upon Captain Jack's tribe were doubtless the cause of the war."[60]

The Indian-rights advocates were aroused by what they believed to be the prejudice that influenced the military and government officials' treatment of the Modocs. The doctrine of the brotherhood of all men and their equal rights before the nation's laws made them especially sensitive to any violation of these principles. Citing the Declaration of Independence and the New Testament as sources for their beliefs, they were certain that they were operating within the framework of universal ultimate truths. There could be no equivocation or compromise: If all men were to receive equal

57. Alfred H. Love, letter to Columbus Delano, June 4, 1873, Secretary of the Interior, Letters Received.
58. *The Evening Bulletin* (Philadelphia), June 10, 1873.
59. *Ibid.*; *The New York Times*, June 10, 1873.
60. *The Press* (Philadelphia), June 10, 1873.

and exact justice, the murderers of the Modoc captives should receive no less severe punishment than the murderers of the peace
commissioners.

Benjamin Coates of Philadelphia voiced this opinion when he
wrote President Grant demanding that the government exert the
"same effort" to secure the murderers of the Modocs that it had exerted to secure the murderers of General Canby and Commissioner
Thomas. "I do not ask . . . for the *'utter extermination'* of all the
border ruffians of Oregon, and the women and children belonging
to them. But I would suggest that the white murderers and the red
murderers have meted out the *same punishment at the same time.*"
Coates then asked Grant if he did not think it right "that no Indian
shall be punished beyond imprisonment—until the white murderers
are taken and punished with them?"[61]

Grant forwarded Coates's letter to Commissioner of Indian
Affairs E. P. Smith for his consideration. Smith, reacting to attacks
on the Indian policy, wrote to the Secretary of the Interior that he
agreed that " 'justice, Christianity, and the rights of man,' demanded
the punishment of these later offenders against law and life." He
added that the murder of the Modoc prisoners who were in the
charge and under the protection of the United States Army "was as
truly a violation of the laws of war as was the treachery of the Modocs
in the assassination of General Canby." Smith then asked Delano to
have the War Department secure the arrest of the murderers of the
Indians and to have them tried by the same military commission that
was then convened to try the Modoc leaders. Then, if the people
charged with attacking the Modocs were found guilty, they should
be punished "at the same time, and in the same manner as the treacherous Modocs."[62] Smith's letter got no further; Secretary Delano
ordered that it be held up. The matter was later turned over to the
United States Secret Service, but there is no record of the culprits
ever being caught or brought to trial.[63]

The murder of the prisoners may have been a blessing to those
Modocs on trial, for it did eliminate any chance that they would be
turned over to the local civil courts. As General Davis told the press,
the atrocity indicated that since the people thought the prisoners
were definitely guilty, a trial by civil law would be a useless farce.[64]

61. Benjamin Coates, letter to President Grant, June 11, 1873, Bureau
of Indian Affairs, Letters Received.
62. Edward P. Smith, letter to Columbus Delano, June 19, 1873, Bureau of Indian Affairs, Letters Sent.
63. H. R. Clum, letter to Secretary Delano, September 23, 1873, in
Modoc War, 329.
64. *The New York Times*, June 13, 1873.

The trial of the Modoc leaders by a military commission was set for July 1, 1873. In this instance, humanitarians were hopeful that sufficient organized pressure on the President and Congress would bring acquittal.

On June 17, Congressman J. K. Luttrell of California, after several days of investigating the Modoc affair where it happened, wrote Delano that he could only conclude "that the war was caused by the wrongful acts of bad white men." The Modocs, who had been forced to slaughter their horses for food, told Luttrell that either they could die of starvation on the reservation or they could have a "speedier death by the bullet in the lava-beds. They chose the latter." Although he favored hanging all those who participated in the murder of the peace commissioners, the congressman pointed out that humanity and justice demanded a thorough investigation of what might well be unprecedented corruption and swindling of the Indians in that area.[65]

Alfred B. Meacham, the wounded survivor of the Modoc peace conference, was convinced that "virtual acquittal or pardon" of the guilty Indians would lead to flagrant disregard of authority by the other tribes. By the same token, he pointed out, the white men who massacred the Modoc prisoners should also be hanged. During his journey to the trial, Meacham, who was representing the Indian Bureau, told reporters in Denver that he was still a firm believer in the Peace Policy. He added that "there are white men in California and Oregon more responsible for the blood of General Canby than Captain Jack himself."[66]

However, it was neither "bad white men" nor Oregon volunteers who were placed on trial before the military commission at Fort Klamath. After five days of examination and testimony, Captain Jack and five other Modoc leaders were found guilty of "murder, in violation of the laws of war" and sentenced to be hanged.[67]

The death sentences gave the humanitarians a positive goal—executive clemency and commutation of the sentences. On June 30, just before the trial, a public meeting had been held at Cooper Union in New York City to discuss those "important facts relative to the Modoc War" not mentioned in the public dispatches of either the civil or military authorities. Those at the meeting adopted a memorial embodying the conclusions of the gathering, and John Beeson presented it to the President. Declaring that the trial and punishment of the Indians would be a "farce and a tragedy, the truthful

65. J. K. Luttrell, letter to Columbus Delano, June 17, 1873, in *Modoc War*, 293–94.

66. *The Denver Weekly Times*, June 25, 1873.

67. General Court Martial Order No. 32, in *Modoc War*, 95–97.

history of which our posterity will blush to read," the memorialists stated that the "so-called Modoc War" was the consequence of misconduct by the whites and the government's failure to fulfill its treaty obligations. Therefore, they concluded, permitting a commission of white officials to decide the fate of the Indians was "extremely unjust." According to the memorial, there were only two possible ways to solve the Modoc difficulty: either an arbitration similar to that which settled the *Alabama* claims between America and England or the government's magnanimous confession of its error and restoration of the Modocs to their rightful home with full restitution for wrongs suffered.[68]

Neither arbitration nor such all-out magnanimity could be offered to the Modocs by a government committed to a peace enforced by its Army and a nonvoluntary reservation system wherein uncooperative tribes were considered hostiles and subject to punishment. As Sherman had telegraphed Canby in March, "Should the peaceful measures fail, and should the Modocs presume too far on the forebearance of the Government, and again resort to deceit and treachery, I trust you will make such good use of the military force that no other tribe will imitate their example, and that no other reservations for them will be necessary except graves among their chosen lava beds."[69]

On July 12, the officers of the Universal Peace Union met with Grant and implored him to retain his Indian Peace Policy and to "deal considerately and mercifully" with the Modoc prisoners. They pointed out that "few of the citizens or soldiers on the Pacific coast are in such a frame of mind as to dispassionately prosecute" the trial and that, in case of conviction, "there will be haste and unfeeling executions, which we most earnestly desire to prevent." The petitioners then expressed their desire to "speak early, before any conviction, in behalf of executive clemency, which we trust you will interpose in such an event."[70] A few days later, Lucretia Mott reiterated the Universal Peace Union's views in a "very satisfactory interview" with the President. Grant praised the workers in the peace cause and assured her "that all the condemned Modocs should not be hung."[71]

At the time of these conferences, no one in the East knew that the trial proceedings had been completed three days before and that

68. John Beeson, Memorial to President Grant, July 18, 1873, *ibid.*, 313–16.

69. General Sherman, telegram to General Canby, March 13, 1873, *ibid.*, 71.

70. Universal Peace Union, Memorial to President Grant, July 12, 1873, *ibid.*, 309–11.

71. Universal Peace Union, "Official Report of the Eighth Annual Meeting," *The Voice of Peace*, I (June, 1874), 36.

the sentences had been pronounced. The findings of the military commission did not officially come before the President for his approval until early August. After a three-week delay, Grant finally approved the sentences, but to the relief of the humanitarians, he stayed the executions until October 3, 1873.[72]

The Indian-rights forces quickly rallied to the cause of clemency. In Philadelphia, a public meeting sponsored by the Universal Peace Union resolved that until the murderers of the Modoc prisoners were arrested, the government should reserve action upon the captives and "not treat one more harshly than another."[73] Two days later, the American Indian Aid Association declared that in view of numerous precedents, a military court had no authority to try the Modoc prisoners. The association suggested that the present Administration preserve the "clean record of the republican party" by declaring a "general amnesty for the Modocs and their white aggressors."[74]

Throughout the months of July and August, the President and the Secretary of the Interior were deluged with letters and petitions asking executive clemency for the Modocs. Many people based their request upon the assumption that the trial was illegal and cited the Milligan case, a Supreme Court decision outlawing military tribunals where civil courts existed. Others maintained that, since Canby was killed while acting as a peace commissioner and not as an officer of the Army in war, a military trial was illegal. Still others thought that, since the government had habitually allowed its military commanders to violate the rules regulating the flag of truce, the Indians could not be held accountable for a similar action.[75]

H. Wallace Atwell, who had covered the Modoc War for the *Sacramento Daily Record* and *The New York Herald,* supported humanitarian contentions that the trial was biased and illegal. He testified that the Indian prisoners were tried without counsel, that the interpreter was unable to translate English idioms or even understand good English, and that the wrongs committed by designing whites, which would have mitigated many of the Modoc offenses, were not even considered at the trial.[76]

72. President Grant, Executive Order to W. W. Belknap, Secretary of War, August 22, 1873, in *Modoc War,* 183.

73. Alfred H. Love, letter to Columbus Delano, August 2, 1873, *ibid.,* 318–19.

74. American Indian Aid Association, Statement on the Modoc War, August 4, 1873, *ibid.,* 321.

75. *Ibid.*

76. H. Wallace Atwell, letter to Columbus Delano, July 30, 1873, in *Modoc War,* 323–24.

By mid-August, the humanitarians were confident that when the President heard all the arguments—particularly the one citing the doubtful legality of the tribunal—he would not order the death sentences carried out. On September 10, their optimism was partially rewarded when Grant issued an executive order commuting the sentences of two of the six convicted Indians to life imprisonment.[77] The fact that the death sentences were primarily designed to deter further hostilities by the Indians, as well as to assuage frontier anger, may have been a factor in the President's modification of the original order. The hanging of four convicted Modocs, instead of six, would not lessen the force of the example, particularly since the two Modocs whose sentences had been commuted were least implicated in the murders. On the other hand, Attorney General George Williams had firmly supported the legality of the trial by a military commission, and his decision was not questioned by any high-ranking officials, civilian or military.[78] The deluge of correspondence and visitations from Indian sympathizers, both individuals and organizations, undoubtedly influenced Grant's decision. After all, the Administration's Indian policy was one of peace and was based upon humanitarian principles. Finally, public indignation had cooled considerably by this time, and as Love had pointed out as early as August 2, many people were expressing a strong sentiment for leniency.

Grant's decision to commute only two of the sentences, however, failed to satisfy the majority of the reformers. Most of them were still firmly convinced that the Modocs were the outraged vicitims of the white man's cruelty and greed. As Benjamin Hallowell, representing a Quaker committee on Indian concerns, gently informed the President:

We will sustain thy action, be it what it may, feeling assured it will be the best that thy official duty to all concerned will permit. We may add, however, that if thy decision shall be in favor of extending *the fullest Executive clemency* to the prisoners, it

77. General Court Martial Order No. 34, *ibid.*, 98.
78. Attorney General Williams based his decision about the legality of the trial on the ruling that all military offenses that do not come within the "Rules and Articles of War" were tried and punished under the common law of war by military commission. He cited several precedents for this action and pointed out that the Milligan case had no parallel here. In the latter case, the courts were open and unobstructed for his prosecution (not the case in Oregon), and neither was the indicted a prisoner of war. Attorney General George H. Williams, letter to President Grant, June 7, 1873, in *Modoc War*, 88–90.

will not only rejoice our hearts . . . but we believe it will ultimately, when all the facts shall be disclosed, receive the warm
approbation of the friends of humanity throughout the world.[79]

Reaction on the frontier to these humanitarian efforts ranged
from bitter sarcasm to open hostility. An Oregon newspaper labeled
the peace commission a "wretched farce, that was conceived in sin
and iniquity, by a few Indian sympathizers." It warned that the people were becoming aroused and were now determined to "hold these
hypocritical Indian worshippers to a strict accountability for their
past conduct in this matter."[80]

Henry Ward Beecher's prayer at Plymouth Church that "justice, tempered by mercy, might be pursued, and that the government might win more by love than by severity" in dealing with the
Modocs drew an angry rebuttal from The Denver Weekly Times.[81]
Its editor observed that prayers for these Indians were correct only
"in the sense of the Ohio volunteer who in the War of 1812 prayed:
'Lord save the soul of that poor Indian,' and then plugged a bullet
hole through the body." He went on to explain, "We have very little
faith in prayer for the Modocs, unless backed by powder and shot.
. . . Therefore while the prayers are being offered, we trust Sherman
will remit no vigilance nor cease warlike preparation, but will strike
a death blow—if he gets a chance."[82]

A month later, annoyed by the humanitarian attempts to release
the Modocs, the editors of the Weekly Times sardonically noted
that although they had always thought the Modocs "murderers,
thieves and bloody devils . . . it certainly cannot be so, when we find
a parcel of civilized men preparing to try every means at their disposal
to save them. We begin to think that the Modocs are Christian gentlemen and ladies, and that the rest of us are cannibles [sic] thirsting
for missionary meat."[83]

On October 3, 1873, Captain Jack, Schonchis, Black Jim, and
Boston Charley were executed at Fort Klamath, Oregon. The re-
maining 153 Modoc captives were quietly and quickly transported to
Fort D. A. Russell in Wyoming Territory and from there to the

79. Executive Committee on Indian Concerns, Baltimore Yearly Meeting, Society of Friends, Memorial to President Grant, September 13, 1873,
ibid., 328.
80. J. Dany of Jacksonville, Oregon, newspaper clipping to Columbus
Delano, March 16, 1873, ibid., 271.
81. The Boston Evening Transcript, April 21, 1873.
82. The Denver Weekly Times, May 14, 1873.
83. Ibid., June 18, 1873.

Quapaw Agency in the Indian Territory. There, under the supervision of the Quakers, they were to be civilized and Christianized.
Although Alfred Love's suggestion of June 4, 1873, that the Modoc
Indians be turned over to the Universal Peace Union for civilization
was not fulfilled, he could rejoice that they were now at least safely
in the hands of the Quaker agents.

By the end of 1873, the Peace Policy, though badly shaken and
still on the defensive, had successfully survived its first real test. In
August, Felix Brunot was overjoyed to receive a letter from Governor
Benjamin Potts of Montana highly praising the "humane policy of
the President towards the Indian tribes." The Governor, who had
been appointed by Grant in 1870, lashed out at these people who
"declaim loudly against its continuance" and added that since the
adoption of the Peace Policy, the previous "frequent incursions from
hostile Indians" had almost ceased.[84] In another frontier territory,
Governor S. H. Elbert expressed the belief that Colorado had seen
its last Indian raid.[85] In October, General John Pope was able to
report that, "with very trifling exceptions," the Department of the
Missouri had experienced no difficulties with the Indians during the
past year.[86]

The humanitarians could still congratulate themselves in spite
of a few setbacks. The Commissioner of Indian Affairs reported substantial progress in Indian civilization and "increasing satisfaction"
in the operation of the agencies by the religious organizations in
1873.[87] The release of Satanta and Big Tree from a Texas prison—the
government's fulfillment of a pledge to the Kiowas in return for the
tribe's good behavior—thoroughly vindicated the successful humanitarian demands for executive clemency in 1871. The Army's part in
the Indian policy was still a sore point, but humanitarians could
point with satisfaction to the cooperation of Army leaders with the
various peace commissioners and, in general, with the Peace Policy
itself.

84. Charles Lewis Slattery, *Felix Reville Brunot, 1820–1898*, 212–13.
85. *The Denver Weekly Times*, November 5, 1873.
86. Secretary of War, *Annual Report of the Secretary of War*, 43d
Cong., 1st sess., 1873–1874, House Exec. Doc. No. 1 (Serial 1597), 42.
87. Commissioner of Indian Affairs, *Annual Report of the Commissioner of Indian Affairs*, 1873, in *Annual Report of the Secretary of the
Interior*, 43d Cong., 1st sess., 1873–1874, House Exec. Doc. No. 1 (Serial
1601), 3, 9.

8

Demand for Further Reform

The Modoc War and the murder of the two peace commissioners did not destroy the Peace Policy, but thereafter, criticism of Indian Bureau officials increased and more complaints about corruption from advocates of Indian rights occurred. In December, 1873, William Welsh, one of the organizers of the Board of Indian Commissioners and its first chairman, told Grant that the powerful "Indian Ring" had recently acquired great influence in the Interior Department. Welsh warned that if the "ring" was not checked, it would undermine the Peace Policy by destroying the confidence of Congress. This, in turn, would hinder the passage of appropriations needed to promote Indian civilization. Grant appointed a commission to investigate the charges, but because it had not been given power to subpoena witnesses or compel production of evidence, it accomplished nothing.

Welsh then presented his case to Grant again, this time in an open letter. The primary target of his accusations, now publicly revealed, was the new Commissioner of Indian Affairs, Edward P. Smith, who had succeeded Francis Walker a few months before. Before being appointed commissioner, Smith had been agent to the Chippewas of Minnesota, and, said Welsh, it was then that he began his fraudulent practices. As an agent, he allegedly had contracted for the sale of immense amounts of timber without the knowledge of the tribes who owned it, without competitive bids or advertising, and at half the market value. Worse still, only a fraction of the money supposedly paid for it had reached the Department of the Interior. Secretary of the Interior Delano and Commissioner of Indian Affairs Walker had approved the sale, but they now claimed to have had no knowledge of the details of the transaction. They had assumed at the time that the sales were legal. According to Welsh, Smith was still engaged in such fraudulent activities as padding expense accounts and making contracts without consulting the Board of Indian Commissioners.[1] The combination of contractors who made up the "Indian Ring," asserted Welsh, seemed to possess

1. William Welsh, *Indian Office: Wrongs Doing and Reforms Needed,* 3–7, 14.

129

greater influence in the Interior Department than did the Board of Indian Commissioners. He claimed that of one-half million dollars in vouchers rejected by the board as fraudulent, illegal, or irregular, nearly all had been paid by order of the Secretary of the Interior.[2]

In order to help eliminate the temptations for wrongdoing among Indian Bureau officials, Welsh suggested a substantial increase in the inadequate salaries paid the agents and the Commissioner of Indian Affairs. He further recommended that the Society of Friends be given control of the entire Indian service but that the other denominations be allowed to retain their present agencies. "There is a devotion to this cause in the Society of Friends that I do not find as marked in any other religious body," he explained, and he added that this plan would not only check demoralization and promote Indian civilization, but also save the government one million dollars a year.[3]

Upon Commissioner Smith's request, the Interior Department investigated Welsh's charges. It found no evidence of fraud, and when Welsh refused to support his allegations before the investigating body, the Commissioner was cleared. Nevertheless, Smith had lost much of the confidence of the Board of Indian Commissioners and the supporters of the Peace Policy.[4]

Welsh had resigned as chairman of the board not long after its founding because of what he believed was its lack of real authority over Indian affairs. This authority, he contended, had been illegally assumed by the Interior Department, acting through the Commissioner of Indian Affairs. In 1870, he had brought thirteen charges against Indian Commissioner Ely Parker, one of which was that he had exceeded his authority because he failed to consult the board. Welsh's attack on Smith appears to have been similarly motivated; in 1873, board members believed that their influence over the Indian Bureau was further deteriorating. As Chairman Felix Brunot's biographer described the problem during 1873, the board's recommendations were ignored, and the Interior Department did not submit many important matters to it at all. The President had supported the commissioners, but it seemed "even he was powerless in the face of the determination of unscrupulous politicians."[5]

The truth of the matter was that the Board of Indian Commissioners had never been granted any actual authority over the func-

2. *Ibid.*, 8.
3. *Ibid.*
4. Henry E. Fritz, *The Movement for Indian Assimilation, 1860–1890*, 153–54.
5. Charles Lewis Slattery, *Felix Reville Brunot, 1820–1898*, 219.

tions of the Interior Department or the Indian Bureau. From the beginning, effective interaction between the board and the department
was a voluntary arrangement that depended largely on the Interior
Department's cooperation. When Indian Commissioner Parker resigned his post in 1870, he claimed that his authority had been
usurped by the commissioners. His resignation was the beginning of a
growing official resistance to humanitarian supervision. This unfortunate conflict between the Indian Bureau and the Board of Indian
Commissioners eventually weakened the Peace Policy.

To preserve the board's effectiveness, William E. Dodge urged the
creation of a department of Indian affairs that would be "distinct
from and independent of the Interior Department, and an able . . .
man at its head."[6] When the President told him that such a solution
would be impossible because of determined congressional opposition,
six of the original board members resigned in June, 1874. After as-
suring Grant of their complete confidence in him and in the objectives
of the Peace Policy, they said that they could not continue a service
as "vexatious and arduous as it is ineffective in the correction of
abuses."[7] The board was not discontinued, but because the new appointments were political in nature, the reformers lost faith in it
and frequently denounced the new commissioners as tools of the
"Indian Ring." This change in the board did not eliminate faith in
the Peace Policy, but the advocates of Indian rights did feel compelled to keep a close and critical scrutiny over Indian affairs.

"Honesty and right dealing" had not been attained throughout
all parts of the Indian service, Alfred Love admitted, but enough
reform had been accomplished to demonstrate that through the "wisdom and justice" of the Peace Policy, the Indian Bureau could become as honest as any other department of government.[8] Love later
wrote that both Negroes and Indians were suffering "untold enormi-
ties" at the hands of the white people, and "yet the cry goes forth
against the victims. . . . May President Grant . . . stay the murderous
hands of our own people, and hold back Sherman, Sheridan [and]
Custer" in order to sustain the Peace Policy.[9]

Love was worried about the Red River War and General Custer's
Black Hills expedition. The outbreak of the Red River War in western Indian Territory and Texas involved the Kiowas and Comanches
of the Central Superintendency. The Quaker agents there had re-

6. Richard Lowitt, *A Merchant Prince of the Nineteenth Century*,
303.
7. Slattery, *Brunot*, 223; Lowitt, *A Merchant Prince*, 302.
8. "Indian Department," *The Voice of Peace*, I (July, 1874), 62–63.
9. *Ibid.*, I (September, 1874), 84.

luctantly called in the Army to round up their hostile charges, which gave the detractors of the Peace Policy an opportunity to demand again the transfer of the Indian Bureau to the War Department. The Black Hills expedition in the Sioux country of Dakota, Love thought, could create serious problems with the Dakota Sioux. The humanitarians considered Custer an Indian exterminator, and most of them did not change their minds, even after they learned of a letter he had written to one of the reformers praising the beneficial effects of "Christianity and Civilization" on his Santee Sioux scouts.[10]

In December, 1874, Bishop Whipple attacked the Administration's conduct of the reservations, where, because of "shameless neglect, the dishonesty of agents and the lack of any wise system of civilization the Indians are destitute and helpless." He warned Smith that the Indian question "will not keep down—at every turn it rises to plague us" and declared that it could be solved only by "justice and fear of God." Whipple then proposed that the existing reservation system be amended by granting every Indian who "gives up his wild life and lives by labor" an inalienable patent for 160 acres of land. Furthermore, the civil laws of the state or territory containing the reservation should be extended over the Indian residents in order to protect both white men and Indians and to serve as a first step toward citizenship.[11]

Although granting lands in severalty had been practiced on several reservations since the late 1850's, the titles had not always been inalienable. Under the Peace Policy, the plan was still on a small scale, but it was receiving increasing attention. In August, 1870, Superintendent Janney noted that the allotment of lands to individual Indians was well under way in the Northern Superintendency.[12] However, the lack of sufficient funds for surveying the lands, construction of homes, and furnishing farm implements, livestock, and seed had prevented the application of the system to more than a relatively small number of Indian families. Reformers and government officials had been working for the extension of civil law over the tribes, but they had made little headway with either this proposal or the one to have a territorial government for Indian Territory. Most congressmen still seemed to think that the education of

10. George A. Custer, letter to The Reverend S. D. Hinman, 1874, in *The Junction City* (Kansas) *Weekly Union*, August 12, 1876.
11. Bishop Whipple, letter to John Q. Smith, December 5, 1874, Bureau of Indian Affairs, Letters Received.
12. Superintendent and the Agents of the Northern Superintendency, Memorial to the President, Secretary of the Interior, and Commissioner of Indian Affairs, August 20, 1867, *ibid.*

the wilder tribes to civilization's intricate legalities was an unsurmountable obstacle to the effective operation of law and government within the reservations.

The humanitarians' criticisms of the Peace Policy and the Indian Bureau officials were, unlike the bitter assaults from the West, aimed at strengthening the program. On the other hand, their complaints about the flaws in the Peace Policy and their charges that officials in the Indian Bureau were corrupt gave the Grant Administration's political opponents an advantage that they were quick to use. Captain William Weir, who had fought under Grant at Vicksburg, wrote the President in 1874 that those in Wisconsin who opposed Grant "have made political captial [sic] by lecturing and writing on the Indian Question."[13]

Criticism of the Peace Policy did bring some results. In 1873, to discourage dishonesty and inefficiency on the part of officials and agents, provision was made for the appointment by the President, with the advice and consent of the Senate, of five inspectors to police the Indian agencies. That same year, Congress passed a law preventing the use of congressional Indian appropriations in advance of the fiscal year and requiring the remission of any unexpended balance to the Treasury.[14] Whipple and other reformers who believed that individual ownership of land by the Indians would accelerate their civilization and eliminate their dependence on annuities were partially satisfied by the passage of the Indian Homestead Act of 1875. The act allowed any Indian who had abandoned his tribal relations to obtain land under the homestead law that had previously applied only to white people.

John Beeson was particularly distressed about attacks upon the Peace Policy by "unprincipled politician[s]." To counteract their propaganda, the reformer volunteered to accompany "worthy representatives" of various tribes on a lecture tour through the major cities of the nation "until the close of the next Presidential campaign." Confident that such a tour would "induce a feeling of brotherhood between the races" and create sentiment for the President's policy, Beeson asked for official authority to invite the participation of selected Indians and for funds to finance the project.[15]

This was not Beeson's first request for official sanction to visit the Indian Territory in behalf of the advancement of Indian civiliza-

13. William Weir, letter to President Grant, February 2, 1874, *ibid.*
14. Laurence F. Schmeckebier, *The Office of Indian Affairs: Its History, Activities, and Organization*, 78.
15. John Beeson, letter to B. R. Cowen, October 9, 1874, Secretary of the Interior, Letters Received.

tion and the Peace Policy. In 1872, in spite of Peter Cooper's personal recommendations, he had been refused appointment as a "visiting commissioner" because of the Indian Bureau's lack of funds. In July, 1873, a similar request was again rejected for the same reason.[16] Still undaunted, Beeson held a series of public meetings in Boston, New York, and Philadelphia to gain support for his latest proposal to send a delegation to the General Council of the tribes of the Indian Territory. By December, 1874, even he was convinced that the aims of the Peace Policy were not being fully realized, and he wanted his delegates to convey the profound regret of the people of the United States for the failure of the government, the Board of Indian Commissioners, and the churches to protect the Indians from "cruel outrage in violation of the most solemn treaties." Finally, the delegates were to reach a mutually agreeable settlement with the Indians of all existing difficulties and to unite with them in a "common effort for human rights, well knowing that if we neglect or trample upon yours, we by so doing imperil our own."[17]

At the Universalist Church in Philadelphia, Beeson told his audience that the "present widespread demoralization in every walk of life is but the harvest from the seed which has been liberally sown in our dealings with the Indians" and declared that the first step in national reform should be complete recognition of the Indians' equal rights.[18] In December, 1874, he wrote to Indian Commissioner Smith and Secretary of State Hamilton Fish explaining that he had already made arrangements to start for the Indian Territory with a delegation of "three Gentlemen and three Ladies so that by Christmas we may present . . . the Spirit of the Gospel of Peace on earth and good will to Men (Indians included)." He reminded Smith that although he had labored for Indian rights for twenty-one years, he had received no money from the government. His urgent plea that now "in behalf of Peace I want help" proved of no avail, and again his appeals were officially rejected.[19]

While Beeson was campaigning for his peace delegation, cther humanitarians were also lecturing in behalf of Indian rights. In May, 1874, at Wendell Phillips' invitation, Alfred B. Meacham, who had

16. John Beeson, letter to John Q. Smith, June 25, 1873, Bureau of Indian Affairs, Letters Received; John Q. Smith, letter to John Beeson, July 7, 1873, Bureau of Indian Affairs, Letters Sent.
17. *The Evening Bulletin* (Philadelphia), December 9, 1874.
18. *Ibid.*
19. John Beeson, letter to John Q. Smith, December 11, 1874, Bureau of Indian Affairs, Letters Received; John Beeson, letter to Hamilton Fish, December 14, 1874, *ibid.*

been wounded during the Modoc attack on the peace commissioners, spoke at Park Street Church in Boston. He described his experiences in the Modoc affair and emphasized the injustices suffered by Captain Jack's rebellious band. Phillips observed, "Never before have we had just such a witness upon the stand. Covered all over with wounds received at the hands of the Indians; having suffered all that man can suffer and still live—that he should yet lift up his voice in their behalf, affords a marvelous instance of fidelity to principle, against every temptation and injury."[20] In a letter to E. S. Tobey, Phillips wrote of Meacham, "I think his entrance next winter on [a] wide lecture tour with this for a topic will largely help our question."[21]

Meacham was born in 1826 in Indiana. His parents had moved there from North Carolina because they abhorred slavery. At the age of nineteen, he had helped to move the Sac and Fox Indians to the reservation assigned them after the Black Hawk War. This experience generated his interest in the Indians and his admiration for them. Later, after he had successfully prospected for gold in California, he married and settled in the Blue Mountain region of Oregon.[22] Meacham was a Republican who backed Grant in 1868, enthusiastically endorsed the Peace Policy, and conferred with the President on Indian management in the spring of 1869. He was then appointed Superintendent of Indian Affairs for Oregon and became involved in the Modoc negotiations. Meacham served as a presidential elector from Oregon in 1872, and by 1874, he was becoming politically prominent in the Northwest. His work "for a friendless race and a bad cause" was proof enough to Westerners that he had gone completely crazy, and it cost him a promising political career.

Meacham's speech in Boston's Park Street Church was only the beginning of his career as an active proponent of Indian rights. He was an eloquent and effective speaker who frequently delivered his lecture on the Modoc tragedy during 1874. In addition to his lectures, Meacham compiled a thick volume that described government relations with the northwestern tribes through the Modoc War and presented his solutions to the Indian problem. "We must recognize the manhood of the Indian," Meacham wrote, "treating him *as a man*, dealing justly and fairly with him, redressing his wrongs, while punishing him for his crimes." Hatred of Indians and a desire for revenge had to be "buried in a common grave," while the people of

20. Theodore A. Bland, *Life of Alfred B. Meacham*, 3.
21. Wendell Phillips, letter to E. S. Tobey, June 30, 1874, in Wendell Phillips Letters, George Hay Stuart Papers.
22. Bland, *Meacham*, 3–7.

the United States should "gather up and care for these people" and uphold the humane policy.[23] In the Introduction to Meacham's book, Wendell Phillips praised the author for trying to reverse the "hideous current of national indifference and injustice" and predicted that the book would do much to vindicate the President's policy.[24]

In the spring of 1875, Meacham brought a delegation of Modoc and Klamath Indians to Philadelphia, where they spoke to a meeting of Alfred Love's Universal Peace Union. In a manner reminiscent of Red Cloud, one Modoc warrior proudly said that the Great Spirit had given this country to the Indians. "Perhaps he intended the white man should be superior to the Indian," he added, "but I do not look at it just that way. We think the Great Spirit made us all; we are all one people, one blood."[25] Meacham and his Indian delegation appeared before Peter Cooper's Indian Commission and other East Coast audiences during the spring and summer of 1875. Motivated by what he described as a "religious conviction of duty, to dispel the animosity against these Indians,"[26] Meacham seldom refused an opportunity to speak. His schedule proved too demanding, and before the end of the year, he suffered a physical breakdown, followed by a nearly fatal illness. By the spring of 1876, he had regained enough strength to continue his crusade for Indian rights. During the next two years, he averaged five lectures a week in the churches of the New York and New England area.[27]

Although Meacham had the sympathetic support of the press, he, like John Beeson, found working for Indian rights distressingly unremunerative. The worker himself had to bear a considerable portion of the expense, in spite of the collections that were often taken and the regular contributions of such interested parties as E. S. Tobey, Wendell Phillips, and the Massachusetts Indian Commission. For example, in May, 1876, the expenses of a meeting at Tremont Temple were more than $100 and were paid by Meacham. His second lecture in Park Street Church cost $50, but it was paid by Tobey and Phillips.[28] By the end of 1875, Beeson had worked for Indian rights for nearly twenty years, but during that time, he had received only

23. Alfred B. Meacham, *Wigwam and War-Path; or the Royal Chief in Chains*, 681–83.
24. *Ibid.*
25. "Interview of the Peace Society with the Modoc and Klamath Indians," *The Voice of Peace*, II (May, 1875), 23.
26. *Ibid.*, 22.
27. Bland, *Meacham*, 8–9.
28. Wendell Phillips, letter to E. S. Tobey, May 31, 1876, in Wendell Phillips Letters, George Hay Stuart Papers.

$2,350. Most of this money, which came from churches, humanitarians like Peter Cooper and Gerrit Smith, and public officials like Senator William Sprague (Republican, Rhode Island),[29] paid only a fraction of the total expense. If men like Meacham, Beeson, and Phillips were "professional philanthropists," a label that was frequently applied in derision by enemies of reform, it could hardly be charged that they had taken up the profession for the wealth to be gained.

While Meacham was speaking in New England about the Modoc tragedy, Wendell Phillips was also giving frequent lectures on the Indian problem. He believed that Grant's policy embodied correct principles, but he thought that it had not yet come up to them. Phillips and many of his colleagues could not reconcile the use of the Army with a policy of peace and justice. He spoke about this inconsistency repeatedly, drawing striking contrasts between the English policy in Canada and the system in the United States. In Canada, a white man could "vault into the saddle and ride from Montreal to the Pacific without a pistol,—where civilization had adopted the Indians as fast as they were reached,—and where the Crown had spent nothing for a hundred years for blood and spoilation." On the other hand, he declared, the United States had spent millions, "only to place our Government on a level with the barbarians it condemned."[30]

Phillips also influenced the appointment of Indian agents who supported the Peace Policy. In November, 1875, he asked Tobey, a member of the Board of Indian Commissioners, to recommend to the President the appointment of Samuel F. Tappan as an agent. "All Grant wants," Phillips surmised, "is some one [sic] to back him up and let him feel he is supported in such an appointment. . . . Grant means well but politicians bear on him hardly."[31]

In the November, 1875, meeting of the Universal Peace Union, Lucretia Mott reported a case of injustice involving the Temecula tribe of the Mission Indians in southern California. She said that white men had driven them from their lands and had then acquired the title. The tribal chief had recently journeyed to Washington to request immediate relief for his people and ask that provision be

29. John Beeson, Address: To the People of the United States, September 23, 1875, Bureau of Indian Affairs, Letters Received.

30. Carlos Martyn, *Wendell Phillips: the Agitator*, 415–16; Wendell Phillips, "Extracts from an Address by Wendell Phillips, at the Academy of Music, Philadelphia," *The Voice of Peace*, II (December, 1875), 141–43.

31. Wendell Phillips, letter to E. S. Tobey, November 8, 1875, in Wendell Phillips Letters, George Hay Stuart Papers.

made for the other Mission Indians who had been dispossessed. Mrs. Mott's publicizing the mistreatment of the Mission Indians eventually led to a concerted attack on the problem.[32]

Otherwise, by the end of 1875, the humanitarians' criticism of the operation of the Peace Policy was diminishing. They made fewer charges of corruption after John Q. Smith replaced Edward P. Smith as Indian Commissioner, and they were even more reassured when they heard about President Grant's promise to a delegation of clergymen. The Peace Policy, he told them, would not be abandoned while he was President and that "it was his hope that, during his administration, it would be so firmly established as to become the necessary policy of his successor."[33]

The reports of satisfactory progress in the civilization of the Indians convinced many critics that they had been mistaken. To support its contention that the civilization of the Indians was not only practicable but was "fairly under way," the Indian Bureau reported that over 42,500 male Indians were undertaking self-support; that over 329,000 acres were under cultivation, a gain of 200,000 acres in five years; and that nearly 10,600 Indian children were attending school. These statistics revealed that the program was accomplishing more than its critics had recognized and more than the rumors of corruption and treaty violations would have indicated. However, the Commissioner warned, without the sympathy and cooperation of the "best citizens of the country" the efforts for civilizing the Indians would be abandoned.[34]

Bishop Whipple, now fully convinced, wrote Grant that "notwithstanding all the claims which have been made the Peace Policy has been a marked success. No act of any President will stand out in brighter relief on the pages of history than your kindness to a perishing race. When this change was made an honest agent was a rare exception. . . . For all this you are held in esteem by thousands of the best men in America. I cannot find words to express my own deep sense of obligation for your perseverance when a less brave man would have faltered."[35] In December, Lydia Maria Child wrote that she liked the President's annual message. "It is characterized by just

32. *The Voice of Peace*, II (December, 1875), 143.

33. *Ibid.*, 144.

34. Commissioner of Indian Affairs, *Annual Report of the Commissioner of Indian Affairs, 1875, Annual Report of the Secretary of the Interior*, 44th Cong., 1st sess., 1875–1876, House Exec. Doc. No. 1 (Serial 1680), 3, 4, 22.

35. Bishop Whipple, letter to President Grant, November 11, 1875, Bureau of Indian Affairs, Letters Received.

and humane sentiments. His course with regard to the Indians particularly pleases me. If such a policy had been instituted years ago, how much bloodshed and money might have been saved!"[36]

The letters of praise were almost immediately followed by other reformers' attacks on the Peace Policy. Their goal was to bring the entire Indian program closer to the humanitarian ideal, and they were afraid that Congress might pass an amendment transferring the Indian Bureau to the War Department.

One of the strongest requests for more reform came early in 1876 from the New York Indian Peace Commission. This new organization may have been affiliated with Peter Cooper's United States Indian Commission, for Cooper, Chancellor Howard Crosby, Profesor B. N. Martin of New York University, and Reverend J. M. Ferris, Secretary of the Board of Missions of the Reformed Church, belonged to both groups. In a pamphlet entitled *A Thorough Digest of the Indian Question*, the Indian Peace Commission insisted that the Indian problem was not yet solved, despite many years of labor, the expenditure of large amounts of money, and the trial of various expedients. They charged that both government officials and philanthropists were guilty of not devising definite, comprehensive measures based on correct principles. The commission then presented for congressional action a bill embodying a detailed program for final solution of the Indian problem. It based its plan on the use of reservations, but these were to be subdivided and adapted to the number of Indians on each reservation and their habits. Thus, each tribe could retain its separate organization until proper education would enable its members to assume the responsibilities of citizenship. Furthermore, facilities would be provided to enable them to become self-supporting as soon as possible, and a system of self-government, courts, and laws would be established.[37]

The New York reformers warned that "no worse fate could befall the Red Man than his transfer to the military." Such a calamity, they maintained, could be prevented if the press, the churches, private citizens, and public officials, as well as all humanitarians, would urge Congress to pass the New York Peace Commission's bill.[38]

In 1871, Colonel Baker's ill-timed attack had led to the defeat of a transfer clause in the Army appropriation bill, but the Modoc War had revived interest in the transfer issue, and at one time, Con-

36. Lydia Maria Child, letter to Sarah Shaw, December 6, 1875, Lydia Maria Child Papers, Houghton Library.
37. New York Indian Peace Commission, *A Thorough Digest of the Indian Question*, 1–3.
38. *Ibid.*, 2.

gress seemed ready to approve the change. The humanitarians again responded. In February, 1874, Alfred Love wrote Secretary of the Interior Delano expressing the Peace Union's strong opposition to control by the War Department.[39] Delano needed no encouragement; he was committed to the Peace Policy. Grant, the Senate, and the Indian Bureau also opposed Army control. The Commissioner of Indian Affairs declared in his report of November, 1875, that the decision depended on what was to be the future treatment of the Indians: "If we intend to have war with them, the Bureau should go to the Secretary of War. If we intend to have peace, it should be in the civil department." The policy of civilization, he added, would be "materially hindered by the presence and example of soldiers," for a standing army and an Indian agency had no common end in view.[40]

With only the House, the War Department, and white people on the frontier favoring transfer, the attempt again failed, but proponents of War Department control were not easily discouraged. In April, 1876, the House again passed a bill that was to go into effect the following July. Under its provisions, Army officers were to take charge of Indian affairs, and the commanders of the various departments were to be the ex officio heads of Indian administration within their respective jurisdictions. This bill recognized a growing competition between Protestants and Catholics for control of certain agencies and stipulated that all religious sects were to have equal rights in the Indian reservations.[41]

Despite the charges of official corruption that the House had brought against Secretary of War Belknap in March, the transfer movement rapidly gained strength. This trend toward control by the War Department may have been influenced by William Welsh's surprising plea in favor of transfer. Welsh was a perfectionist who had demonstrated his impatience for reform by suddenly resigning from the Board of Indian Commissioners because he thought it did not have enough power to accomplish its purpose. His subsequent investigations of Indian Bureau officials and the government's seeming reluctance to respond to his revelations of corruption may have influenced his decision to support transfer. At any rate, Welsh was the only reformer who did.

On May 22, Felix Brunot wrote William E. Dodge that he knew of no "prominent working friend of the Indians who agrees with Mr.

39. Alfred H. Love, letter to Columbus Delano, February 11, 1874, Bureau of Indian Affairs, Letters Received.
40. *Annual Report of the Commissioner of Indian Affairs*, 1875, 18–19.
41. *The Nation*, XXII (April 27, 1876), 269.

Welsh in his recommendation of the transfer." Furthermore, military control was opposed by every religious denomination working among the Indians. "I am fully convinced," Brunot concluded, "that the transfer would not be in the interest, either of justice, economy, humanity, civilization, Christianity, or even honesty of administration."[42] His letter was published in all the leading papers of the East to offset Welsh's highly publicized proposal.

Bishop Whipple warned the new Secretary of the Interior, Zachary Chandler, that Army control would be nothing less than outright condemnation of the Peace Policy. "The change of the Bureau now," he wrote, "will entail on us untold evil & cost millions in war."[43] In June, the Board of Foreign Missions of the Reformed Church of New York informed Chandler that their own experience in operating an Indian agency under the Peace Policy had shown them the wisdom of civil management, and they added, "Any change therein is earnestly deprecated."[44]

Congressmen lined up on the transfer bill, in the spring of 1876, in close proximity to their previous stands on the Peace Policy. However, those who did change seemed to be politically motivated—at this point, more Republicans opposed transfer, and more Democrats favored it. Although proponents had enough strength to get the bill through the House, they lost in the Senate. They would again raise the issue later in the year.

According to Indian Commissioner Smith, 1875 "should have been marked for bloody conflicts," but it had been one of the quietest on the western Plains in a long time.[45] Relative peace had come despite the settlers and cattlemen who were surrounding the reservations, hide hunters who were slaughtering the buffalo herds, gold seekers who were swarming over the Black Hills, and a network of railroads that was being constructed throughout the West. Many people believed that placing the Indians on reservations and instituting the civilization program had greatly reduced the chances of large-scale warfare.

However, real peace depended upon the cooperation of all the tribes in the government's program, and such complete harmony was not yet the case. In his annual report, Commissioner Smith noted that the government would probably try to compel the northern

42. Slattery, *Brunot*, 227–31.
43. Bishop Whipple, letter to Zachary Chandler, May 29, 1876, Bureau of Indian Affairs, Letters Received.
44. Board of Foreign Missions of the Reformed Church, New York, letter to Zachary Chandler, June 16, 1876, *ibid.*
45. *Annual Report of the Commissioner of Indian Affairs*, 1875, 506.

"non-treaty Sioux," a large band that ranged eastern Wyoming and Montana, "to cease marauding and settle down." The Commissioner complained that these Indians had not yet acknowledged the Federal Government except by "snatching rations occasionally at an agency." This assembly of several Sioux bands and some Northern Cheyennes was rapidly growing in size because "outlaws from the several agencies . . . attached themselves to these . . . hostiles."[46]

These "non-cooperating" Indians, whose leaders were Sitting Bull and Crazy Horse, either had refused to be put on reservations or had left them for several reasons. A large number of Indians believed that their nomadic culture was superior and wanted no part of the comparatively sedentary agricultural life of the reservations. They were strongly influenced by tribal religious and warrior traditions, and if they did recognize the hopelessness of their cause, they preferred going down fighting to living the degraded life of a squaw. These Indians ridiculed those on reservations, destroyed their crops, and even murdered them on occasion. The inflammatory ridicule of the reservation Indians drew many glory-seeking young braves into the hostile camps.

Giving up their way of life meant giving up their freedom, and the mobile, buffalo-hunting Plains tribes were especially averse to such a radical change. They did not understand and would not have cared that the change from hunting to agriculture was a necessary and significant step in the progression from savagery to civilization. Besides, the government's legendary faithlessness in fulfilling treaty obligations on time and as prescribed impelled many Indians to rebel against the reservation system.

Commissioner Smith admitted that forcing these Indians to live on reservations might cause some conflict, but fortunately these bands could not muster more than 500 warriors at any given time. "I am led . . . to repeat with increased confidence," he added, "that a general Indian war is never to occur in the United States."[47] This confidence was the prelude to one of the greatest military defeats, as well as casualty tolls, that the Army suffered in an engagement with the Indians.

In December, the Commissioner sent messages to the hostile bands asking them to move to a reservation before January 31, 1876. They were warned that if they refused to come in by that time, they would be turned over to the War Department for punishment. From December 12 to February 4, 1876, agents of the Interior Department tried to bring in the nontreaty bands and thus to avert probable

46. *Ibid.*, 507.
47. *Ibid.*

hardship and bloodshed. The negotiations were fruitless and served only to notify the hostiles that troops were soon to be sent.

On March 1, a force of 600 cavalry and 2 companies of infantry under the command of General George Crook set out from Fort Laramie in Wyoming Territory. After seventeen days of difficult marching in weather so cold the mercury congealed in the thermometers, the expedition struck what they thought was Crazy Horse's village on the Powder River. As the Indians retreated, the troops dashed into the camp, burned 105 lodges, destroyed ammunition and other supplies, and captured the horse herd. This operation did not seriously cripple the band, for the following morning the Indians surprised the troops and recovered the horses. Frostbitten and exhausted, the troops returned to Fort Laramie.[48]

Because of the inclement weather, military activity was not resumed until May. At this time, the Army initiated a larger operation that called for General Crook to attack from the south, General Alfred Terry from the east, and Colonel John Gibbon from the west. At the Rosebud River on June 17, Crook met a large war party. After a desperate battle in which the Army suffered thirty-three casualties, the General retreated to his supply camp several miles to the south, where he settled down to await reinforcements.

Meanwhile, Terry had ordered Lieutenant Colonel George A. Custer to move the Seventh Cavalry toward a reported Indian camp on the Little Big Horn River and to prevent the Indians' escape. On June 25, Custer's column made contact with the village, which proved to be much larger than anticipated by either military reconnaissance or Indian Bureau estimates. Perhaps as many as 15,000 Sioux were concentrated along a five-mile stretch of the river, and as many as 5,000 were fighting men. Outnumbered by perhaps as much as 10 to 1 and divided into three widely separated commands, the troopers had little chance even for survival.

In the afternoon, the five troops of Custer's immediate command met thousands of charging warriors. For nearly two hours, the one-sided battle raged, but before the choking clouds of dust and powder smoke had time to drift away, all of Custer's troopers lay dead along the slopes and ridges of the Little Big Horn. Meanwhile, five miles upstream, Custer's supporting column under Major Marcus Reno had sustained heavy losses and had been forced back across the river. The survivors, who were joined shortly afterward by Captain Frederick Benteen's troops, entrenched themselves on a high bluff. There,

48. General Phillip Sheridan, Report, *Annual Report of the Secretary of War*, 44th Cong., 2d sess., 1876–1877, House Exec. Doc. No. 1 (Serial 1742), 834.

under attack by the Indians and tortured by heat and thirst, they managed to hold off the enemy until the arrival of Terry's column on the evening of June 26.[49]

The public and government officials did not believe the early reports of the catastrophe, but by July 7, the reports had been definitely confirmed. The public's reaction was a mixture of fear, anger, and vengeance. In frontier towns, residents eagerly offered their services "to avenge Custer and exterminate the Sioux."[50] A Boston paper noted that the massacre "has inflamed the communities nearest the Indians, and, indeed, the whole country. . . . 'Remember Custer' is the watchword of the whole frontier from Iowa to Utah."[51] A newspaper correspondent telegraphed from Salt Lake City, "All the Union Pacific Railroad, from Cheyenne westward, and eastward, too, is alive with the excitement of Indian warfare."[52] From as far away as Oregon came an appeal to the President for protection from the possible spread of hostilities.[53] Senator Algernon Paddock (Republican, Nebraska) introduced a bill to authorize raising five regiments of frontier Indian fighters;[54] in the House, William Phillips (Republican, Kansas) proposed a similar bill.[55]

Again, as in 1873, the Indian Peace Policy was the target for much of the nation's wrath. Throughout the Plains and Rocky Mountain region, newspapers carried editorials denouncing the Quaker method.[56] *The Boulder* (Colo.) *News* blamed the tragedy on the "false philanthropic sentiment of the East," which had brought about the "reprehensible Indian policy of the government." Following this jibe at Eastern humanitarians, the editor turned on the Indians, who were the "same cruel, revengeful savage, yesterday, to-day, and—till extermination. They are the same savage [sic] they were when Lord Chatham, in Parliament, painted them as 'these horrible hell-hounds of savage war—hell-hounds, I say, of savage war.' " The editor then recommended that the Indians be treated as individual citizens, not as tribes set apart on reservations. "Those capable of being civilized would survive—those incapable had better perish, they are of no use in creation."[57]

49. *Ibid.*, 442–43; Charles Kuhlman, *Legend into History*, 175–213; Edgar I. Stewart, *Custer's Luck*, 408–95.
50. *The New York Times*, July 12, 1876.
51. *The Boston Evening Transcript*, July 8, 1876.
52. *The Boston Daily Advertiser*, July 22, 1876.
53. *The New York Times*, July 9, 1876.
54. *The Boston Daily Advertiser*, July 8, 1876.
55. *Kansas State Record* (Topeka), July 17, 1876.
56. *The New York Times*, July 12, 1876.
57. *The Boulder* (Colorado) *News*, July 7, 1876.

The bitterness of people in the West toward the government's Indian policy even extended to criticism of the Army, which was particularly vulnerable after the disastrous defeat of the Seventh Cavalry. The frontier population had castigated the Army on previous occasions for not taking more aggressive action toward the Indians, but now that the much-desired offensive operation had been crushed, Westerners maligned the Army itself as inept and bungling. In Deadwood, Dakota Territory, the residents sneeringly asked what, after the enormous expense to the taxpayers, the Army had done all summer. To express their displeasure at the Army's failure, they dispatched a petition to Washington demanding the removal of General Crook from his command.[58] When Senator Paddock of Nebraska introduced his frontier Indian-fighter bill in Congress, he explained that volunteers could "do the job better than the army."[59] When, despite the pressures for frontier regiments, General Sherman and Secretary of War Belknap deemed them unnecessary, Congress rejected Paddock's and Phillips' bills and authorized an increase in the regular Army by 2,500 enlisted men.[60]

Western reaction to the tragedy was as expected, but advocates of Indian rights were shocked when Easterners, even some who had professed support for the Peace Policy, demanded severe punishment and a change in policy. As *The New York Times* remarked, many people in the East seemed to have had their patience exhausted and to think that the Indians must now be exterminated "as though they were so many mad dogs."[61] E. L. Godkin, editor of *The Nation*, declared bluntly, "Our philanthropy and our hostility tend to about the same end, and this is destruction of the Indian race." Grant's attempt to improve the Indian policy had been worthy in all respects, but now, he concluded, the "missionary expedient may be said to have failed."[62] To prevent the "constant repetition" of such tragedies as the Custer Massacre, *Harper's Weekly* urged the adoption of a totally new Indian policy, one that was intelligent, moral, and efficient.[63]

As in 1873, those Eastern editors who supported Grant defended the Peace Policy, and those who were against Grant attacked it. *The Boston Evening Transcript* believed that the hostile bands should

58. *The New York Times,* October 12, 1876.
59. *The Boston Daily Advertiser,* July 8, 1876.
60. Robert G. Athearn, *William Tecumseh Sherman and the Settlement of the West,* 310.
61. *The New York Times,* July 12, 1876.
62. *The Nation,* XXIII (July 13, 1876), 21.
63. "A National Disgrace," *Harper's Weekly,* XX, 1023 (August 5, 1876), 630.

suffer stern punishment but that the government should continue the Peace Policy for all friendly Indians, "who would be exposed to the . . . blind rage of race prejudice, in case of the general conflagration on the border that some thoughtless people seem to desire."[64] *The Boston Daily Advertiser* also upheld the Peace Policy, but it criticized the government's administration of it and attacked Congress for modifying the policy under pressure of the "Indian Ring."[65]

Most Eastern papers that remained loyal to the Peace Policy defended the military operations against the Sioux as a necessary adjunct to the policy. *The New York Times* explained that the Sioux were a much more dangerous and determined foe than most people realized and that under the leadership of Sitting Bull, the tribe had actually "invited war" by its hostile actions.[66] *The Boston Evening Transcript* reminded critics that the Army was acting only as police for the Indian Bureau's Peace Policy—"There is no inhumanity or anti-Peace Policy about it."[67] The Washington *Republican* and *Washington Star* took similar positions, but the *Brooklyn Eagle* blamed President Grant, the Grant Republicans, and the Peace Policy for the disaster.[68] The *Baltimore Gazette* also held the Administration responsible and demanded an investigation, while the *New York World* and the Philadelphia *Times* rebuked Grant's policy of exterminating the Sioux.[69]

Most reformers saw the Army as the real evil in the tragedy and as a major obstacle to the successful operation of the civilization program. At a meeting of the American Board of Missions in Hartford, Connecticut, the delegates debated the subject of Indian policy vigorously. The American Board of Missions took an active interest in Indian affairs during the 1870's and 1880's. Its president was Mark Hopkins, also president of Williams College, and its vice president was William E. Dodge of the Board of Indian Commissioners (until June, 1874). Dr. Leonard Bacon, founder of the New York *Independent*, spoke for most of the delegates when he attacked the Army's part in Grant's program. Custer and his wrongful "policy" symbolized the Army's attitude, he observed; the late General had once said that there "ought to be one Indian war, and then no more Indians. It was

64. *The Boston Evening Transcript*, July 6, 8, 1876.
65. *The Boston Daily Advertiser*, July 10, 1876.
66. *The New York Times*, July 7, 1876.
67. *The Boston Evening Transcript*, July 10, 1876.
68. *Brooklyn Eagle*, in *The Boston Evening Transcript*, July 10, 1876.
69. Richard R. MacMahon, *The Anglo-Saxon and the North American Indian*, 40.

this spirit that actuated him when he went to massacre and was massacred."[70]

The Army had been one of Wendell Phillips' favorite targets, and now he attacked it with a vengeance. In a letter to the editor of *The Boston Evening Transcript*, Phillips criticized the phrase "Custer Massacre." "What kind of war is it, where if we kill the enemy, it is death; if he kills us, it is a massacre?" he asked, and he charged that the real Custer Massacre occurred in 1868 when the General attacked a peaceful Cheyenne village on the Washita and shot sleeping women and unarmed men. Phillips then directed a letter to General Sherman asking him to either confirm or deny the charge that he advised exterminating the Indians. They had been "butchered by our soldiers," he continued, "with brutal and detestable cruelty . . . we have violated every rule of civilized war, massacring women and children with worse than savage brutality."[71]

Sherman wrote to Samuel Tappan denying that he had ever advocated extermination and challenged the citation of any act or utterance of his in favor of that policy. The Indians should be protected and cared for while they were on the reservation, he explained, but if they left, then they must be punished.[72] Sherman's answer was not altogether satisfying, for the Army's policy of classifying every Indian who was not on a reservation as hostile and subject to military action had been an anathema to reformers for several years.

Throughout the fall and winter of 1876, in writings and lectures, Phillips pursued his antimilitary theme. Under Army restraint, the tribes were provoked to useless revenge, robbed of their lands, and decimated by whisky and bullets. Custer would have been better employed in restoring law and order in the South, but, instead, he was obeying the orders of a government "whose barbarous policy had cost hundreds of millions, many lives, and more dishonour."[73]

Even such a loyal supporter as Bishop Whipple felt compelled to express his conviction that the Indian policy was in need of further reform. In a long letter to Grant, he pointed out that although the Peace Policy had done more for the civilization of the Indians than any previous government efforts, it still was fettered by all the faults and traditions of the old policy. Corruption and dishonesty among the agents was now a rarity, but, he said, the Indians as yet had no government or law, treaties were still being violated, and the na-

70. *The New York Times*, October 6, 1876.
71. MacMahon, *The Anglo-Saxon*, 41–44.
72. *The New York Times*, July 22, 1876.
73. Lorenzo Sears, *Wendell Phillips, Orator and Agitator*, 303.

tion was still persisting in a policy that always ended in massacre and war.[74]

Many other religious leaders and organizations, disillusioned about what appeared to be a complete reversion to an Indian policy based on military force, became sharply critical of the Administration's program. As late as December, 1876, E. Whittlesey, new Chairman of the Board of Indian Commissioners, complained that even though this was the first really Christian effort to "elevate and save a long wronged race," it was almost impossible to find a religious paper that cordially supported the Peace Policy.[75] However, most religious criticism was primarily directed at the Army, not the basic principles of the Peace Policy.

Not all humanitarians criticized the operation of the Administration's Indian program. On July 10, the Universal Peace Union met in Philadelphia to hear addresses by Lucretia Mott and Julia Ward Howe opposing war and capital punishment. Among the resolutions adopted was one counseling the government to adhere to the Peace Policy in its dealings with the Indians. Those who attended the meeting sent a petition to the President pleading for just and humane treatment of the Sioux and asking him to veto any bill for transfer of the Indian Bureau to the War Department. The following day, Alfred Meacham said that the Modoc War had been in "no possible sense" a result of the Peace Policy and that the present Sioux War had not been caused by "peace men, or Quakers, or Sunday-school sentimentalists."[76]

The Peace Policy came under another assault by congressmen of both parties who represented the Plains and Rocky Mountain regions, and more people from east of the Mississippi also criticized it. Staunch advocates like Senators Henry L. Dawes and William Windom insisted that the Peace Policy was the only solution, but in the frontier West at least, the Indian question was more than ever a political issue.

Following the Custer Massacre, most reformers continued to believe that military control of Indian affairs would destroy the Peace Policy and probably the Indians. They also believed that further reforms were needed, but most agreed with Bishop Whipple that it was impossible to "make a bad bank note good by changing

74. Bishop Whipple, letter to President Grant, July 31, 1876, Bureau of Indian Affairs, Letters Received.

75. E Whittlesey, letter to The Reverend H. M. Dextor, December, 1876, Board of Indian Commissioners, Incoming Corespondence, 1869–1890.

76. *The Boston Daily Advertiser*, July 11, 1876; *The New York Times*, July 12, 1876.

pockets."[77] The Peace Policy must continue to govern Indian relations.

The question of military control in 1876, however, was influenced by more than the tragedy on the Little Big Horn and the shortcomings of the Peace Policy—1876 was a presidential election year, and the transfer question suddenly revived.

77. Whipple, letter to Grant, July 31, 1876, Bureau of Indian Affairs, Letters Received.

9

The Critical Years, 1876–1879

In contrast to the Republican platforms of 1868 and 1872, the national platform of the Republican party of 1876 failed to mention either the Indians or Indian policy. The Democratic platform, too, did not mention this issue. Both major parties carefully avoided a formal commitment on the Indian question, but that did not mean that political leaders believed the problem was solved. With the controversial Sioux campaign under way, the Custer Massacre, and increasing charges of corruption in the Indian service, the Republican strategy seemed to be silence. However, Republican leaders appear to have been considering a thorough revision of Grant's policy at some future time. The platform's references to "equality" and "inalienable rights" and its statement that "unless these truths are cheerfully obeyed, or, if need be, vigorously enforced, the work of the Republican party is unfinished" could be applied to all races.[1] At least this approach left the Hayes Administration more free to do what it pleased on Indian policy.

On the other hand, the Democrats, who had been demanding a new policy, had offered few precise plans for it, and the party platform and subsequent events indicated that no distinct Democratic Indian policy had evolved. Besides, there were other good campaign issues in 1876: the South and Reconstruction, civil service and currency reform, hard times and government scandals. Although an editor for *The New York Times* noticed in the summer's political discourses that the recent massacre and Indian war were being used as a "new argument" against the Republican party and a "fresh charge" in the indictment against Grant, Indian policy slipped behind the other national issues as the political campaign progressed.[2] This lack of emphasis occurred despite the publication of such pamphlets as Richard R. MacMahon's *The Anglo-Saxon and the North American Indian*. Scoring the Peace Policy as bloodthirsty and merciless, and drawing heavily on Wendell Phillips' criticisms after the Custer Massacre, MacMahon blamed Grant's Administration and concluded that "the public good demands a change of party."[3]

1. *The Boulder* (Colorado) *News*, June 30, 1876.
2. *The New York Times*, July 30, 1876.
3. Richard R. MacMahon, *The Anglo-Saxon and the North American Indian*, 49.

This apparent disinterest did not hold true in Congress or in the border states and territories. In Congress, the transfer question, an offspring of problems with the Indian policy, was very much alive, and in the frontier West, the Peace Policy was still a favorite target. The House of Representatives had passed the transfer bill of April, 1876, but the Senate had defeated it. Unable to secure its passage before the close of the session, the Democratic House used the Custer tragedy to point out that Republican senators had blocked transfer and that the House had temporarily yielded in order to permit unimpeded prosecution of the Sioux War.[4]

The Liberal Republicans had merged with regular Republicans now that Rutherford B. Hayes was the Republican party's candidate. Carl Schurz enthusiastically campaigned for Hayes and declared that the Democratic party, because it stood in the way of reconciliation with the South, was the "party of reaction."[5] This consolidation of the regulars and the Liberals did not affect Indian policy in 1876, but it would have a significant bearing on future policy under President Hayes. Under the leadership of Carl Schurz, a liberal who was interested in reform, the government's Indian policy would soon undergo a new phase of controversy, reorganization, and reform.

The reformers' disillusionment about the Sioux campaign and their suspicion that corruption still lingered in the Indian system did not panic them into junking the Peace Policy. They still had faith in its basic principles, but they wanted a thorough cleansing of its faults and then the full-fledged application of a purified, true policy of peace. Hayes and a new set of government officials might be able to make the changes and rejuvenate the Indian program. Like the Liberals, who were concerned with corruption in government and reforming civil service, the Indian-rights advocates endorsed the new Republican candidate. Lydia Maria Child, Bishop Whipple, and Wendell Phillips were pleased with Hayes, but Peter Cooper decided to become his own candidate. As the nominee of the Greenback party, he became so absorbed in the paper-money panacea for the nation's financial ills that he had little time for the Indian problem. Consequently, he did not emphasize it during the campaign, but he did return to Indian-rights work in 1877.

Indian policy was a political issue in some areas of the West, where transfer was again proposed as the solution. However, with the exceptions of Texas and Montana, the Republican party was victorious throughout the trans-Missouri region. This cannot be interpreted as a clear indication of Indian policy sentiment; some

4. Loring Benson Priest, *Uncle Sam's Stepchildren: The Reformation of United States Indian Policy, 1865–1887,* 19–20.
5. *The New York Times,* October 21, 1876.

successful Republican congressional candidates called for abandoning Grant's Peace Policy, others upheld it, and Democrat William
Steele, who campaigned against the policy in Wyoming, was defeated. Local issues and political affiliation were probably more important to most voters than their traditional discontent with the
Peace Policy. There were a few scattered indications in 1876 that a
change of viewpoint was taking place in the West. *The Junction City*
(Ks.) *Weekly Union,* a consistent advocate of extermination, edi-
torialized in July, 1876, "The true method of treating with the wild
Indians is to civilize them. . . . That this can be done there is no
reasonable doubt. . . . The people of the United States . . . will re-
quire strong proof of the error of the 'Peace Policy' before they will
consent to the murder of women and children as advocated . . .
under the policy known as 'extermination.' "[6]

The election of Hayes marked the end of a pioneer era in post-
Civil War reform of the Indian policy. By this time, the Peace Policy
had been in operation nearly eight years. As the first definite program
aimed at civilizing the Indians and the final solution of the problem,
it had been inaugurated with cautious optimism. Although it had
been blamed for tragedies, it had survived for the two terms of the
Grant Administration. After 1873, increasing criticism and skepticism frequently weakened its effectiveness, and from its beginning,
the sectional division in Congress had been a serious handicap. Many
humanitarians had made charges of dishonesty in the Indian Bureau
and had decried what they considered the Army's too frequent use of
force. Many people in the frontier West had repeatedly expressed
their antipathy for the principles of the policy. However, the Peace
Policy was still in full operation when Hayes took office in March,
1877.

Grant's Indian program had made considerable progress in
founding schools and educating Indian children. It had established
the agency and reservation system for the Plains tribes, and the Indians had tremendously increased their agricultural production.
Ending the notorious treaty system and passing the Indian Homestead Act were other steps in the right direction, but in 1877, even
the most enthusiastic supporters of the Peace Policy recognized that
these achievements would only begin to make the Indians civilized,
self-supporting members of society.

Although most Indian-rights workers had supported Hayes, his
Administration had barely begun when it faced new doubts. Neither
Hayes nor Carl Schurz, who was appointed Secretary of the Interior,

6. *The Junction City* (Kansas) *Weekly Union,* July 16, 1876.

had clearly given his views on the Indian question or the Peace Policy. Schurz's announcement that changes would be made in the Indian policy ordinarily would not have been foreboding, but he had indicated that he opposed church participation in the Indian program. Such liberal journals as *The Nation* agreed with him, and state and national political leaders were against the selection of agents by the churches.

Shortly after the inauguration, Alfred Love, Lucretia Mott, and Henry Child, who were representing the Universal Peace Union, petitioned the new President to continue and perfect the Indian Peace Policy. "A very great improvement in the condition of the Indians, in the peace of the country, and in the fulfillment of our obligations as Christians, was effected during the late administration," they said, and they asked that "every encouragement be offered for good men and women" to become teachers to the Indians.[7]

In April, 1877, the Central Superintendency's Friends Committee on Indian Affairs told Hayes of their confidence that within a few years, all the tribes under their care would "cease to be a source of trouble or great expense to the Government, and that in due time they may be converted into useful citizens of the country." Although the Friends believed that much progress had been made in Christianizing and civilizing the Indians, the "work of elevating a people from a savage to a civilized condition cannot be done in a day." The Quaker committee then reminded the President that they had not asked for this "stewardship" and they were not asking that it be continued in their hands, "but if the President should desire it, we are ready and willing to serve our Government as heretofore."[8] The Friends committee primarily wanted to know Hayes's attitude toward continuing the Peace Policy and the Quakers' participation in Indian work. Hayes reassured them that he was well satisfied with the existing situation and that he was not considering a change in policy.[9]

Meanwhile, several humanitarians were trying to renew public and official enthusiasm for the existing policy. Stanley Pumphrey, a Quaker reformer from England, began a series of lectures on Indian civilization during the spring of 1877. He consistently stressed the controversial view that the Indians were capable of being civilized. They could be civilized only if they were insulated from the govern-

7. Alfred H. Love, letter to President Hayes, [Spring] 1877, Bureau of Indian Affairs, Letters Received.
8. Associated Executive Committee of Friends on Indian Affairs, Address to President Hayes, April 4, 1877, *ibid*.
9. Rayner Wickersham Kelsey, *Friends and the Indians, 1655–1917*, 184.

ment's injustice and the white settlers' invasion of the reservations. Where they had a fair chance, the Indians actually had increased in population since 1865. His claims rebutted the predictions of those opponents of the Peace Policy who had assumed that the number of Indians would inevitably decline to insignificance. These opponents maintained that the divine destiny of the Anglo-Saxons and the inherent inferiority of the Indians were enough to make any effort to educate the doomed savages a ridiculous waste. If extermination was inevitable, then, as Samuel Bowles had once suggested, the government should only "smooth and make decent the pathway to his grave."[10] On the other hand, *The Nation* asserted that when Congress and the public appreciated Pumphrey's report on the increased number of Indians, the government would initiate even more progressive and permanent reforms in the Indian policy.[11]

While Pumphrey was lecturing on civilization of the Indian, John Greenleaf Whittier was becoming more interested in the Indian-rights movement. Whittier had given much attention to the "noble savage" in his writings, but until the 1870's, his reform work had been for the Negroes. In February, 1870, he wrote approvingly of the Quakers' activity for the Indians and the freedmen, and later that year, he made a large contribution to the Hampton Institute for the education of both Indians and Negroes.[12] In May, 1877, in an essay entitled "Indian Civilization," Whittier maintained that the people of the United States could ignore neither the present condition nor the future prospects of the Indians. "Apart from all considerations of justice and duty, a purely selfish regard to our own well-being" should compel the public's attention to the Indians' situation. Since the suffering and neglect of one part of the community must affect all others, a common responsibility rested upon each and every citizen. Whittier strongly urged the continuation of the Peace Policy because the progress of the Indians' education, civilization, and conversion to Christianity had been of a "most encouraging nature." If civilizing the Indians was ever a doubtful problem, he declared, "it has been practically solved."[13]

Whittier based his contention that the Indians were capable of

10. Samuel Bowles, *Our New West*, 158.

11. *The Nation*, XXV (October 18, 1877), 242. Stanley Pumphrey was born in Worcester, England, in 1837. In September, 1875, he came to the United States to work for the rights of the freedmen and the Indians and dedicated himself to these causes until his death in 1881.

12. *The Bond of Peace*, III, 4 (April, 1870), 33; *The Standard*, I, 3 (July, 1870), 160.

13. John Greenleaf Whittier, *The Works of John Greenleaf Whittier*, VII, 233.

civilization on the currently popular doctrine of cultural evolution and the civilizing power of Christianity. The wildest of the Indians, he theorized, were like the northern barbarians who swooped down upon Christian Europe. Yet the descendants of those "human butchers are now among the best exponents of the humanizing influences of the gospel of Christ."[14] Thus, he concluded, the Indian was no more inferior in the capacity for improvement than the Norse ancestors of present-day Danes and Norwegians.[15]

Throughout his life, Whittier felt profound sympathy for both the American Indians and the Negroes. According to the poet and journalist Richard Henry Stoddard, two of the most prominent characteristics of Whittier's writing were its "antislavery element" and his belief in "a poetical side to Indian life." Before the Civil War, he usually wrote either metrical Indian romances or antislavery essays. Like most prewar humanitarians, he soon became completely absorbed in the abolitionist movement, and in 1838 and 1839, he edited the *Pennsylvania Freeman*, a Philadelphia antislavery journal. After a mob sacked and burned his office, he became the editor of the "Anti-Slavery Reports" and the *Middlesex Standard* (Lowell, Mass.).[16] Whittier was, above all, a Christian humanist. His appeal was to "universal humanity," which made his outlook very close to that of most of his contemporaries who worked for Indian rights.

While Pumphrey and Whittier were laboring to persuade the public to support the Peace Policy, Bishop Whipple again directed one of his lengthy letters to the President. During the past few years, the Bishop had alternately praised and criticized Grant's Indian policy, but after the Sioux War of 1876 and the election of Hayes, he became increasingly denunciatory. In May, 1877, he observed that the "difficulties which surround the Indian system are almost insuperable, simply because of our wretched Indian policy which leaves Indians without government, personal rights of property, [and] incentives to labor."[17] The following September, he said that, as President, Hayes had full power to reform the Indian policy. "It [the Indian policy] has been a byeword [sic] and reproach to our people, an inexhaustible source of profligate expenditure and has brought to Indians and whites a perrenial [sic] harvest of sorrow, degradation, and blood." Whipple then asserted that the Indian

14. *Ibid.*
15. *Ibid.*, 234.
16. R. H. Stoddard, "John Greenleaf Whittier," *Appleton's Journal*, V, 107 (April 15, 1871), 432–33.
17. Bishop Whipple, letter to W. R. Rogers, May 19, 1877, Bureau of Indian Affairs, Letters Reecived.

system was a "governmental almshouse to educate savage paupers—
we expect to accomplish civilization for wild Indians under circumstances which would wreck any civilized nation on the Earth." He
proposed that the President publicize the "glaring defects of our
present policy" and ask Congress to redress the evils by securing
for the Indians property rights, government protection, civil law, and
the rewards of labor instead of idleness.[18]

John Beeson seconded Whipple's criticism a month later. Beeson
wrote to Hayes complaining of the failure of the Indian policy and
suggesting that the new President might be the man "to espouse the
rights of the Aboriginal race as Lincoln did the African." Good motives and ample funds were not enough; if Hayes did not use different methods, "it will be as the past, *wasted* and *useless.*" The Congress should investigate the causes of the wars being waged against
Chief Joseph and Sitting Bull before it approved military appropriations to cover the cost. Congressional discussion of the investigation,
Beeson added, would let the people know the right and wrong of
the present Indian conflicts.[19]

Alfred B. Meacham and his assistant, Theodore Bland, lectured
throughout the Midwest in the summer of 1877 in support of a reformed Peace Policy. Upon his return to the East, Meacham began
work on a journal promoting a "true Indian 'policy.'" The first
issue of *The Council Fire* was published on January 1, 1878. Meanwhile, he lectured in Washington, D. C., to audiences that included
congressmen, Army officers, and public officials. He aroused so much
interest in his cause that he decided to move the journal to the Capital, where he could exert more immediate and effective influence.[20]

In the spring of 1877, the United States Indian Commission
brought charges of irregularities against Samuel A. Galpin, the Chief
Clerk of the Indian Bureau.[21] In response to such charges and spread-
ing criticism, Secretary Schurz launched an investigation of the Indian Bureau and the agencies. In his report of January, 1878, he
blamed Galpin for much of the "cupidity, inefficiency, and . . . bare-
footed dishonesty" that had been uncovered, and he promptly dis-
charged him and several other suspected employees. This action and
Schurz's earlier dismissal of Indian Commissioner John Q. Smith
amounted to a thorough housecleaning that left few unchastened.

18. Bishop Whipple, letter to President Hayes, September 28, 1877,
ibid.
19. John Beeson, letter to President Hayes, October 15, 1877, *ibid.*
20. Theodore A. Bland, *Life of Alfred B. Meacham*, 9.
21. *Congressional Record*, 46th Cong., 3d sess., 1880–1881, Part 3, 2108.

The next step Schurz planned was a complete reorganization of the Indian agencies.[22]

Throughout the fall of 1877 and the spring of 1878, Hayes received many letters and memorials proposing changes in the Indian policy. The majority strongly urged the government to extend the rights and privileges of United States citizens to the Indians, encourage the Indians to use the Indian Homestead Act, and expand education. These suggestions had been originally incorporated into Grant's Peace Policy as ultimate objectives, and the Homestead act had been passed in 1875. The act had not been widely used, however, because it required the payment of certain prescribed fees and commissions and because it required the Interior Department to maintain a fund for this purpose.[23] As the American Missionary Association pointed out in December, 1877, the humanitarians' goal was an Indian policy that would convert the "wards of the nation" into responsible and intelligent citizens.[24] The more ardent advocates of Indian rights thought that the civilization program was not progressing rapidly enough toward this end. Now that the corruption was being rectified, they increasingly criticized what appeared to be growing governmental lethargy in applying and expanding the Peace Policy. By the end of Grant's term, Indian-rights advocates were becoming uneasy, and after six months of the Hayes Administration, they were convinced that the earlier official enthusiasm had cooled perceptibly.

In order to dispel the humanitarians' fears and doubts, the President, in his first annual message, dwelt at length upon the Indian problem and promised to preserve peace with the Indians by a "just and humane policy." His strong recommendations for citizenship and privileges of the Homestead act for all Indians who broke their tribal relationships pleased the humanitarians.[25]

The Hayes Administration's Indian policy had been formulated by Secretary Schurz between March and November, 1877. Schurz's program on the surface seemed to be a continuation and extension of Grant's, but in actual fact, it was overhauling the previous policy by gradually eliminating church participation in Indian affairs. For

22. Claude Moore Fuess, *Carl Schurz, Reformer*, 255.

23. Laurence F. Schmeckebier, *The Office of Indian Affairs: Its History, Activities, and Organization*, 76.

24. American Missionary Association, Memorial to the President, Secretary of the Interior, and Commissioner of Indian Affairs, December 13, 1877, Bureau of Indian Affairs, Letters Received.

25. James D. Richardson, ed., *A Compilation of the Messages and Papers of the Presidents, 1789–1902*, 1908 ed., VII, 475–76.

several years, politicians had resented the loss of patronage, and Indian Bureau officials had thought that the churches were interfering in government affairs.[26] The change of administrations in 1877 seemed a propitious time for Congress to reinstate the old system of political appointments. Schurz, who believed that the entire Indian program would operate most efficiently when it was directly under the government's control, agreed that the churches should not have the power they did. Despite the fears of the humanitarians, Schurz's policy was primarily a change in operation; it was not an abandonment of the original objectives of the Peace Policy.

In the fall of 1877, the new Commissioner of Indian Affairs, E. A. Hayt, took office. One of his first acts was to notify the Quakers of the Central Superintendency that he considered many of them inefficient and some of them even dishonest. Shortly afterward, he deprived the Friends of several agencies and abolished the office of Central Superintendent. The Quakers and President Hayes met and tentatively agreed upon continuing the old program, but the agreement proved to be illusory. The President had unbounded confidence in Secretary Schurz and was reluctant to circumvent the Interior Department's program for reorganization. Consequently, the Indian Commissioner continued the policy of removing the churches.[27]

A similar situation soon confronted the Friends of the Northern Superintendency. In January, 1878, the Senate did not confirm four of the six agents nominated by the Quakers and appointed by the President because Senators Alvin Saunders and Algernon Paddock of Nebraska opposed them. Both senators were Republicans and had recently indicated sympathy for the Indian cause but apparently were no longer able or willing to resist patronage pressures. They objected on the grounds that the Quaker appointees were not residents of their state. The Nebraska people, they maintained, were entitled to this patronage. By taking advantage of the courtesy of the Senate, any senator could influence agency appointments within his particular state and thereby seriously impede the old Peace-Policy system.[28] In addition, Indian Commissioner Hayt had shown his extreme reluctance to accept the agents proposed by the Friends or any other denomination.[29]

Modification of the policy, unhampered by any laws or regula-

26. Priest, *Uncle Sam's Stepchildren*, 36–38.
27. Kelsey, *Friends and the Indians*, 184.
28. Samuel M. Janney, *Memoirs of Samuel M. Janney*, 303; *The Press* (Philadelphia), April 12, 1878.
29. *The New York Times*, May 18, 1879.

tions protecting the churches' function in the program, proceeded quietly and efficiently. As a result, orders from Commissioner Hayt and noncooperation by agency employees who had been appointed by the Indian Bureau negated the work of the agents.[30] Furthermore, the churches gradually lost an official voice in Indian affairs.[31] During the summer of 1879, the Quakers severed all official connections with the Interior Department and asked their agents to resign from both the Northern and Central superintendencies. Other denominations also withdrew, and by 1880, church control of the Peace Policy no longer existed.

Secretary Schurz knew that a sudden and forthright stand against church participation would bring an enormous amount of criticism from religious and Indian-rights groups. To avert this criticism and prevent possible obstruction of his plan, he ignored some complaints and questions and evaded answering others for months and even years.[32] These devious tactics did eliminate church control, but many religious leaders and Indian-rights advocates never forgave the Secretary. Their opposition to Schurz would reach a climax during the controversy about removing the Ponca Indians.

As the influence of the churches was declining, demands for transfer of Indian affairs to the War Department were growing. In Congress, the issue again was largely one of partisan and sectional politics. The Democrats strongly supported transfer as their solution to the shortcomings of the civilization program that was operating under the Interior Department's jurisdiction. The end of Grant's Administration and the increasing criticism of the Indian policy made many politicians think that a change to military control might be nearly as popular as the inauguration of the original Peace Policy had been in 1869. Such a radical change would imply that Grant's policy had been no more than a misguided, if not a disastrous, experiment. Political propaganda against the Peace Policy would then be much more credible, and one of the few bright spots remaining on Grant's administrative record would be badly tarnished.

The advocates of transfer failed to realize the strength of Eastern opposition to military control. Most of the humanitarians and most of the churches supported civilian control. In Congress, the Republicans usually backed their own Administration's program, and with a majority of Republicans in the Senate, they constituted a nearly impassable barrier to passage of a transfer bill in any form. Secretary Schurz also opposed control by the War De-

30. Kelsey, *Friends and the Indians*, 196.
31. Priest, *Uncle Sam's Stepchildren*, 37.
32. *Ibid.*, 38.

partment. Although many people on the Western frontier still appeared to favor the change, their Republican representatives usually supported the Administration in this matter.[33]

None of the Indian-rights advocates would support transfer, although William Welsh had urged such a move in 1876.[34] The Quakers had accepted the use of the Army as a temporarily necessary measure for controlling the wild tribes. They clearly hoped that the Army would leave as soon as the civilization program had taught the Indians to be more tractable. Then, a truly peaceful program could be established without having to offer peace with one hand and wield the sword with the other.

Although the Friends were willing to work with the Army in the operation of the Peace Policy, at no time did they agree to the transfer of Indian affairs to the War Department. In a memorial to Hayes in October, 1877, the American Board of Foreign Missions expressed views almost identical to those held by the Quakers.[35] In general, most of the religious bodies working with the Indian Bureau agreed.

Like the churches, the independent reform organizations decidedly opposed transfer. In 1876, Peter Cooper's New York Indian Peace Commission had protested placing the Indians under War Department supervision, for "war measures can never civilize or elevate individuals or nations." These influential New York reformers thought that a military system of government would destroy the Indians by war, disease, or demoralization.[36]

The congressional debate on the Army appropriation bill in the spring of 1878 renewed the transfer controversy. The agitation within the House for the addition of a transfer amendment to the bill invoked an immediate humanitarian response. The United States Indian Commission memorialized Congress asking that civil control be retained, because Indians justly treated were always peaceful—"therefore there is no need of soldiers to prevent their raids upon the Whites."[37] In February, 1878, Peter Cooper and John Beeson helped to form the Ladies' National League to Protect the

33. *Ibid.*, 24–25.

34. Charles Lewis Slattery, *Felix Reville Brunot, 1820–1898*, 227.

35. American Board of Foreign Missions, Memorial in behalf of the Indian tribes to President Hayes, October 23, 1877, Bureau of Indian Affairs, Letters Received.

36. "Indian Department," *The Voice of Peace*, II (February, 1876), 165–66.

37. United States Indian Commission, Memorial to Congress, [Spring] 1878, Bureau of Indian Affairs, Letters Received.

Indians, which lost no time in opposing the War Department's jurisdiction. On March 25, the members resolved that placing the Indians under the Army's "demoralizing contact and control" would be unjust.[38]

Meanwhile, Alfred Love's Universal Peace Union told Congress that jurisdiction by the War Department was "incompatible with the conditions which involve the spread of the arts of civilization, the observance of true religious sentiment and the establishment of peace." The solution to the problem was the formation of a separate and distinct department of Indian affairs.[39] This solution had been proposed for several years by those reformers who felt that neither the War nor the Interior Department could successfully handle a task of such magnitude and complexity. The Peace Union was not deviating from its faith in the Peace Policy itself; in fact, they asserted that "all the past and present Indian troubles" were the results of "flagrant departures from the plighted faith and boasted Peace Policy of the United States." Senator Hannibal Hamlin (Republican, Maine) and Representative Charles O'Neill (Republican, Pennsylvania) presented the Peace Union's memorial to Congress, and their doing so indicated the continued working relationship between Republican congressmen who supported the Peace Policy and Indian-rights workers.[40]

In September, 1877, Bishop Whipple wrote President Hayes that he opposed the War Department's control on the grounds that the Army was not trained for the patient labor necessary to educate the Indians. He then reminded Hayes that during the fifty years that the Army had controlled Indian affairs, the results were such that the whole nation had demanded reform.[41]

After helping to organize the Ladies' National League, John Beeson took on the transfer issue. He spoke to church congregations, private organizations, and public meetings, contacted influential public men, and distributed leaflets, newspaper stories, and petitions to Congress. His appearance before the Society of Spiritualists in New York City was typical. He read a memorial, which he planned to present to Congress, asking that the Indians not be transferred from the civil to the military power. He then launched into an

38. "Justice for the Indians," *The Voice of Peace*, V (May, 1878), 30.
39. Universal Peace Union, "Public Action of the Universal Peace Union," *ibid.* (April, 1878), 14.
40. Universal Peace Union, "Official Report of the Twelfth Anniversary Meeting," *ibid.* (July, 1878), 58.
41. Bishop Whipple, letter to President Hayes, September 28, 1877.

attack on the Army and told his audience that the Indian wars with the Modocs and Sitting Bull were the "direct result of aggressive military interference."[42]

Beeson sent a copy of the United States Indian Commission's memorial opposing transfer to President Hayes, at the same time warning him about "a growing (perhaps dangerous) eliment [sic] of radicalism called communists which is disposed to affiliate with the Indian cause, and will be greatly increased by the needless use of Millitary [sic] against them."[43] By the end of April, 1878, Beeson had secured the promises of several large New York and Brooklyn churches, including that of Henry Ward Beecher, to use their influence against transfer. On May 1, he wrote Hayes that if a veto was necessary to prevent such a move, he would be "well sustained in giving it."[44]

Despite the opposition, Representative Alfred Scales (Democrat, North Carolina), Chairman of the House Committee on Indian Affairs, was able to muster enough support by the end of May to attach a transfer amendment to the Army appropriation bill. To forestall action on the measure, the Senate demanded the appointment of a joint congressional committee to investigate the matter. The House Democrats, faced by a determined Republican Senate, agreed to this proposal, and a committee of three senators and five representatives began their investigation in the summer of 1878.[45]

While the congressional committee examined the Indian problem—a slow and tedious task that involved not only checking the operations of the Indian Bureau and the Army, but also inspecting military posts and agencies on the frontier—criticism was mounting. In October, John Beeson complained to Indian Commissioner Hayt of the "vast amount of *Red Tape* used to prevent instead of promote Justic [sic]." He decried the growing apathy of the Eastern public and the leaders in both religion and politics, and he said that it was up to the Indian Commissioner to tell the people that the Indians' rights were "as great and inalienable as their own."[46]

Unlike Beeson and his Indian-rights colleagues, E. L. Godkin, editor of *The Nation*, supported Schurz's elimination of church influence and attacked the methods of Grant's Peace Policy. Turning

42. Newspaper clipping, Miscellaneous File, 1878, Bureau of Indian Affairs, Letters Received.

43. John Beeson, letter to President Hayes, [ca. March] 1878, Bureau of Indian Affairs, Letters Received.

44. John Beeson, letter to President Hayes, May 1, 1878, *ibid.*

45. Priest, *Uncle Sam's Stepchildren*, 20.

46. John Beeson, letter to E. A. Hayt, October 27, 1878, Bureau of Indians Affairs, Letters Received.

the job over to religious denominations was a confession that the government was unable to discharge one of its most important functions through its own agents, and Grant "might almost as well have handed over the management of the Treasury to the Bible Society, and called on the Board of Foreign Missions to conduct the Post Office."[47] Godkin was speaking for the new order when he advocated complete control of Indian affairs by elected or appointed civil officials whose integrity would be ensured by new reform measures that affected the civil service.

Westerners, too, renewed their sniping at the Indian policy. Probably the majority still favored transfer, but by this time, many border settlers had lost patience with the Army as well as the government. Then, too, with the extermination of Custer's command by the Sioux still fresh in their minds, frontier people had yet to regain confidence in the Army's ability to handle the tribes. Thomas Hindman of Buffalo, Kansas, wrote the President in October, 1878, that most of the people in western Kansas and eastern Colorado were "greatly incensed & exasperated against the government on account of the mismanagement" of Indian affairs, and he warned of their "diminished respect, & even contempt" for a government that spent millions to provide for and protect the Indians while it ignored the rights, welfare, and even lives of its "loyal and long tried" citizens. He complained bitterly of "our handful of inefficient soldiers now on the frontier" and their officers, who refrained from punishing hostile Indians because of the danger involved and who avoided "suppressing and taming" the Indians because the Army could be further reduced in size when the Indians were subjugated. As it was, he added, the Army might as well be distributed among the large cities of the East, "where they are much needed to Suppress and keep in order the . . . villainous & communistic elements of Society that infest populous places." To solve the Indian problem, Hindman urged that the settlers be deputized as United States marshals and armed with the latest repeating rifles and plenty of ammunition. Such a force, he believed, could "render the Indians harmless in one year" and self-supporting in ten years.[48]

Such viewpoints offered little encouragement for control by either the War or the Interior Department. By 1878, more support seemed to have developed for the creation of a separate department of Indian affairs. A plan to that end had already been frequently

47. "General Grant's Indian Policy," *The Nation*, XXVIII (January 9, 1879), 22.

48. Thomas Hindman, letter to President Hayes, October 13, 1878, Bureau of Indian Affairs, Letters Received.

recommended by many humanitarian leaders and organizations. Alfred Love, Felix Brunot, Bishop Whipple, the anthropologist Lewis H. Morgan, and other reformers thought it was a logical way out of the growing dilemma.

Meanwhile, the joint congressional committee, which had received a great number of petitions, letters, and memorials from reformers, was forced to limit itself to official papers and documents only. The last nonofficial paper it accepted was a memorial from Lucretia Mott's Pennsylvania Peace Society, a branch of the Universal Peace Union. In opposing transfer and upholding the policy of peace and civilization, the society emphasized that giving the "sword-power" a voice in legislation would hurt the growth of free institutions.[49]

The Army was not often in a position to express its viewpoints, but in December, 1878, General Nelson Miles took advantage of an interview for the *Washington Post* to criticize the Interior Department. "I have no doubt that Mr. Schurz is trying to improve the service, and that Mr. Chandler followed a similar course," Miles told the *Post* reporter, "but that they have not succeeded entirely is made evident by the constant revelation of new frauds. . . . Under the War Department system that would be remedied." Schurz immediately asked Miles for specific information about the new frauds and reminded him that his cooperation would facilitate efforts to improve the Indian service.[50] The General's reply indicated that he had apparently based his allegations more on rumor than on official reports. He took pains to state that there was nothing personal in his remarks and that both Chandler and Schurz had "accomplished very much to eradicate evils which had existed under their predecessors."[51] The publication of such correspondence in the press helped secure public support for continuing the Interior Department's jurisdiction.

Critics frequently observed that the weakness of the existing system was that the Secretary of the Interior did not have the means for controlling and protecting the rights of the Indians. Furthermore, any system of reform that he inaugurated could be reversed by his successor. In response to this argument, the advocates of the Peace Policy contended that the small frontier Army did not have

49. Pennsylvania Peace Society, "Official Report of the Twelfth Anniversary Meeting," *The Voice of Peace*, V (January, 1879), 149.

50. Quoted in Carl Schurz, letter to General Nelson A. Miles, December 26, 1878, Bureau of Indian Affairs, Letters Received and Letters Sent.

51. General Nelson A. Miles, letter to Carl Schurz, January 16, 1879, *ibid.*

the means to control and protect the Indians. The ease with which secretaries might be changed was also a way to oust a bad official or system, and although the Indian Bureau might be under political control, it was by that very fact more responsive to demands of the public and humanitarians.

During the congressional investigation, Schurz declared that military management of the Indian Bureau, prior to 1849, had been "disgracefully lax and slovenly." He further asserted that honesty was not always the rule in the Army, and his observations left no doubt about his stand on the transfer question. The Secretary was supported by Indian Commissioner Hayt, who confided that he was "personally aware that the Indians were opposed to the proposed change," and by A. B. Meacham, who testified that one half of the Indians needed no form of military supervision and that they regarded the Army as an oppressor.[52]

Meacham conducted a tireless campaign against military control in the columns of *The Council Fire*. The hundreds of copies of the periodical that were freely distributed to congressmen at the height of the controversy proved to be very effective. His speeches on the subject often inspired his audiences to draw up memorials to Congress earnestly protesting transfer. Meacham's thesis was the straightforward one used by all the reformers: The War Department's control meant extermination of the Indians. In January, 1879, he brought a delegation of Indians to Washington to speak for their "rights and liberties." One of them was Chief Joseph, a renowned Nez Percé leader who had recently gained the admiration of the nation for leading his small band's heroic but futile struggle to stop the Army from moving them from their tribal homeland. The outnumbered Indians had frequently defeated and outmaneuvered the troops, which lent considerable antimilitary value to Chief Joseph's appearance in Washington.[53]

In his annual message of December 2, 1878, President Hayes emphasized that "greater reliance must be placed on humane and civilizing agencies for the ultimate solution of what is called the

52. *The Nation*, XXVII (December 12, 1878), 358. The various agency reports to the Indian Bureau from 1875 to 1878 indicated that many tribes were apparently opposed to transfer. For instance, in March, 1878, the five Civilized Tribes of Indian Territory sent to Congress a memorial against transfer because an "inevitable consequence" would be the "wholesale breaking up of the work of civilizing and Christianizing the Indians." *The Press* (Philadelphia), March 11, 1878.

53. "Indians in Washington and Their Interview," *The Voice of Peace*, V (February, 1879), 164; *The Christian Register* (Boston), February 1, 1879.

Indian problem." He reminded Congress that because the Indians were the original owners of the soil, "we owe it to them as a moral duty to help them in attaining at least that degree of civilization which they may be able to reach." In referring to the investigation by the joint congressional committee, Hayes expressed his hope that "in the decision of so important a question the views expressed above may not be lost sight of."[54] Little doubt now remained that the President also favored the Interior Department's control.

In spite of the formidable array of opposition to transfer, the congressional committee, still governed largely by partisan considerations, split on the issue. The four Democratic members condemned in the strongest terms the whole of the past management of Indian affairs, asserted that church control under the Peace Policy was a practical acknowledgement that the Indian Bureau was incapable of handling its affairs, and advocated immediate transfer to War Department control. The four Republican committeemen insisted upon continuing the present policy of reform and improvement and condemned military control. To the satisfaction of many reformers, the Republicans recommended a separate and distinct Indian department, the head of which would be a member of the Cabinet.[55]

However, the equal division within the committee, which dramatized the basic difficulties confronting a satisfactory solution to the problem, served only to nullify the conclusions of both factions. As Loring Benson Priest has concluded, the failure to reach an acceptable decision was itself significant, for the opponents of transfer had been granted an important delay.[56] From that time on, the decreasing danger of large-scale Indian warfare and the extensive reforms undertaken by Schurz in the Interior Department rapidly weakened arguments for transfer.

By far the most unusual piece of antitransfer propaganda was published by the Universal Peace Union in September, 1879. Purportedly, it was a letter from Sitting Bull, who was then a refugee in Canada. In June, 1876, the letter stated, the Indians had sent a flag of truce as Custer approached the village on the Little Big Horn, but the brave who carried it had been shot down like a dog. It implored the Great Spirit to "save the whites from distribution and annuities to be made under the sword of officers and soldiers! We call the representatives of the Great Father sent to us 'Fathers.' We think they are queer fathers, always armed to meet their children. . . .

54. James D. Richardson, ed., *A Compilation of Messages and Papers of the Presidents*, 1897–1917 ed., IX, 4455–56.
55. *The Nation*, XXVIII (February 6, 1879), 75, 93.
56. Priest, *Uncle Sam's Stepchildren*, 22.

We desire peace, but we cannot have peace as long as we are pursued by army men, who seem to be bound to drive us into [a] fight, when we desire anything else. We desire to see ourselves educated in the medicine of life—religion of the black gown."[57] The authenticity of the letter has never been established.

In February, 1879, the House defeated several measures to effect transfer, and for all practical purposes, the issue never again seriously threatened to gain congressional approval. With the defeat of transfer, the humanitarians were certain that they had scored another victory for the cause of Indian progress and civilization. Even more important was the additional impetus given to Secretary Schurz's reformation of the Indian Bureau. The much-needed reform and reorganization, although it reduced church participation to an unofficial and voluntary status, permitted advocates of the Peace Policy to defend the existing system with considerably more credibility. Reforming the Indian Bureau was an indispensable part of the fight against military control.[58]

57. "Sitting Bull," *The Voice of Peace*, VI (September, 1879), 86.
58. Priest, *Uncle Sam's Stepchildren*, 22.

10

The Ponca Controversy

The concentration of all Western Indian tribes upon a few large reservations was an essential part of the Grant Administration's Indian policy. This policy had been strongly supported by Western settlers, particularly those settlers in areas from which the Indians would be removed. As time went on, however, the population in the Western states and territories grew rapidly, and people began to protest when the government proposed that any additional tribes move to neighboring reservations. Furthermore, most railroad promoters opposed any change for fear it would interfere with projected lines. Bishop Whipple, Alfred Love, John Beeson, and many other humanitarians also objected to this policy because they thought it would force tribes to live in unfamiliar regions and perhaps to be located among old tribal enemies. Finally, the Indians themselves firmly opposed being removed.

With such an array of opponents, the Grant Administration proceeded slowly with the removal plan. By the fall of 1876, there were some 76 separate reservations, excluding 28 in the Indian Territory. This situation was in contrast with Grant's original plan to concentrate all the Indians in two large areas on public lands north of Nebraska and south of Kansas.[1] By 1876, this plan had been modified so that three, and possibly four, large reservations were proposed. These were the Indian Territory, the White Earth Reservation in northern Minnesota, the Yakima Reservation in southern Washington Territory, and possibly a fourth in Colorado or Arizona.[2]

In his report of October 30, 1876, Indian Commissioner John Q. Smith asserted that the policy of concentration of the tribes on a few reservations would remove much of the difficulty surrounding the Indian question. Many agencies would be abolished, which would reduce the expense. The aggregate boundary lines between

1. Loring Benson Priest, *Uncle Sam's Stepchildren: The Reformation of United States Indian Policy, 1865–1887*, 6.
2. Commissioner of Indian Affairs, *Annual Report of the Commissioner of Indian Affairs*, 1876, *Annual Report of the Secretary of the Interior*, 44th Cong., 2d sess., 1876–1877, House Exec. Doc. No. 1 (Serial 1749), vii.

the reservations and the country occupied by white people would be greatly shortened, and the contact between the races would be reduced. The sale of liquor and arms could be more effectively prevented; white encroachment on Indian Territory could be more easily controlled; a far smaller military force would be needed; and generally, the Indians could be more efficiently aided and controlled by the government. Finally—and this appealed especially to settlers—the government could sell large amounts of newly opened land for settlement, and the money from the sales could be used to defray the expense of removing the Indians.[3]

During 1876, the government accelerated its removal program. It completed the removal of the Pawnees from Nebraska to Indian Territory, began negotiations with the Red Cloud and Spotted Tail Sioux for a similar move, and took steps to settle the Poncas in the same area. On the surface, moving the Poncas appeared to be not only logical but necessary. Their reservation in the southeast corner of Dakota Territory was frequently raided by the neighboring Sioux, who resented the Poncas' living on lands included in the permanent Sioux reservation.

This unpleasant predicament was the aftermath of a government blunder. In drawing up the Sioux Treaty of 1868, the Indian Bureau had ceded to the Sioux 96,000 acres that the Treaty of March, 1865, had granted to the Poncas. Since the Treaty of 1868 was still in force in 1877 and the Sioux demanded possession of the area, the Interior Department claimed it had no alternative but to remove the Poncas. The Sioux were a powerful, warlike tribe, and moving the small and more docile Ponca tribe appeared much more expedient. In addition, the situation gave the Indian Bureau an excuse to carry out its plan to settle as many tribes as possible in Indian Territory.

The Sioux attacks had made the Poncas resist civilization, and Commissioner Smith was confident that the proposed removal would benefit the Poncas. Furthermore, the vacated lands would provide a suitable home for some wild bands of Sioux. Congress had approved funds for the operation, but unfortunately, the sum appropriated was inadequate. Moreover, the plan could not be put into effect until the Poncas consented.[4]

At first, the Poncas refused even to discuss the matter. Finally, the government persuaded them to send a delegation of 10 chiefs to inspect the lands set aside for them in Indian Territory. The pros-

3. *Ibid.*, ix.
4. *Ibid.*, xvii.

pects so disheartened 8 of the delegates that they returned home on foot before reaching the destination. The 2 remaining chiefs completed the journey and, upon the urgings of the accompanying Indian Bureau officials, selected an area for settlement. Meanwhile, the tribe had split over the issue. The minority, who favored moving, were attacked and terrorized. Finally, of 717 tribesmen, only 170 were willing to begin the trek south, and these required military protection. After a miserable journey of 59 days in stormy, cold weather, the contingent finally reached its new reservation. Fortunately, according to Indian Inspector Kemble, the Poncas seemed "exceedingly well pleased" with their new home.[5]

Meanwhile, the Indian Bureau had ordered the refractory portion of the tribe removed at once. The Poncas learned that they had to move, and they were asked whether they "would go peaceably or by force." Realizing the futility of further resistance, they sullenly agreed. A succession of disasters marred the 65 day trek of the second party. Their march also was hampered by heavy rain storms, mud, and high water, but in addition, many became seriously ill. To compound the misery, a tornado struck the camp in southern Nebraska and caused one death, several serious injuries, and considerable damage to wagons and supplies. As the journey continued, deaths from illness began to multiply; by July 2, after 47 days on the road, nine Indians had been buried along the way. At this point, one Ponca brave tried to kill the head chief of the tribe. After two hours of turmoil that threatened to break out in open revolt, the Army quelled the disturbance and ordered the disgruntled rebel back to the Omaha Agency.[6]

These later arrivals were far from satisfied with their new reservation. They had inadequate housing and suffered from fatigue, oppressive heat, and malaria—a disease new to this northern tribe. The Poncas asked to visit the President in Washington, and in the fall of 1877, a delegation met with President Hayes. They asked to be allowed either to return to their old reservation in Dakota or to join their kinsmen, the Omahas, in Nebraska. The President said they could do neither because removing any Indians *from* Indian Territory was both unwise and impossible. Such a move would be directly contrary to the government's policy of concentration. How-

    5. Commissioner of Indian Affairs, *Annual Report of the Commissioner of Indian Affairs*, 1877, *Annual Report of the Secretary of the Interior*, 45th Cong., 2d sess., 1877–1878, House Exec. Doc. No. 1 (Serial 1800), 21–22.

    6. E. A. Howard, Agent, report, August 25, 1877, *Annual Report of the Commissioner of Indian Affairs*, 1877, 97–99.

ever, the disappointed delegates were told they could select a permanent home in a more desirable location.[7]

The Poncas' experience did bring about a modification of the original reservation program. As Indian Commissioner Hayt reported on November 1, 1877, the new policy would still embrace a steady concentration of the smaller bands on the large reservations, but there would be a "discontinuance of the removal of the northern Indians to the Indian Territory. This last is essential to the well-being of the Indians, since the effect of the change of climate to which they are subjected by such removals tells with fatal effect upon their health and longevity."[8] The Commissioner's decision did not take effect until after the defeated survivors of the Nez Percé War of 1877 were transported to the Indian Territory in the summer of 1878. Largely overshadowed by the Ponca affair, the tragedy of the Nez Percé removal did not attract reform attention until later. As with the Poncas, the mortality from disease was severe.

In his annual report for 1878, Hayt admitted that the Poncas had been wronged, and he asked that restitution be made "as far as it is in the powers of the government to do so." They had received no compensation for the violation of the Treaty of 1865 or for the homes and agricultural implements that they had left behind. The government could, and should, make immediate payment for these, but, he added, the "removal inflicted a far greater injury upon the Poncas, for which no reparation can be made—the loss by death of many of their number, caused by a change in climate."[9] On February 3, 1879, the Interior Department presented a bill to Congress "for the relief of the Ponca tribe." This bill granted them permanent title to their chosen tract in Indian Territory and $140,000 in reparations. They were to use $82,000 to purchase their new reservation from the Cherokees; the Indian Bureau would invest the balance for them in government bonds.[10]

Meanwhile, the Poncas were becoming increasingly unhappy. Malarial fever and chills caused severe suffering and so many deaths that by the end of the first year a census of the tribe showed a decrease

7. *Annual Report of the Commissioner of Indian Affairs,* 1877, 23.
8. *Ibid.,* 2.
9. Commissioner of Indian Affairs, *Annual Report of the Commissioner of Indian Affairs,* 1878, *Annual Report of the Secretary of the Interior,* 45th Cong., 3d sess., 1878–1879, House Exec. Doc. No. 1 (Serial 1850), xxxvi–xxxvii.
10. Commissioner of Indian Affairs, *Annual Report of the Commissioner of Indian Affairs,* 1879, *Annual Report of the Secretary of the Interior,* 46th Cong., 2d sess., 1879–1880, House Exec. Doc. No. 1 (Serial 1910), xiv.

from 684 to 639 persons. These figures presented an alarming contrast with the total of 717 that left the Dakota reservation the previous year.[11] Late in December, 1878, Standing Bear, one of the principal chiefs of the tribe, saw his last son die from malaria. Now completely certain that only one course would end the suffering and misery, he placed the body of his child in an old wagon and, with thirty other Poncas, began the long trek north to Dakota. By early spring, the party managed to reach the Omaha reservation in Nebraska, where the Omahas welcomed them.[12]

However, the government had no intention of permitting such a brazen flouting of its authority. Commissioner Hayt observed, "I am sure Congress will not consent to send all these Indians back North. We must reconcile them to stay . . . in the Indian Territory."[13] In May, General Crook was ordered to arrest the runaway Poncas and escort them back to the Indian Territory.

By this time, newspaper accounts of the tribulations of Standing Bear and his fellow tribesmen were attracting national attention. The Indian-rights advocates in particular reacted as strongly as they had to the Piegan Massacre in 1870. Mary C. Morgan, a representative of the Indian Hope Association of New York, implored Mrs. Rutherford B. Hayes to "speak a word for the wretched Indians." Alluding to the indifference of high-ranking officials, she asked, "*Who* can read the speeches of the Ponca Chiefs at Omaha & not feel a throb of *indignation* at the cold blooded [*sic*] injustice & cruelties?" The forced removal of the tribe to a "poisonous climate," she asserted, made the whites just as guilty of murder "as tho' inflicted with knife or gun. My God! it seems to me, if *I* were situated as *you* are, I would exert every energy in my nature" to bring justice to them. "If you *would* only use your influence for the noble work of ameliorating evil & wretchedness."[14]

Not all of the demands for justice were as passionately stated as Mary Morgan's, but the same anger and indignation had infected not only the humanitarian ranks but also the general public. The Poncas' case was not the first involving hardship and tragedy. The

11. William H. Whiteman, Agent, report, August 31, 1878, *Annual Report of the Commissioner of Indian Affairs*, 1878, 65.

12. Earl W. Hayter, "The Ponca Removal," *North Dakota Historical Quarterly*, VI, 4 (July, 1932), 271; Thomas Henry Tibbles, *Buckskin and Blanket Days*, 194–95.

13. Zylyff [Wendell Phillips], *The Ponca Chiefs*, 66.

14. Mary C. Morgan, letter to Mrs. Rutherford B. Hayes, April 3, 1879, Bureau of Indian Affairs, Letters Received.

public was still aware of the costly war resulting from the attempted Nez Percé removal in 1877 and the unsuccessful flight of Dull Knife's Cheyennes from Indian Territory to their old homes in Dakota in 1878, which ended with the Fort Robinson Massacre of the captured band. The humanitarians thought the Ponca removal represented the culmination of a series of injustices. Also, by 1879, the usually apathetic public had been sufficiently swayed by Indian-rights propaganda and newspaper reports to react with remarkable vigor. The result was a powerful and prolonged renewal of interest in the Indian problem that would culminate in a second major reform movement in Indian policy.

The Poncas received widespread support for their refusal to return to the Indian Territory. Surprisingly, residents of the Dakota Territory and Nebraska were among the foremost agitators for restoration of the tribe to their old home. In a petition to the Senate, the pastors of Yankton, Dakota Territory, asked that the Poncas be allowed to return for the sake of justice and their general welfare. Also, their return might prevent another Indian war, and finally, "their former white neighbors on the border, who remonstrated against their removal, would feel safer if they were allowed to return, because they would stand between them and the Sioux."[15]

Republican Senators Paddock of Nebraska and Henry M. Teller of Colorado supported the petition. Paddock had opposed the Ponca removal in 1878 because he was a friend of the Indian "so far as it is practicable to be at this juncture" and because he opposed any further Indian removals unless the Indians agreed. Teller, serving his second year in the Senate, favored a civilization policy. He had opposed the Ponca removal because it was "a shame and disgrace to this nation."[16] With influential friends in both East and West, the Poncas had a better chance for justice.

The mixture of humanitarian altruism and practicality in the Yankton petition may also have motivated a group of citizens from Omaha, Nebraska (the Omaha Committee) to make the first organized efforts to secure justice for the Poncas. With the counsel of several prominent Omaha lawyers, Standing Bear brought suit before Judge Elmer Dundy of the United States District Court for a writ of habeas corpus. For the Indian-rights advocates the case was especially significant. Not only were Westerners taking a leading part in the Indians' defense, but also, as John Beeson pointed out at a meeting of the Universal Peace Union in Philadelphia, the decision

15. *Congressional Record*, 46th Cong., 1st sess., 1879, IX, Part 1, 716.
16. *Ibid.*, 45th Cong., 2d sess., 1877–1878, VII, Part 4, 3239–40, 3311.

was important "as a test whether the government has a legal right to remove Indians anywhere in violation of their treaties."[17]

On May 19, 1879, Judge Dundy ruled that an Indian was a person within the meaning of the habeas corpus act and thus was entitled to sue a writ of habeas corpus in the Federal courts. Dundy further ruled that because the right of expatriation was a "natural, inherent, and inalienable right," it extended to the Indians as well as white people. His concluding statement made Dundy the Indian-rights hero of the hour:

> In time of peace no authority, civil or military, exists for transporting Indians from one section of the country to another, without the consent of the Indians, nor to confine them to any particular reservation against their will, and where officers of the government attempt to do this, and arrest and hold Indians who are at peace with the government, for the purpose of removing them to, and confining them on a reservation in the Indian Territory, they will be released on habeas corpus.[18]

After this victory, the Omaha Committee was even more determined to see that the Poncas received full justice. In June, 1879, the committee sent Reverend Thomas H. Tibbles, an assistant editor of the *Omaha Daily Herald* who had helped to organize the Ponca movement, to the East Coast to secure money and backing for the cause. They wanted to bring suit in the Supreme Court for the recovery of the land in Dakota and then transport the Poncas in the Indian Territory back to the original reservation. In addition, they hoped that the legal and civil status of the Indians could be clarified.

After Dundy's decision, the United States District Attorney immediately appealed the case to the Federal Circuit Court. While they awaited a hearing on the appeal, Standing Bear and his followers were not allowed to settle upon any Indian reservation because they were no longer wards of the government. Consequently, they were forced to stay on an island in the Niobrara River, a part of the old reservation that had been overlooked in the Treaty of 1868. Because it was too late to plant crops and employment was difficult to find, the Poncas had to depend on the charity of the Omaha Committee.[19]

Thomas Tibbles was a native of Ohio. When he was a young man, he had drifted westward and eventually reached eastern Kansas during the turbulent 1850's. He became a member of John Brown's

17. Universal Peace Union, "Official Report of the Thirteenth Anniversary Meeting," *The Voice of Peace*, VI (June, 1879), 39.
18. Zylyff, *Ponca Chiefs*, 106–7.
19. Ruth Odell, *Helen Hunt Jackson*, 161–62.

antislavery company and participated in the local Underground Railroad until the Civil War. He served as a scout on the Plains during the war and then became an itinerant preacher. After preaching for eight years, he took a job for the Omaha *Daily Bee* but moved to the *Omaha Daily Herald* in 1876.

The Poncas' attempt to resist the might of the Federal Government had won Tibbles' admiration. His many years of close association with the Plains tribes—he claimed to be one of the few white members of the Sioux Soldier Lodge—prompted his identification with the Indians. When Secretary Schurz had failed to respond to his widely publicized criticism of the Interior Department's orders to return the Poncas to Indian Territory by force, Tibbles was convinced that he was "in for another fight on the very same principle" that had carried him to Bleeding Kansas in 1856, namely "that before the law all men are equal."[20]

Tibbles' lecture tour in the East was a success, especially in Boston, where he received the enthusiastic support of Edward Everett Hale and Wendell Phillips. Phillips encouraged him to continue the fight for Indian rights and promised any service that he could render, but he warned Tibbles that he would "have to endure and suffer and drink the cup of bitterness" before the battle would be won. Urged on by interested Boston philanthropists, Tibbles arranged a second lecture tour soon after he returned to Omaha in September.[21] This time, to ensure greater success, he planned to take Chief Standing Bear and two young Omaha Indians—Susette LaFlesche, whose Indian name was Bright Eyes, and her brother, Wood Carver. Bright Eyes had been well educated in a New Jersey school, and although she was only part Indian, she was intensely interested in the Indians' welfare. She was to act as interpreter for Standing Bear. The lecture tour, Tibbles hoped, would not only arouse additional sympathy for the wronged Poncas, but also raise funds to support the homeless northern band and defray the expense of lawsuits brought to recover their Dakota lands.[22]

Tibbles and his party arrived in Boston on October 29 and immediately became the objects of great popular attention and adulation. The enthusiasm shown for the Indian cause at the lectures and receptions recalled the triumphant tour of Red Cloud and the Sioux chiefs in 1871. Boston, which *The Nation* called the "philanthropic center of the country," was particularly receptive to the complaints of wronged Indians, and the Ponca tour was no exception. After

20. Tibbles, *Buckskin and Blanket Days*, 199.
21. *Ibid.*, 209–11.
22. Odell, *Helen Hunt Jackson*, 158, 162.

hearing the testimony of Standing Bear and Bright Eyes, the merchants of Boston called a public meeting, and a committee was appointed to investigate the wrongs suffered by the Ponca Indians and
the general management of all the Indian tribes. The committee of
five consisted of Massachusetts Governor Thomas Talbot, Boston
Mayor Frederick Prince, and three other prominent Bostonians.

At the first meeting, the committee unanimously resolved that
since the Poncas had been unlawfully deprived of their lands, it was
the government's duty to restore their homes and property to them.
It was further resolved that since the Indians were "persons" under
the law, they were protected by the provisions of the Constitution
and could not be deprived of "life, liberty, or property without due
process of law." Also, they should be amenable to the law and
possess the rights accorded to people of every nationality, race, or
color residing within the nation.[23] These resolutions expressed the
prevailing humanitarian feeling in November, 1879. These or similar principles soon became the code of operation for Ponca sympathizers throughout the nation.

By the end of November, Tibbles' campaign in Boston was
flourishing. Many people had become involved in the Ponca cause,
and they had raised nearly $7,000 to finance the Supreme Court case.
However, when an anonymous benefactor offered to donate $3,000 to
make up the deficit if Secretary Schurz would support the movement,
complications occurred. Schurz was evasive at first, but it was obvious
that he did not approve of the suit or the demands for an investigation of the Ponca problem. The Secretary's adamancy touched off a
controversy between some reformers and the Interior Department
that was not settled until the Ponca case had been closed and a new
Administration had taken office.

The dispute started when a letter from Helen Hunt Jackson
was published in *The New York Tribune* on December 15, 1879.
In this letter, Mrs. Jackson unmercifully criticized the Secretary for
opposing the Ponca suit. Schurz telegraphed an angry reply to the
Tribune that left no doubt where he stood on the matter.[24] In 1879,
Helen Hunt Jackson was widely known for her prose and poetical
works, but up to that time she had never identified herself with any
reform movement. She had been born in Massachusetts and had
moved to Colorado Springs in 1873 on the advice of her physician.

23. Zylyff, *Ponca Chiefs*, inside back cover. The committee, in November, 1879, adopted the name "The Boston Merchants Committee on the
Removal of the Ponca Indians."
24. Odell, *Helen Hunt Jackson*, 162–63; *The Nation*, XXX (February
12, 1880), 105–6.

She married a Quaker businessman from Colorado Springs and lived in Colorado until her death in 1885. In November, 1879, while visiting literary friends in Boston, she attended one of Tibbles' Indian-rights lectures. She "was fired with the indignation that was to be the motivating factor in everything she did or said or thought or wrote for the rest of her life."[25] Mrs. Jackson was one of many humanitarians who took the Ponca wrongs to heart. As Martha Goddard of Boston wrote to Schurz on December 19, the condition of the Indians was the "great question now, and you would be surprised if you knew how much people here think about it & care for it, not passionately, or with any political afterthought, but earnestly, and as a matter of humanity & justice & national honor, as they cared for the emancipation of the slaves."[26]

Mrs. Jackson sent her second attack directly to the Secretary. On January 9, 1880, she wrote Schurz that if he approved of the Poncas bringing suit to recover their lands, they would have all the money they needed immediately. If he did not approve, would he be willing to give the reasons for his disapproval? She asked him to state these reasons "in clear and explicit form."[27] Eight days later, Schurz's reply came in the manner requested. He told Mrs. Jackson that he believed the collection of money for a Supreme Court case was "useless" because, as the Supreme Court repeatedly had decided, an Indian tribe could not sue the United States or a state in the Federal courts. Therefore, collecting money and paying attorneys to do a thing that could not be done would be foolish. Schurz then suggested that instead of wasting their money on a court case, they would accomplish much more by donating it to new Indian schools like Hampton and Carlisle. The solution to the problem of Indian lands, he concluded, was to settle them in severalty and give individual titles in fee simple. The Indians would then hold their lands by the same title by which white men held theirs and would have the same standing in the courts and the same legal protection of their property.[28]

On the same day that Secretary Schurz was composing his reply to Mrs. Jackson, she wrote to a close friend, "I think I feel as you must have felt in the old abolition days. I cannot think of anything else. . . . I believe the time is drawing near for a great change in our

---

25. Odell, *Helen Hunt Jackson*, 152–53.

26. Martha Goddard, letter to Secretary Schurz, December 19, 1879, in Carl Schurz Letters, Carl Schurz Papers, Vol. 56.

27. Helen Hunt Jackson, letter to Carl Schurz, January 9, 1880, in Helen Hunt Jackson Letters, Carl Schurz Papers, Vol. 57.

28. Carl Schurz, letter to Helen Hunt Jackson, January 15, 1880, *ibid.*

policy toward the Indians. In some respects, it seems to me, he is really worse off than the slaves." She also said that she would soon begin her research at the Astor Library on a history of the government's injustice toward the Indians.[29]

Shortly after receiving Schurz's letter of January 17, Mrs. Jackson replied with a series of pointed questions that were intended to force the Secretary's hand. She asked if he would be in favor of the Poncas recovering their lands by process of law, "provided it were practicable." Then—if his only objection to bringing suit was that it "would be futile"—could he not agree, if reputable lawyers were ready to undertake the case, to see the attempt made in the courts and the question settled? "If it is, as you think, a futile effort, it will be shown so. If it is, as the friends and lawyers of the Poncas think, a practicable thing, a great wrong will be righted."[30] Although there were other questions, forthright answers to these questions would indicate where the Secretary stood on the Indians' rights and the reform cause.

The Secretary's reply indicated no change in his original attitude. He did point out that *if* an Indian tribe could legally maintain an action in the Federal courts to assert its rights, he would not object to it. On the other hand, he objected to the collection of money from public-spirited persons "ostensibly for the benefit of the Indians, but in fact for the benefit of attorneys and others" who were to be paid for testing a question that the Supreme Court already had clearly decided. Schurz warned that processing such a suit would actually hurt the Indian-rights movement. If the movement were so conducted that it resulted "only in putting money into pockets of private individuals, without any benefit to the Indians, the collapse will be as hurtful as it seems to be inevitable." Such an ignominious end, he added, would deter the "sincere friends of the Indians" from further efforts of that kind and thus seriously cripple future welfare projects for them. He then observed that a number of severalty bills were before Congress, and the passage of one would do more than any court decision to secure for the Indian the "practical enjoyment of his property."[31]

The New York Tribune and *The Boston Daily Advertiser* published extracts from the Jackson-Schurz correspondence, and in those cities, the verbal duel fomented considerable excitement. *The New York Times* observed that Secretary Schurz had left the impression

29. Thomas Wentworth Higginson, *Contemporaries,* 155.
30. Helen Hunt Jackson, letter to Carl Schurz, January 22, 1880, in Helen Hunt Jackson Letters, Carl Schurz Papers, Vol. 57.
31. Helen Hunt Jackson, *A Century of Dishonor,* 365–66.

that he did not approve of the movement to secure legal rights for the Poncas. As for his solution to the Indian problem, which advocated lands in severalty, the *Times* expressed regret that he did not show how "giving to an Indian of 160 acres of land can clothe him with civil rights which he does not now possess, and which the Secretary thinks that the courts cannot give him."[32] While the *Times* sided with the humanitarian forces, *The Nation* supported Schurz's conclusion as the more logical one.[33] To show his support, Clinton B. Fisk of the Board of Indian Commissioners wrote to the Secretary on January 29, "Your plans are the only ones that will bring peace & justice."[34] On the other hand, the Philadelphia *Telegraph* charged that Schurz was contesting the admission of Indians to the protection of the courts and that he was trying to impede the friends of the Indians who wished Judge Dundy's decision confirmed by the Supreme Court. The Secretary vehemently replied that these allegations were untrue and that he recognized Judge Dundy's decision "as good and did not contest it at all." Furthermore, he did not contest the Indians' right to go into court; he had simply showed that, as the law stood, an Indian tribe had no standing in the court. Schurz then reminded Dunbar Lockwood, editor of the *Telegraph*, that as a result of the Ponca controversy, he had introduced legislative provisions in Congress for opening the courts to the Indians on an equal basis with white people.[35]

Another attack on the Administration's Indian policy came in a book entitled *The Ponca Chiefs*. The book, which had an Introduction by Bright Eyes, was written by Wendell Phillips under the pseudonym of Zylyff. It contained a merciless critique: The wrongs and sufferings inflicted upon the Poncas were a "fair specimen of the system of injustice, oppression, and robbery which the Government calls 'its Indian policy.'" Through this policy, the Government had become "incompetent, cruel, faithless," and having "systematically and shamelessly" violated its most solemn promises, it had "earned the contempt and detestation of all honest men and distrust and hate of the Indian tribes."[36]

During the winter of 1879–1880, Interior Department officials received a tremendous amount of criticism, but another side to the

32. *The New York Times*, February 21, 1880, in Jackson, *A Century of Dishonor*, 368.
33. *The Nation*, XXX (February 12, 1880), 105.
34. Clinton B. Fisk, letter to Secretary Schurz, January 29, 1880, in Carl Schurz Letters, Carl Schurz Papers, Vol. 58.
35. Carl Schurz, letter to E. Dunbar Lockwood, April 1, 1880, Carl Schurz Papers, Vol. 60.
36. Zylyff, *Ponca Chiefs*, iii.

Ponca furor renewed the Secretary's optimism. From Philadelphia, Mrs. Mary Longstreth wrote Schurz, "We are now gladdened by the prospect of better things through a humane and righteous policy, and an improved public sentiment."[37] Shortly after the publication of Schurz's first letter, Indian Commissioner Fisk reported from New York City that the discussion of the Ponca question in New York was "awakening thoughtful men to the importance of making common cause with yourself in pushing for proper legislation."[38] In February, William E. Dodge told the Secretary that there was then more feeling in the best circles about the Indians than he had ever known. Dodge said he fully supported Schurz's "lands in severalty" plan and his educational program for the Indians.[39] Several months later, Dodge presented a Presbyterian committee's memorial to the government requesting the further extension of these principles.[40]

In Chicago, the American Missionary Association passed resolutions supporting a program very similar to that endorsed by the Interior Secretary. The association advocated securing for the Indians equal consideration in the courts, the ownership of land in severalty, and the full rights of United States citizenship. Fisk assured Schurz that the "best elements in New England and the North West" would support such a platform.[41] From Sacramento, California, word came that the Secretary's Indian policy had received the "most hearty approval from the best elements of the Pacific Coast."[42] Even in Boston, the Boston Merchants Committee on the Removal of the Ponca Indians admitted that they had been impressed with the zeal and honesty of the Indian agents, especially since the introduction of the radical reforms under Grant. The committee then recommended a series of measures that accorded closely with Schurz's program to solve the Indian problem.[43] The basic difference between the Interior Department's plan and the proposals of most humanitarians was the humanitarians' emphasis on full citizenship for all the tribes. Schurz

37. Mrs. Mary Longstreth, letter to Carl Schurz, February 9, 1880, in Carl Schurz Letters, Carl Schurz Papers, Vol. 58.

38. Clinton B. Fisk, letter to Carl Schurz, December 22, 1879, in Carl Schurz Letters, Carl Schurz Papers, Vol. 56.

39. William E. Dodge, letter to Carl Schurz, February 6, 1880, in Carl Schurz Letters, Carl Schurz Papers, Vol. 58.

40. D. Stuart Dodge, *Memorials of William E. Dodge*, 179.

41. Fisk, letter to Schurz, December 22, 1879.

42. Emma Allison, letter to Secretary Schurz, January 12, 1880, in Carl Schurz Letters, Carl Schurz Papers, Vol. 57.

43. The Boston Merchants Committee on the Removal of the Ponca Indians, *The Indian Question*, 4, 12.

believed that individual ownership of land and equal rights before the courts must come first.

As far as the advocates of Indian rights were concerned, Judge Dundy's decision was only the beginning of litigation involving the civil rights and land ownership of the Ponca tribe and, by implication, all other Indians as well. On April 3, 1880, the attorneys for the Omaha Ponca Indian Committee initiated a series of court cases aimed at establishing the Poncas' title to their old reservation lands. At the same time, the case of *John Elk vs. Charles Wilkins* began in the Circuit Court of the Nebraska District to determine the rights of the Indians under the Fourteenth Amendment.[44]

Meanwhile, a Senate committee that had been appointed to investigate the Ponca removal reported that a "great wrong had been done to the Ponca Indians" and recommended restoration of their old lands and ample reparation.[45] Encouraged by the Senate committee's condemnation of the government's treatment of the Poncas and the committee's approval of any procedure that would right the flagrant wrong, the Omaha Committee devised a new plan. Since only the Supreme Court had jurisdiction in the Indian Territory, the committee concluded that the only way to test the case in the courts would be to induce the Poncas in the Indian Territory to cross the border into Kansas.[46]

At the request of the committee, Tibbles arranged a secret visit to the Ponca band in the Indian Territory. In June, 1880, he reached the Ponca Agency and met the chiefs of the tribe. Following the committee's instructions, Tibbles informed them that since they had been illegally removed, they had a legal right to return home; that the Omaha Committee would help them get back to their old lands; and that if they were arrested, the committee would undertake to test the matter in the United States District Court in Kansas. When the

44. Jackson, *A Century of Dishonor*, 373–74. On December 14, 1870, the Senate Judiciary Committee had concluded that the Fourteenth Amendment had "no effect whatever upon the status of the Indian tribes within the limits of the United States" and that the Indians were excluded because they were not citizens. Senate, Committee on the Judiciary, *The Effect of the Fourteenth Amendment upon the Indian Tribes*, 41st Cong., 3d sess., 1870–1871, Senate Report No. 268 (Serial 1443), I, 10.

45. James D. Richardson, ed., *A Compilation of the Messages and Papers of the Presidents*, 1897–1917 ed., X, 4584.

46. Jackson, *A Century of Dishonor*, 370; Senate, *Testimony Before the Select Committee on Removal of Northern Cheyennes as to the Removal and Situation of the Ponca Indians*, 46th Cong., 3d sess., 1880–1881, Senate Miscell. Doc. No. 49 (Serial 1944), 37. Hereafter cited as *Removal of the Poncas*.

chiefs expressed reluctance and asked for time to consider the matter, Tibbles explained that it would be a long time before the courts could settle it by suits in Dakota and Nebraska and that it would be nearly a year before Congress could act on the case.[47] According to him, the Indians said they were afraid they might be killed if they left the reservation without permission. However, before they reached a final decision, Tibbles was arrested by authority of an order from Washington, thoroughly questioned, then forcibly ejected from the reservation, and warned of more severe treatment if he returned.[48]

The dramatically conceived plot to rescue the Poncas from their oppressors failed in rather ignominious fashion, but the publicity it received may have done more to help the Indians' cause than another test case. At any rate, the public appeared more strongly than ever to favor the Indians. As *The New York Tribune* pointed out, "The Indian Department may as well understand at once that the Ponca case has passed out of their control. It is a matter of simple justice which the people are determined to see righted."[49]

Shortly after the Tibbles affair, the Indian Bureau issued an order stating that any Ponca who left the Indian Territory and took with him any property would be arrested for stealing. Because they could not travel to Dakota without food and transportation, Helen Hunt Jackson observed, this order kept them imprisoned as effectively as a military guard. The order seemed to belie the Indian Bureau's report that the Poncas were so content that it would be very difficult for anyone to induce them to leave their new home.[50]

In October, 1880, the Secretary of the Interior received a memorial signed by the chiefs and headmen of the Ponca Agency in the Indian Territory asking title to that reservation and indicating their willingness to give up their rights to the Dakota lands. On the surface, this message appeared to verify the Indian Bureau's assertions of Ponca contentment. However, the statement made it clear that all were not satisfied, for it said, "Our young men are unsettled and hard to control, while they think we have a right to our land in Dakota."[51] The publication of the memorial in the press again stirred up public and humanitarian indignation.

President Hayes, in his annual message of December 6, 1880, outlined an Indian program containing the features that reformers had been demanding for the past decade. It consisted of three major

47. *Ibid.*, 38; Tibbles, *Buckskin and Blanket Days*, 226.
48. Jackson, *A Century of Dishonor*, 371.
49. *Ibid.*
50. *Ibid.*, 372.
51. *Removal of the Poncas*, 16.

provisions and one objective. It provided for allotment in severalty, with the fee-simple title inalienable for a certain period; equal protection under the law; and "vigorous prosecution" of Indian education. Its aim was to prepare for the "gradual merging of our Indian population in the great body of American citizenship."[52] It said nothing about ending the forcible reservation system, the particular anathema of reformers like Alfred Love, Wendell Phillips, and Helen Hunt Jackson. The policy, which Secretary Schurz had drawn up, was essentially the one he had been trying to effect during the past year. The features were not new; all had been objectives under Grant's Peace Policy. Schurz's policy differed in that its primary emphasis was on allotment in severalty. Schurz believed that individual ownership of land and an agricultural vocation were necessary conditions for civilization. When an Indian became an independent farmer who owned the soil he tilled and who knew the essentials of reading, writing the English language, and arithmetic, he would be ready to become a full-fledged citizen. This belief was thoroughly Jeffersonian in concept, but it also embodied the current theory of cultural evolution—that mankind's progress upward naturally evolved from hunting, to herding, and finally to farming.[53] To achieve the civilization of the Indians in the shortest time possible, the herding stage must be artificially by-passed. This idea partly explains the reason that the Indian policy makers so often opposed encouraging the Plains tribes to adopt a pastoral economy, as Lewis Henry Morgan advocated.

Officials of the Indian Bureau and the Interior Department still thought that the forcible reservation system, even with its removals, was a necessary preliminary to allotment in severalty, but as a result of the Ponca and Nez Percé resistance, Indian Commissioner Hayt had proposed a modification of the policy in October, 1877. The Indian-rights workers considered the Ponca case a living example of the hated system. Many of them regarded Schurz's conservative and legalistic approach to the Indian problem as mere obstinacy or even antihumanitarianism.

The outcry that followed the Ponca memorial of October brought further government action. On December 18, 1880, President Hayes appointed a special commission composed of Generals George

52. Richardson, *Messages and Papers*, 1897–1917 ed., X, 4576–77.
53. Anthropologist A. L. Kroeber maintains that this concept was a "pseudo-philosophical guess aiming to supersede actual history" and that masses of scholarly and scientific evidence contradict it. In fact, he adds, the theory has been traced back to speculations made by the Sumerians of Lower Mesopotamia 5,000 years ago. A. L. Kroeber, *Anthropology*, 278.

Crook and Nelson A. Miles and two well-known civilians, William Stickney and Walter Allen. The commission thoroughly investigated both Ponca bands and reported their findings on January 25, 1881. The report agreed with the Senate's conclusion that the Poncas had been unjustly treated, but it confirmed the Indian Bureau's contention that the band in the Indian Territory unanimously desired to stay in their new home. On the other hand, it revealed that Standing Bear's band was just as determined to remain in Dakota. Since Congress had failed to pass the Ponca bill of February, 1879, the commission recommended that Congress enact immediate legislation making ample reparations for losses incurred by removal.[54]

Meanwhile, a delegation of Ponca chiefs from Indian Territory—the authors of the memorial of October 25, 1880—arrived in Washington to discuss the confirmation of title to their new lands, the relinquishment of the old reservation, and indemnification for their losses. The Boston Indian Citizenship Association, of which Governor John D. Long of Massachusetts and Helen Hunt Jackson were members, was highly suspicious of the sudden conversion of the once-recalcitrant band. Long's and Jackson's denunciations of Schurz were so frequent and violent that they aroused *The Nation,* which supported the Secretary. Godkin's periodical was especially critical of Tibbles and labeled him the "chief authority for stories of oppression and suffering, known to be exaggerated, if not intentional falsifications." This statement appeared after Tibbles had charged that Schurz had used threats to deter the Ponca delegates from speaking their minds freely, that he had prevented the representatives of the Dakota Poncas, who were also in Washington, from seeing them, and that he had purposely garbled the memorial of October 25, which expressed their willingness to sell their Dakota lands. He had misused the memorial in order to furnish Congress a basis for making amends and settling the issue in a way that would follow his policy.[55]

On February 1, 1881, President Hayes sent a special message to Congress recommending that the Poncas be allowed to select individual allotments on whichever reservation they chose. He also urged that the government make full compensation for all relinquished lands and for the losses incurred by them in their removal to the Indian Territory. "In short," he concluded, "nothing should be left undone to show the Indians that the Government of the United States regards their rights as equally sacred with those of its citizens." Finally, he said that the aim of the policy should be to place the Indians

54. Richardson, *Messages and Papers,* 1897–1917 ed., X, 4585.
55. *The Nation,* XXXII (January 6, 1881), 3.

on the same footing with the other inhabitants of the country as rapidly as practicable—to give them the rights and responsibilities of citizenship.[56]

The President's recommendation for the solution of the Ponca controversy was not only an attempt to secure justice for the wronged Indians, but also a compromise designed to support the Secretary of the Interior's removal program and to eliminate the detested nonvoluntary reservation system. However, indignation had so increased during the winter of 1880–1881 that the reformers thought compromise more a defeat than a victory. Many of them, particularly those in Boston, were now certain that Secretary Schurz had been at least deceptive in his dealings with the Indian Territory Poncas, who really had not wanted to stay but acceded to the government's demands because of threats and intimidation. Unlike the congressional squabbles about the transfer issue, partisan politics were apparently not involved. Early in 1881, the Indian-rights advocates concentrated on Secretary Schurz, who they thought personified antireform sentiment.

In January, 1881, Helen Hunt Jackson's *A Century of Dishonor* was published in New York. The book was a passionate and one-sided history of the government's "repeated violations of faith with the Indians." Mrs. Jackson had spent several months of arduous research in the Astor Library, but she had been seeking those factual materials that would fill in and support her preconceived thesis. The best that can be said for this work as a history of United States Government-Indian relations is that it told for the first time the story of the white men's perfidy and wrongdoing to the Indians. It is not a balanced, objective account, but it did have a purpose—to "appeal to the heart and conscience of the American people." In the Introduction, Mrs. Jackson called for the Congress of 1880 to "cover itself with a lustre of glory, as the first to cut short our nation's record of cruelties and perjuries! the first to attempt to redeem the name of the United States from the stain of a century of dishonor!"[57] As Albert Keiser noted many years later, it was "propaganda in a noble cause."[58]

The influence of *A Century of Dishonor* can be only surmised. The author saw that copies were distributed to every member of Congress, and with the publicity occasioned by the Jackson-Schurz correspondence, it was widely enough read by the public and the humanitarians to stimulate demands for further reform. Herbert Welsh, Secretary of the Indian Rights Association, wrote in 1890 that *A Century of Dishonor* and *Ramona*, which was published in

56. Richardson, *Messages and Papers*, 1897–1917 ed., X, 4585–86.
57. Jackson, *A Century of Dishonor*, 30–31.
58. Albert Keiser, *The Indian in American Literature*, 250.

1884, "have spread knowledge and aroused sympathy where ignorance and indifference to our Indian policy existed before."[59] In 1929, historian Ralph Henry Gabriel said that *A Century of Dishonor* was widely read during the 1880's and made a powerful impression on its readers, among them President Grover Cleveland.[60] However, Mrs. Jackson's biographer, Ruth Odell, asserts that Congress paid no attention to her book, although it was mentioned once during the debates on the Indian appropriation bill.[61] Nevertheless, historians have generally considered it one of the high points in the Indian-rights crusade.

In December, 1880, Massachusetts Senator Henry L. Dawes began to oppose Schurz. Dawes did not agree with the Secretary on the allotment-in-severalty bill that was before the Senate. But, as he announced to that body in January, he was willing to support the imperfect bill because it would help to bring the Indians "from a state of barbarism into civilization."[62]

The Senator broke with Schurz, not so much over Schurz's handling of the Ponca case, but over his failure to bring to justice the murderers of Chief Standing Bear's brother, Big Snake. In a speech before the Senate on January 31, 1881, Dawes virtually accused the government of having planned and carried out the assassination of Big Snake in the fall of 1879. The Interior Department reported that he had been killed while resisting arrest for making a threat on the agent's life. There was no evidence to support the allegation that the Indian's death had been prearranged; nevertheless, the Senator described Big Snake as a hero resisting the tyranny of the government. It was a relief, he observed, to find that the department's methods were not American in origin but bore "too striking a resemblance to the modes of an imperial government carried on by espionage and arbitrary power. They are methods which I believe to be unique, and which I trust will never be naturalized" (an allusion to the Secretary's German birth, a popular target for his detractors).[63] Dawes then presented a petition from Standing Bear's Poncas protesting the ratification of the sale of the Dakota lands and declaring their "purpose and

59. Herbert Welsh, "The Indian Question Past and Present," *The New England Magazine*, III, 2 (October, 1890), 263.

60. Ralph Henry Gabriel, *The Lure of the Frontier, A Story of Race Conflict*, 270.

61. *Congressional Record*, 47th Cong., 1st sess., 1881–1882, XIII, Part 2, 2418.

62. *Ibid.*, 46th Cong., 3d sess., 1880–1881, XI, Part 2, 940.

63. *Ibid.*, II, Part 2, 1057–58.

desire to live upon the same land," which could not be sold without their consent.[64]

Schurz immediately retaliated in an open letter, in which he not only refuted Dawes's charges with characteristic thoroughness, but also struck a sharp blow at his Indian-rights enemies. Many sincere humanitarians had taken a warm interest in the fate of the Ponca tribe, but other agitators of a different class had endeavored to "turn the movement for the benefit of the Indians into one for the blackening of the character of one they choose to represent as a tyrannical oppressor." These agitators were "philanthropy hunting for a sensation," and the people who supported them, he said, provided another example of how easily honest people, in "following such a lead with the dangerous assurance of half knowledge, permit themselves to be made tools for the pursuit of questionable ends."[65]

Dawes's unwarranted attack and Schurz's reply brought Schurz sympathy and support. Edward Eggleston, a novelist and historian from Indiana, and The Reverend James Freeman Clarke, a clergyman from Massachusetts, sent messages of congratulations and confidence.[66] E. L. Godkin of *The Nation* conjectured that the Boston movement to have the Poncas taken back to Dakota might have been instigated by "simple-minded and humane white men who want the Indian Territory thrown open for 'development.' "[67]

Meanwhile, the desertions from the anti-Schurz faction were increasing. In March, Helen Hunt Jackson was shocked to find that her friend William Hayes Ward and the philanthropist and historian Baxter Perry Smith had switched to support Schurz.[68] Mrs. Jackson was still unable to see anything to praise in the Secretary. Fearing that others might become admirers of Schurz, Mrs. Jackson wrote identical letters to Henry Wadsworth Longfellow and Oliver Wendell Holmes criticizing Schurz's position on the Indian question. He was guilty of "such malignity towards innocent people and such astound-

---

64. *Ibid.*, 1058.

65. Carl Schurz, letter to Henry L. Dawes, February 7, 1881, in Frederic Bancroft, ed., *Speeches, Correspondence and Political Papers of Carl Schurz,* IV, 102.

66. Edward Eggleston, letter to Carl Schurz, February 22, 1881, *ibid.,* 114; James Freeman Clarke, letter to Carl Schurz, February 17, 1881, *ibid.*

67. *The Nation,* XXXII (February 17, 1881), 103; *ibid.,* February 24, 1881, 125–26.

68. William Hayes Ward was a Congregational clergyman and Orientalist who taught Latin at Ripon College for a time. In 1868, he joined the editorial staff of the New York *Independent* and became chief editor in 1896.

ing and wholesale lying," she concluded, that "every true friend of the Indians ought to help in denouncing both him and his methods." She sent each of them a copy of *A Century of Dishonor* in order that they might see that it "was not . . . a superficial study of this subject" and "not based on any partisan showings of facts."[69]

The fanatic opposition to Schurz was confined largely to the Boston area and to those closely associated with the Ponca cause. The other philanthropic centers, like New York and Philadelphia, generally gave unqualified support to the Interior Department's program. The majority of the veteran Indian-rights advocates also remained loyal throughout the controversy. William Welsh and William E. Dodge had often expressed satisfaction with the Secretary's reforms and his positive approach to the Indian problem. So, too, did Bishop Whipple, who observed that he had never found an officer of the government "more ready to examine the wrongs done to the Indians."[70]

By the winter of 1880–1881, the peak of the Ponca controversy, many of the humanitarian reformers who had started the movement were no longer living or had retired from active participation in the work for Indian rights. William Lloyd Garrison had died in May, 1879; Samuel Janney, in April, 1880; Lydia M. Child, in October; and Lucretia Mott, in November of the same year. Peter Cooper, who celebrated his ninetieth birthday on February 12, 1881, had virtually retired from active reform work, but such venerable reformers as Wendell Phillips, John Beeson, and Alfred Love were still working for humane treatment of the Indians. On December 3, 1880, at Tremont Temple in Boston, Phillips made an eloquent appeal for contributions to the Ponca cause. As might be expected, Phillips fully supported Mrs. Jackson's and Governor Long's demands for justice at any cost.[71]

John Beeson and Alfred Love, both working through the Universal Peace Union, were still steadfastly opposing the forcible reservation system and the use of the Army. However, when a delega-

69. Helen Hunt Jackson, letter to Henry Wadsworth Longfellow, March 2, 1881, Helen (Fiske) Hunt Jackson Papers, 1830–1885; Helen Hunt Jackson, letter to Oliver Wendell Holmes, March 2, 1881, *ibid.*

70. Claude Moore Fuess, *Carl Schurz, Reformer*, 266.

71. Ruth Odell notes in *Helen Hunt Jackson*, 157, that Joaquin Miller once said that Mrs. Jackson persuaded Wendell Phillips "to take the platform for the Indians as he had for the Negroes." This may have been true with regard to the Poncas, but it was not true for the Indians in general. Phillips had been active in this field since 1868, long before Mrs. Jackson had taken any interest in Indian-rights work.

tion of the Peace Union visited the President in May, 1879, Love told him of their "strong support and appreciation" for his prevention of encroachments on the Indian Territory and for his observance of Indian treaties. Hayes expressed his gratitude and promised that his Administration would meet the Indian problem "with honesty and with integrity."[72] President Hayes's open sympathy with Indian-rights objectives helped to maintain the allegiance of most reformers to his policy.

On March 3, 1881, Congress appropriated the sum of $165,000 to be used to compensate the Ponca tribe for the losses sustained by removal, to secure their lands on either the old or new reservation, and to settle all matters of difference between them and the government.[73] The following August, the Sioux agreed to return the old Dakota reservation to Standing Bear's Poncas.[74] With the satisfactory and peaceful settlement of the Ponca land and reparations claims, the three-year controversy came to an end.

On March 4, 1881, Schurz resigned as Secretary of the Interior to become editor in chief of Henry Villard's New York *Evening Post.* Schurz was no longer a public official, but he was not allowed to forget the dispute. Subsequent research completely cleared him of any guilt, but the Ponca case occasionally rose up to haunt him for the rest of his life. Helen Hunt Jackson was never able to forgive him for what she considered his hypocritical and tyrannical role with respect to Indian-policy reform. Six weeks after Schurz's resignation, she wrote to Edward Abbot that "it is naturally exasperating to those who *know* that he alone has been the chief obstacle for the last four years in the way of any substantial ameliorating of the Indians' state, to see him heralded and cited as the best champion the Indians possess.—I do not believe there are many instances in history of a man so bad willing himself accepted as so good!"[75] In May, 1883, she wrote to Secretary of the Interior H. M. Teller of Colorado. She was grateful

72. Universal Peace Union, "Official Report of the Thirteenth Anniversary Meeting," 39, 41.

73. Hayter, "The Ponca Removal," 274.

74. The Ponca Agreement, August 20, 1881, Secretary of the Interior, Letters Received. The satisfactory conclusion to the Ponca case opened the door to a sympathetic hearing of the appeals of Nez Percé Chief Joseph for the return of his unhappy people to their Idaho homeland. By 1885, so much nationwide compassion and humanitarian pressure had been aroused that the Indian Bureau agreed to return the Nez Percés to a reservation in northeastern Washington.

75. Helen Hunt Jackson, letter to Edward Abbot, April 23, 1881, Helen (Fiske) Hunt Jackson Papers, 1830–1885.

for his "prompt and vigorous action" in alleviating the wrongs of the Mission Indians of California, but she felt compelled to remind Teller that "if Schurz had paid any attention" to the reports on these problems, "much of the present suffering and confusion would have been saved."[76]

Schurz was apparently unable to comprehend the passionate dislike held for him and his policies by those Bostonians who had worked for the Poncas. At a dinner given in his honor by his admirers in Boston, he alluded to the strange circumstance in which his best motives had been impugned by those with whom he had "an identity of general purpose."[77] The Secretary may have been so engrossed in effecting thoroughgoing reforms that he did not fully know of the latent distrust that humanitarians had begun to feel before the Ponca controversy. His ouster of the churches from the Indian program did not arouse open hostility, but it had seriously depleted potential support for him. Primarily, it was Schurz's seemingly heartless and arbitrary methods of handling the Ponca case that had made him the personal target of so much violent criticism. At any rate, Tibbles and the Omaha Committee had found it easy to conclude that the Secretary was not only obstinate and unreasonable, but perhaps even a tool of the "Indian Ring." Tibbles publicized this latter notion in a mediocre novel entitled *Hidden Power, A Secret History of the Indian Ring*, which purported to show how the "ring" controlled the Interior Department and the Indian Bureau. The novel also defended the Army and advocated turning over to that body the distribution of Indian annuities.[78]

Such thinking was carefully encouraged by General George Crook and other Army officials, who sensed that this assault on the Interior Department would help the transfer issue. Tibbles' lectures and the pleas of Standing Bear and Bright Eyes were enough to convince a great many Eastern humanitarians that Schurz had caused all the injustice attributed to the Indian policy. Further, Schurz could not always restrain his angry outbursts against sensation-hunting philanthropists, a practice that only increased the opposition.

One result of the unfortunate controversy was the marriage of Tibbles and Bright Eyes in the summer of 1881. Alonzo Bell, Assistant Secretary of the Interior, humorously wrote to Schurz that he very much feared that

76. Helen Hunt Jackson, letter to H. M. Teller, May 9, 1883, Secretary of the Interior, Letters Received.

77. *The Nation*, XXXII (March 24, 1881), 196.

78. Thomas Henry Tibbles, *Hidden Power, A Secret History of the Indian Ring*, 353.

this last act of the pale-face is in the line of other wrongs perpetrated upon this most unfortunate band of Indians, and that
the confiding Indian maiden will some day feel that the fate of
Big Snake was preferable to the unhappy one which she has
chosen. Will Dawes hold the Department responsible for this?
Will Governor Long add it to his long list of indictments? Let
us hope that both may take a rose-colored view of the union between the dusky daughter of the forest and the gay professional
philanthropist who buried all the wrongs of her race in a greater
one upon herself. I fear poor Bright Eyes has made a mistake,
but I am willing to forgive her if the act effectually disposed of
Tibbles. Even so great a sacrifice may be rare economy if it gives
the Nation a rest from the vexatious borings of the Tibbles
school of philanthropy.[79]

79. Alonzo Bell, letter to Carl Schurz, August 4, 1881, in Bancroft,
Speeches . . . of Carl Schurz, IV, 147–48.

11

A Resurgence of Reform Zeal

While the Interior Department, the Indian Bureau, and the Indian-rights advocates were absorbed in the Ponca problem, events on the western Colorado frontier were rapidly moving toward a crisis. In the fall of 1869, an agency had been established for the Northern Ute tribe on the White River in northwestern Colorado. Army agents had control during its first six years, then in 1875, it had been placed under the Unitarian Church, and Reverend E. H. Danforth was appointed agent. Under the civilization program, Danforth introduced the Utes to farming, an occupation that they regarded with decided distaste. Little progress was made in this direction until 1879, when a new agent, Nathan C. Meeker, moved the agency to a fertile valley a few miles away, established an irrigation system, and began plowing and fencing.[1] Many of the Utes strongly objected to the move and the resulting destruction of the new location's lush pasture. By the summer of 1879, Meeker had persuaded some of the Indians to fence, plow, and dig irrigation ditches, but he had had to use continual persuasion. As time went on, the Utes exhibited an increasingly "bad humor" toward the agent and his farming program.[2]

Meeker's lack of understanding of the Indians and his objections to their long hunting excursions away from the reservation and their purchase of rifles added to the growing discontent at the White River Agency. The government's frequent failure to make prompt delivery of annuity supplies aggravated the tense situation. Then, several mining camps were located on the reservation in direct violation of treaty provisions. Signs of impending trouble increased after the son of a Ute chief was killed near the present town of Fraser, Colorado. In early September, despite the growing hostility, Meeker insisted that additional pasture land be plowed under. The Indians threatened violence if he did not back down, and when he refused, Johnson, the

1. Well known as a poet before the Civil War, Meeker served as a correspondent for Horace Greeley's *The New York Tribune* during the war. He was later given an assignment in the West, where he became enthusiastic about the possibiilties of a colony in Colorado. Greeley agreed to back the venture, and in 1870, the town of Greeley, Colorado, was founded. Wilson Rockwell, *The Utes, A Forgotten People*, 111–12.

2. *Ibid.*, 114.

leader of the Ute opposition, beat Meeker unmercifully. On September 10, Meeker sent a message to Indian Commissioner Hayt asking for immediate protection.[3]

Five days later, Major T. T. Thornburg set out from Fort Steele, Wyoming, with 140 men and 33 supply wagons. When the detachment was within 25 miles of the Ute reservation, a well-armed party of 100 Ute warriors suddenly fired upon it from ambush. The first volley killed Major Thornburg and several men and wounded all but one officer. Captain Payne took over command and, using dead horses and supply wagons, quickly improvised defensive works. The Indians entrenched themselves on the surrounding bluffs and continued to fire into the besieged party. Fortunately, a courier reached Rawlins, Wyoming, without being detected—after riding 160 miles in 28 hours—and secured reinforcements. The rescue party reached Payne's beleaguered troops on October 5. On the same day, a message from Ute Chief Ouray ordered the Indians to cease fighting, which ended the six-day battle.[4]

The ambush of Thornburg's force was only a part of the bloodletting. On September 29, upon receiving word that Thornburg's troops were approaching, the Indians attacked the White River Agency. They killed Meeker and the other agency employees, looted and burned the buildings, and carried three women and two children into captivity. The Utes' reaction against the months of dissatisfaction and sternly imposed restrictions was violent and thorough. The rebellion had been long in the making, and the warning signs would have been obvious to a more experienced and less obstinate man than Agent Meeker.

In March, 1879, John Beeson had written to President Hayes about the presence of gold miners on the Ute reservation and warned him that unless the "strong arm of the Government stops these outrages, the sceens [sic] which sent Gen's Canby, and Custer, and hundreds of brave Men of both Races to premature graves, will occur upon a large scale. War is *certain*, while the unchecked love of gain prompts the Whites, and the Love of family and home prompts the Indians, and the Government does not restrain the one nor protect the other."[5] According to Commissioner Hayt, opening the mining

---

3. Commissioner of Indian Affairs, *Annual Report of the Commissioner of Indian Affairs, 1879, Annual Report of the Secretary of the Interior,* 46th Cong., 2d sess., 1879–1880, House Exec. Doc. No. 1 (Serial 1910), xxviii–xxx.

4. *Ibid.,* xxxii–xxxiii; Rockwell, *The Utes,* 122–31.

5. John Beeson, letter to President Hayes, March 7, 1879, Bureau of Indian Affairs, Letters Received.

camps in violation of treaty provisions "greatly irritated the Utes, and was undoubtedly one of the causes which eventually led to active hostilities."[6] Still, nothing was done to halt the mining operations or remove the miners. On the contrary, Hayt recommended in his report of November 1, 1879, that the Utes be removed to the Indian Territory and that the title to their Colorado lands, some 12,000,000 acres, be extinguished "without injustice to the Indians and without violating the plighted faith of the Government."[7]

Alfred Love quickly came to the defense of the Utes, declaring his opposition to removal and asserting that neither Congress nor the people of Colorado had ever asked the transfer of these Indians to Indian Territory. He then criticized General Sherman for his alleged remark that now " 'we must punish these Indians, and avenge the dead.' . . . What language from a person who is intrusted with so much of the history and reputation of this country! . . . What a standard for our nation; what a lesson for our children." Love then attacked the government for keeping "such a man as Sherman in a dominant and representative position" and called it a discredit to "our common morality, and our advanced civilization."[8] No reformer had so castigated the General since the Custer Massacre in 1876. Many observers may have thought that Love might well be equal to Wendell Phillips when it came to criticizing military leaders.

Soon after the cessation of hostilities, Secretary Schurz dispatched a special agent to negotiate with the rebellious Utes. The agent was to secure a permanent peace agreement, obtain the release of the captives, and at the same time, squelch a projected movement for extermination of the tribe by angry Colorado citizens.[9] The Indians were defiant at first but finally agreed to the agent's demands if he would guarantee that the Army would not be used against them. This condition was granted, and the captives were released. A special commission was then appointed by the Secretary of the Interior and the Secretary of War to investigate the uprising and determine the guilty parties.[10]

6. *Annual Report of the Commissioner of Indians Affairs*, 1879, xxi.
7. *Ibid.*, xxxvii.
8. Alfred H. Love, "We Must Avenge the Dead," *The Voice of Peace*, VI (November, 1879), 139; Sherman's telegram to Sheridan of October 13, 1879, to which Love was evidently referring, stated, "The murderers of Agent Meeker and the employees must be punished, as also those who fought and killed Major Thornburgh and men." *The Denver Daily Times*, October 13, 1879.
9. Claude Moore Fuess, *Carl Schurz, Reformer*, 265.
10. *Annual Report of the Commissioner of Indian Affairs*, 1879, xxxv.

Upon the testimony of the women who had been captured, twelve White River Utes were charged with having participated in the massacre. The Indians would not corroborate the testimony, but Chief Ouray promised to deliver the alleged participants—if the trial could take place in Washintgon, D. C. "The people of Colorado are not friendly," he explained, "and a fair trial here . . . is not to be expected."[11] After they were unable to ascertain or apprehend the malefactors, the commission was ordered to bring a number of the Ute chiefs and headmen to Washington to testify before a congressional investigating committee.[12]

Meanwhile, many theories fixing the blame for the Ute outbreak were being tossed to the public. Western spokesmen claimed that Congress and the Indian Bureau were at fault for not removing the Utes before the trouble began. Secretary Schurz countered that the trouble arose from the encroachments of white settlers, particularly miners prospecting for gold and silver. The massacre itself, he maintained, was instigated by the appearance of Thornburg's troops, not from lack of good faith on the part of the government.[13] Indian Commissioner Hayt also blamed the miners and the presence of the troops, but he agreed with Westerners that a primary cause was the failure of Congress to appropriate the money due the Utes in accordance with the Treaty of 1873.[14] Upon hearing Schurz's analysis, Governor Frederick W. Pitkin of Colorado responded heatedly that neither miners nor settlers had made encroachments on the Ute reservation.[15] New Mexico's Governor Lew Wallace, who corroborated Pitkin's statement, exclaimed to a reporter that he would like to see some of that Indian civilization that Schurz kept mentioning. "The eastern people still adhere to their Quaker doctrine," he added bitterly, "and know but little of the Indian practically. They sympathize with the 'poor Indian,' and consider him a terribly abused creature."[16]

In the winter of 1879–1880, many of the most active Indian-rights workers were so completely absorbed in the Ponca dispute that they gave the Ute uprising comparatively little attention. However, Alfred Love's Peace Union and Lucretia Mott's Pennsylvania Peace Society implored the government to treat the Ute delegation with "impartial justice" and to show them the "magnanimity of true

11. *The Denver Daily Times*, December 8, 1879.
12. Rockwell, *The Utes*, 164.
13. *The Denver Daily Times*, October 4, 1879.
14. *Ibid.*, October 3, 1879.
15. *Ibid.*, October 4, 1879.
16. *Ibid.*, October 13, 1879.

civilization and Christianity."[17] Both Easterners and Westerners sent letters to Schurz's office asking that justice and mercy be accorded the erring tribe. In Colorado, the widespread friendship and respect for Chief Ouray greatly tempered the anger there, but as on previous similar occasions, the frontier people were thoroughly exasperated with Eastern residents for their inability to perceive the "innate cussedness of the Indians." They were even more upset about the prevalent Eastern belief that the Utes had gone to war because they had been grievously wronged by the whites. However, now that the war was over, most people agreed with Secretary Schurz—punish the guilty but deal justly with the Ute delegation in Washington and the tribe in general.

The difference between the Western public and the Eastern advocates of Indian rights hinged upon their respective concepts of justice for the Indians. To Westerners, acquiring reservation land was just because rebelling tribes had forfeited their rights of ownership. The reformers often had accused the frontiersmen of fomenting Indian wars in order to dispossess the Indians of their property, a charge that Westerners vehemently denied. The frontier population was not guilty of starting the Ute War, but the conflict had barely ended when the Colorado press began speculating about opening the White River Agency to settlement. On October 14, 1879, *The Denver Daily Times* noted that "now is the best opportunity we shall ever have for the extinguishment" of the Ute title. "It is of far more importance that these lands should be made to yield up their treasures of mineral and bounteous harvests from the soil for the benefit of mankind, than that a few hundred idle and worthless savages should be maintained at the public expense."[18]

But the Coloradans met determined opposition from other Western residents who objected to the relocation of the "warlike" Utes in or near their respective states or territories. Thus, with the support of the Interior Secretary, a joint resolution was drawn up in Congress stipulating that the Ute Indians were to be kept within the boundaries of Colorado, preferably on a small reservation in the southwestern part of the state.[19] This action satisfied Western con-

17. "The Peace Movement," *The Voice of Peace*, VI (January, 1880), 171. The executive meeting of the Pennsylvania Peace Society on January 7, 1880, was the last such meeting attended by Lucretia Mott. She was not strong enough to remain throughout the session, but she retained a lively interest in its work until her death the following October. Anna Davis Hollowell, ed., *James and Lucretia Mott. Life and Letters*, 461.

18. *The Denver Daily Times*, October 14, 1879.

19. *Ibid.*, December 14, 1879.

gressmen, although it was only partially observed in the final settlement.

The Ute congressional investigation of January, 1880, turned up little additional information about the uprising and massacre, let alone the whereabouts of the guilty Indians. The only participant punished was the confessed leader of the attack on the agency, a headman by the name of Douglas. He was sentenced to imprisonment at Fort Leavenworth but was freed after serving a few months.[20] The investigating committee made more substantial progress in determining the future status of the Ute reservation. On March 6, the Indian Bureau reached an agreement with the Ute delegation in Washington. Under its terms, the Uncompahgre Utes were to be located near the Unitah Agency in northeastern Utah; the rebellious White River Utes, on the Unitah Agency; and the southern band, on their old reservation in southwestern Colorado. Each band would have its lands allotted in severalty as soon as Congress passed the necessary laws; houses, agricultural implements, and cattle would be furnished; and schools would be established and maintained. Finally, with the cession to the United States of the vacated Ute reservation, the land-hungry miners and settlers were appeased. Congress approved the agreement on June 15, 1880.[21]

The commission of five agents appointed by President Hayes to carry out the provisions of the Ute agreement included Alfred B. Meacham, editor of *The Council Fire*. Meacham devoted nearly two years of exhausting labor to the removal and pacification of the Utes. He returned to Washington in October, 1881, in very feeble health. He never fully recovered, but he continued to edit *The Council Fire* until his death in February, 1882.

The Ponca controversy, the Nez Percé War, and the Ute uprising aroused a widespread public interest in the Indian problem. The result was a renewal of enthusiasm for reform and the formation of numerous new Indian-rights organizations throughout the East. The year 1879 marked the birth of a second major reform movement in Indian policy that was to ultimately bring about passage of the Dawes severalty act. Men and women who often had had little previous experience in reform work supported this new movement. Most of these neophytes knew of the prewar reform movements and the anti-slavery crusade only as history. Their viewpoints were still strongly

20. Rockwell, *The Utes*, 164–65.

21. Commissioner of Indian Affairs, *Annual Report of the Commissioner of Indian Affairs*, 1880, *Annual Report of the Secretary of the Interior*, 46th Cong., 3d sess., 1880–1881, House Exec. Doc. No. 1 (Serial 1959), 194–95; Theodore A. Bland, *Life of Alfred B. Meacham*, 12, 24.

colored by the transcendentalist concepts of "self-evident truths," but they were basically products of the new school of Christian utilitarianism, the "social gospel."

The elevation of the Indians from savagery to civilization by the application of the New Testament principle of the brotherhood of man had always formed the foundation of the post-Civil War movement for the reform of Indian policy. Thus, these new reformers differed from their predecessors only in degree. Less emphasis on the spiritual and more on the material and mental improvement of the race characterized what they called the "modern popular movement" on behalf of the Indians. The new reformers did more educational work among the tribes, helped to build homes, and gave medical care in order to "hasten their civilization, Christianization and enfranchisement." The two keys to these goals, they believed, were education and the abolition of the reservation system through ownership of property. The emphasis had changed, but the ultimate objectives were identical with the 1868–1878 decade of reform.

Among the first of the Indian-rights organizations to be produced by the Ponca furor was the Boston Indian Citizenship Association. Organized in late 1879, it was under the leadership of Massachusetts Republican Governor John D. Long, Helen Hunt Jackson, and Senator Henry L. Dawes. Governor Long was an active reformer who had worked for prohibition, woman's suffrage, world peace, and now Indian rights. Senator Dawes was an intelligent, dignified Yankee lawyer who had been in Congress since 1857. He became interested in Indian policy after the adoption of the Peace Policy in 1869 and was one of its most devoted supporters. As chairman of the Senate Committee on Indian Affairs, he used his influence to promote Indian education and the severalty plan.

The purpose of the Boston association was ostensibly to promote the Indians' equality in the courts and the rights of citizenship, but many contemporaries thought that criticism of Schurz was its primary objective. However, members of the association soon realized that if they wanted real accomplishments, they had to work with the government rather than against it. After the Secretary's resignation in March, 1881, Dawes observed that "an open conflict with this new administration, as with the last, on the Indian policy, must be avoided if possible, or we shall be very much disabled."[22] After the settlement of the Ponca case, the Boston association concentrated on securing the political and civil rights of all Indians.[23]

22. Loring Benson Priest, *Uncle Sam's Stepchildren: The Reformation of United States Indian Policy, 1865–1887*, 79.
23. Herbert Welsh, "The Indian Question Past and Present," *The New England Magazine*, III, 2 (October, 1890), 264.

One of the most active and influential of the Indian-rights groups during the 1880's was the Women's National Indian Association of Philadelphia. It was organized in December, 1879, in order to bring about specific fundamental reforms. This association noted that the Indians had neither protection under the law nor any rights that white men had to respect; furthermore, they were still subject to enforced removal. Led by Miss Mary Bonney and Mrs. Amelia Quinton and encouraged by Mrs. John Jacob Astor, the association launched a campaign to inform the public of the needs, capabilities, and progress of the Indians. It stimulated popular interest in the subject by circulating pamphlets and petitions, encouraging newspaper articles, and holding public meetings. It sent petitions and memorials to Congress for legislative action on Indian education, civil rights, citizenship and for land in severalty.[24]

The association's activities did not stop at publicity and petitions. It raised money to send workers to the reservations to assist the Indians in home building, to establish hospitals, and to teach in the schools. By 1886, the Women's National Indian Association had established 60 branch organizations in 27 states, through which it was exerting effective pressure in Washington. As Senator Dawes once observed, "The new Indian policy of the government . . . was born of and nursed by the women of this Association."[25]

Among the association's branches, the Connecticut Indian Association was second only to the parent body in activity. Organized in Hartford in 1881, it was an outgrowth of an earlier but smaller and more informal Indian-rights group that had begun operations in October, 1880. Harriet Beecher Stowe was a vice president of the association, and her presence added greatly to its prestige not only among the humanitarians, but with the Board of Indian Commissioners and with some members of Congress. Board Chairman Clinton Fisk wrote to Mrs. Stowe in April, 1888, to congratulate her on her alliance with that "vigorous, working body of Yankee women who constitute the Connecticut Indian Association. They do things well." He then asked for the association's continuing efforts "to help the poor Indian."[26] The objectives of the Women's National Indian Association and its branches—education, civilization, civil rights, and ultimately full citizenship—were identical wth those of the Interior Department and the Indian Bureau. These objectives, and the gen-

24. Francis A. Goodale, ed., *The Literature of Philanthropy*, 117–18.
25. *Ibid.*, 118; Amelia S. Quinton, *Proceedings of the Third Annual Lake Mohonk Conference of Friends of the Indian*, 46.
26. Clinton Fisk, letter to Harriet Beecher Stowe, April 3, 1888, in Ellen Terry Johnson, *Historical Sketch of the Connecticut Indian Association*, 64.

eral agreement about the merits of allotment of land in severalty and
the eventual abolition of the reservation system, made the efforts of
these organizations especially welcome to government officials. In the
decade of the 1880's, the Interior Department and the Indian Bureau
regarded the work of individual humanitarians and their organizations with growing respect and appreciation.

By 1880, an election year, Indian policy had lost its political
significance. This development was a sign of progress, for it marked
the elimination of much of the political partisanship that had often
hindered and confused legislation on Indian affairs in previous
years. Most people at this time realized that the Indian problem was
a national problem and that it was a bipartisan responsibility. Time
and experience had fostered a general agreement on methods and
objectives during the preceding decade. This agreement, and the
realization that cooperation would accomplish more than criticism,
created a spirit of unity that had been noticeably lacking since 1874
and that distinguished the new movement from the first one.

Herbert Welsh, a nephew of William Welsh, founded a third
major organization, the Indian Rights Association, in December,
1882. According to historian Ralph Henry Gabriel, Welsh had become convinced of the need for more reform after reading Helen
Hunt Jackson's *A Century of Dishonor*,[27] but his visit to Bishop
William Hare's Episcopalian Sioux mission may have provided the
impetus. The association became as respected as Peter Cooper's
United States Indian Commission had been in the early years of
Grant's Peace Policy. Welsh was certain that the Indians could be
civilized and that injustice and inefficiency had impeded their progress, and he thought the "right use of government" was the solution.
To him, the government was a powerful tool that, if used properly
by the people of the nation, could accomplish the task of "civilizing
and regenerating the Indian." The government's leaders, he pointed
out, "cannot know enough to handle this tremendous power over the
Indian wisely and well, unless steadily out of the people comes an
influence, a voice telling them to do their duty and how to do it."[28]
The association grew rapidly, and by 1890, it claimed 1600 members
and many branches throughout the East and Midwest. By using the
well-tested techniques of publication, oratory, and memorials to Congress and government leaders, the Indian Rights Association exerted
a powerful influence on formulating and applying Indian policy.

In order to be most effective, the various rights organizations had

27. Ralph Henry Gabriel, *The Lure of the Frontier, A Story of Race
Conflict*, 27.
28. Herbert Welsh, "The Indian Question Past and Present," 265–66.

to resolve their differences and agree on the policy to be pursued. The opportunity for cooperative effort came at the annual gatherings of Indian workers at the Conference of the Friends of the Indians at Lake Mohonk, New York. Initiated by the Quaker brothers Albert and Alfred Smiley in 1883, the meetings were designed to facilitate unified action that would more effectively achieve reforms. The conference was closely associated with the Board of Indian Commissioners; Albert was a commissioner, and the conference's first president was Board Chairman General Fisk. Representatives of most of the Indian-rights organizations regularly attended the annual week-long meetings to discuss every phase of the Indian service and propose reform measures. During the following years, the conference was able to exert sufficient influence on public sentiment, Indian Bureau officials, and Congress to transform many of its recommendations into legislation.[29]

The winter of 1878–1879 brought a new problem to the attention of the Indian-rights humanitarians—one that would be especially vexing to the Federal Government. In April, 1879, the Commissioner of Indian Affairs notified President Hayes that the Indian Bureau had discovered an elaborate plan for the forcible acquisition of lands in the Indian Territory. The unlawful movement of settlers into the area from the surrounding states was so widespread that the government inaugurated prompt and vigorous countermeasures to prevent serious trouble with the Indian inhabitants. On April 26, President Hayes issued a proclamation in which he warned all persons against settling in the Indian Territory and notified trespassers that they would be speedily removed, by military force if necessary. Troops were immediately dispatched to the border areas to prevent further intrusion, and those invaders who had failed to heed the presidential proclamation were ejected. This attempt to settle the Indian Territory was only the beginning of a problem that was to plague government authorities for more than a decade.[30]

Such a gross violation of reservation rights that had been granted to the Indians in perpetuity by solemn treaty aroused humanitarian interest. On May 3, 1879, Alfred Love and other delegates representing the Universal Peace Union met with President Hayes to appeal for the establishment of an international tribunal of arbitration. After this discussion, they voiced their strong support and appreciation for his prevention of encroachment on the Indian Territory. Hayes, obviously pleased, responded, "It is certainly a gratifi-

29. Frederick E. Partington, *The Story of Mohonk*, 27–29.
30. *Annual Report of the Commissioner of Indian Affairs*, 1879, xliv, 188.

cation to me to hear that you take sides with us in that matter. The stand we have taken will be made a fact."[31]

Preserving the inviolability of the Indian Territory was already a touchy issue among the citizens of the adjoining states. Schemes to open these lands to white settlers had been urged in Congress since 1866, and the pressure became even more formidable when the managers of three railroads operating in the area began to support the proposals. Following Hayes's proclamation, the New Orleans *Times* noted that "thousands of people now in Kansas and Missouri" were awaiting a favorable opportunity to move into the territory and that treaties, soldiers, and presidential proclamations were not enough to stop them. Meanwhile, Senator George Vest (Democrat, Missouri) said that he was planning to introduce a bill that would permit organization of the territory for admission as a state.[32] The Indian-rights organizations, the President, the Indian Bureau, and most of the Indian inhabitants opposed these treaty-breaking invasions and the proposals for statehood, but unfortunately, Congress was unable to come to any such agreement.[33]

Fully aware of this weak link, the Women's National Indian Association published a plea for "hundreds of thousands" of petitions "for speedy and effective Congressional action which shall forever render impossible the execution of these schemes, not only against all the rights of the Indians, but also destructive to our honor as a treaty-fulfilling nation."[34] In 1880 and again in January, 1881, the association sent petitions to Congress protesting the violation of Indian treaties and opposing Vest's bill. Bearing 32,000 signatures from all the states and territories, these petitions and others from the branch societies and other Indian-rights organizations helped to delay the legalized invasion of the Indian Territory.[35]

The illegal settlers were not easily discouraged. Each year, despite periodic presidential proclamations and military removal, thousands of settlers invaded the rich Indian lands. In 1884, 6,000 to

31. Universal Peace Union, "Official Report of the Thirteenth Anniversary Meeting," *The Voice of Peace*, VI (June, 1879), 41.

32. Women's National Indian Association, *An Earnest Petition Needed*, 3.

33. For example, the Creeks sent a committee to Washington to protest the opening of the Indian Territory and to maintain that the sentiment of the tribe was almost unanimously against Vest's bill. *The Press* (Philadelphia), January 2, 1880.

34. Women's National Indian Association, *Earnest Petition*, 3.

35. *Congressional Record*, 46th Cong., 3d sess., 1880–1881, II, Part 2, 1073.

10,000 claims were reported to have been surveyed and staked on the Cherokee lands alone.[36]

The first defeat for advocates of Indian rights came in 1885, when Congress authorized the President to open negotiations with the Cherokees, Creeks, and Seminoles for the purpose of opening to settlement some unassigned lands in Indian Territory.[37] The Creeks agreed to sell the western half of their domain to the Federal Government, and in April, 1889, those public lands not owned by the tribes were opened to settlement. The Oklahoma Territory was formed in 1890 from this western part of the Indian Territory and the public strip known as no man's land.

Protecting the Indians' land rights was an important goal in the Indian-rights program of the 1880's, but educating the Indians was, if anything, even more important. Proficiency in the English language and in vocational arts, which everyone considered a necessary step to civilization and citizenship, had progressed slowly during the 1870's. Although churches and other organizations had given money to supplement insufficient government appropriations, the educational program of the Peace Policy had been seriously hindered by a shortage of funds. In 1879, the Carlisle Indian Industrial School had been established in Pennsylvania through the efforts of Captain Richard Pratt. No money was appropriated for its operation until 1881; however, the demand for Indian school facilities that year was so great that the Indian Bureau exceeded its $75,000 appropriation by $50,000.[38]

Increasing educational appropriations and expanding school facilities were primary humanitarian objectives during the 1880's. Shortly after Hiram Price became Commissioner of Indian Affairs in 1881, William E. Dodge reminded him that if any Indians were to be saved from destruction by the advancing emigration and railroads, their children must be educated so that they could become citizens.[39] By 1882, Congress was fully awakened to the importance

36. Commissioner of Indian Affairs, *Annual Report of the Commissioner of Indian Affairs, 1884, Annual Report of the Secretary of the Interior,* 48th Cong., 2d sess., 1884–1885, House Exec. Doc. No. 1 (Serial 2287), xl.

37. Commissioner of Indian Affairs, *Annual Report of the Commissioner of Indian Affairs, 1885, Annual Report of the Secretary of the Interior,* 49th Cong., 1st sess., 1885–1886, House Exec. Doc. No. 1 (Serial 2379), xxix.

38. *Ibid.,* xc.

39. William E. Dodge, letter to Hiram Price, May 23, 1881, Bureau of Indian Affairs, Letters Received.

of the Interior Department's program for Indian education. Accordingly, the Indian Appropriation Bill for 1883 designated $150,000 "for support of industrial-schools and for educational purposes for the Indian tribes" and another $67,500 for the Carlisle Industrial School. Also, for the first time, it appropriated money for S. C. Armstrong's Indian school at Hampton, Virginia, and the Indian industrial school at Forest Grove, Oregon. In addition, it authorized the establishment of training schools in the Indian Territory and Nebraska. Finally, an act of May, 1882, created the office of Indian School Superintendent, and a veteran Indian agent, James M. Haworth, was appointed superintendent.[40]

The action of Congress in 1882 was a tremendous step forward in Indian education, and the reformers enthusiastically supported the movement. At an Indian-rights meeting in Boston, John Greenleaf Whittier said that the "westward setting tide of immigration is everywhere sweeping over the lines of the reservations. . . . The entire question will soon resolve itself into the single alternative of education and civilization or extermination." He reported that school experiments had shown that the Indians could be enlightened and civilized; therefore, what was needed was "more support for existing schools and new ones opened without delay."[41]

The Indian Rights Association petitioned Congress in February, 1884, asking that unexpended funds in the Plains Indian tribes' Treasury accounts be spent exclusively for their education "as rapidly as can be without waste or extravagance." The petitioners reminded Congress that some of the agencies still had no schools. "If these schools are earnestly and intelligently supported by the Government," they asserted, "the progress of these Indians will be steady toward the condition of law-abiding and self-supporting citizens."[42]

Practical assistance came from many organizations like the Connecticut Indian Association. The association's funds built homes for married students who were graduating and helped others through professional schools.[43] During the fiscal year 1885, religious and humanitarian organizations donated thousands of dollars to supplement the sum appropriated by Congress for the support of the Indian

40. "Report of the Indian School Superintendent," *Annual Report of the Commissioner of Indian Affairs*, 1885, xc, xcii, lxx.
41. John Greenleaf Whittier, *The Works of John Greenleaf Whittier*, VII, 238–39.
42. Indian Rights Association, petition to Congress, February 20, 1884, Bureau of Indian Affairs, Letters Received.
43. Mrs. J. C. Kinney, letter to Hiram Price, October 27, 1884, Bureau of Indian Affairs, Letters Received; Connecticut Indian Association pamphlet (n.p., n.d.), *ibid.*

boarding schools maintained by the churches under a government contract. They also expended nearly $80,000 for the operation of mission schools that they alone supported, and they gave large contributions to Carlisle and other training institutions. Indian sympathizers contributed almost $72,000 for building schoolhouses on the reservations; the congressional appropriation was $40,000 for both building and repair. Indian Bureau officials said that despite increased government appropriations, the religious and humanitarian organizations' assistance to Indian education was essential for preventing curtailment of the educational program. Indian Superintendent John Oberly reported in November, 1885, "All persons who know what has been done by Christian effort in Indian educational work, must heartily agree in saying that this effort should not be permitted to relax."[44] The reformers concurred, but they believed that still more Federal money was needed. Within the next three months, John Beeson, the Indian Rights Association, the Women's National Indian Association, the Northern New Jersey Baptist and Presbyterian ministers, and Mrs. John Jacob Astor and "other ladies of New York"[45] sent to Congress petitions for an increase in appropriations for Indian education.

The improved cooperation between the Interior Department and the Indian-rights advocates was especially apparent in the case of the Mission Indians of southern California. The 3,000 Indians under the jurisdiction of the Mission Agency were a peaceable, industrious people whose long contact with the Spanish had brought them to a high degree of acculturation. The rapid settlement of the area from 1848 on had driven many of these Indians from the more desirable lands. Eventually, executive orders from Grant and Hayes set aside a few, small, unsettled tracts for the permanent use and occupation of the Indians. Since the Civil War, white settlers had wanted to eject the Mission Indians from these areas. Even more serious, growing numbers of settlers were encroaching upon these Indian lands, both within and outside the reservations.

Agents' reports of the situation and memorials from religious societies and Indian advocates in California finally brought government action. In July, 1882, the Interior Department appointed Helen Hunt Jackson special agent and instructed her to investigate the condition of the Mission Indians and to survey the possibilities of establishing additional reservations for the growing numbers of land-

44. "Report of the Indian School Superintendent," *Annual Report of the Commissioner of Indian Affairs*, 1885, cxxiv, cxxv.

45. *Congressional Record*, 48th Cong., 1st sess., 1883–1884, XV, Parts 2, 3, 4, 1549, 2173, 2452, 3952, 4654.

less bands. She had already spent the previous winter in California collecting material on these Indians for *The Century Magazine*. By 1882, she had acquired a nationwide reputation as an authority on the Mission bands, as well as Indians in general, so her appointment by Secretary Henry M. Teller not only illustrated the renewed harmony between reformers and the government, but also showed her competency for the task. Her recommendations for removing all white settlers from the reservations and patenting these lands to the Indian occupants were approved by the Interior Department, which submitted immediately a bill to Congress to secure these provisions.[46]

The bill for the relief of the Mission Indians was first submitted to Congress in January, 1884, and was passed by the Senate in that year and again in 1886. The House reported favorably on the measure, but it took no action. However, the Indian Bureau was granted the authority to remove white settlers from the Indian reservation lands by military force.[47] Congress did pass an appropriation bill enabling the Indians to homestead land without payment of a fee, which had been a serious barrier to extensive use of the Indian Homestead Act of 1875.

The plight of the Mission Indians affected Mrs. Jackson as deeply as the Poncas' predicament had. Like the Poncas, some Mission Indians were being forced to move because speculators had acquired title to their lands. Upon completion of her tour in May, 1883, she wrote to Thomas Bailey Aldrich that her opinion of human nature had "come down 100 per ct. in the last thirty days. Such heart sickening fraud, violence, cruelty as we have unearthed here—I did not believe could exist in civilized communities and 'in the name of the law.' " She was certain that the situation had all the elements for another book that would reveal the miserable conditions of the Indians more forcefully than *A Century of Dishonor* and that would reach more people. "If I could write a story that would do for the Indians a thousandth part of what *Uncle Tom's Cabin* did for the Negro," she said, "I would be thankful the rest of my life."[48]

46. Commissioner of Indian Affairs, *Annual Report of the Commissioner of Indian Affairs, 1883, Annual Report of the Secretary of the Interior*, 48th Cong., 1st sess., 1883–1884, House Exec. Doc. No. 1 (Serial 2191), xlv, xlvi; *Annual Report of the Commissioner of Indian Affairs, 1884*, xxxvii.

47. Commissioner of Indian Affairs, *Annual Report of the Commissioner of Indian Affairs, 1887, Annual Report of the Secretary of the Interior*, 50th Cong., 1st sess., 1887–1888, House Exec. Doc. No. 1 (Serial 2542), li.

48. Helen Hunt Jackson, letters to Thomas Bailey Aldrich, April 1 and May 4, 1883, Helen (Fiske) Hunt Jackson Papers, 1830–1885.

In New York, during the winter of 1883–1884, Mrs. Jackson wrote *Ramona*, a novel based on the misfortunes of the Mission Indians in California. According to Mrs. Jackson, it contained a "big dose of information on the Indian question" that she hoped would make readers "burn with indignation and protest our wrongs to the Indian." Even the actual writing itself had been an "extraordinary experience," almost as if it had come as a revelation, and "I am not without superstition about it," she told Aldrich.[49]

Ramona first appeared in serial form in the *Christian Union* in June, 1884. It depicted the decaying Indian and Mexican culture being swept away by the "relentless, onrushing wave" of Anglo-Saxon civilization.[50] The story was an instant success, and it probably deserved Herbert Welsh's observation in 1890 that it helped greatly to enlighten the public on the Indian problem.[51] Shortly before her death from cancer in August, 1885, Mrs. Jackson wrote to a friend, "You have never fully realized how for the last four years my whole heart has been full of the Indian cause. . . . The change in public feeling on the Indian question in the last three years is marvelous; an Indian Rights Association [is] in every large city in the land." One of her last letters was to President Cleveland expressing her gratitude for what he had done to uphold the rights of the Indians and pleading with him to continue these efforts.[52] Her efforts to secure justice and humanity for the Indians made her name the symbol of the Indian-rights movement of the entire post-Civil War era.

A year earlier, on February 2, 1884, Wendell Phillips had succumbed to angina pectoris at the age of seventy-two. Phillips would not be remembered for his Indian-rights work; he had become too indelibly associated with the antislavery crusade. Consequently, when the Wendell Phillips Hall Association was formed in 1891 for the purpose of erecting a memorial educational building to commemorate his life and public service, the building was described as a monument to the antislavery movement.[53] At Phillips' first memorial observance in Boston in 1911, ex-slave Archibald Grimke did praise the reformer's interest in every good cause—Irish freedom, the Indians, the Chinese, labor, woman's suffrage, and temperance—"but for us, the colored people . . . , he had a love and sympathy sur-

49. Helen Hunt Jackson, letters to Thomas Bailey Aldrich, December 1, 1884, January 20, 1885, *ibid.*

50. Albert Keiser, *The Indian in American Literature*, 251–52.

51. Welsh, "The Indian Question Past and Present," 263.

52. Thomas Wentworth Higginson, *Contemporaries*, 161, 166–67.

53. Wendell Phillips, *The Freedom Speech of Wendell Phillips, Faneuil Hall, December 8, 1837*, Preface.

passing the love and sympathy of woman. He was, indeed, our own, our beautiful, our devoted and great-hearted friend and champion."[54] Phillips' identification with his first and greatest reform cause unfortunately blurred the memory of his sixteen-year effort for the Indians. He was the last of the prominent abolitionists who had become deeply involved in work for Indian rights.

Ironically, John Beeson, who had been working for the Indians since 1854, was still hardly known to the general public in the 1880's, and he is even less remembered at the present time. He was as sincere, as fervent, and as hard working as Phillips, but he could not match Phillips' forty years of national leadership in abolitionism and reform or his gifted oratory. Neither could he hope to achieve Mrs. Jackson's literary fame. Beeson had an obvious struggle even to scrawl his awkward correspondence, which was often damaged by the frequent misspellings, whereas Mrs. Jackson was a smooth, persuasive, and gifted writer.

Beeson was known and generally respected in Washington, D. C., New York City, Philadelphia, and other philanthropic centers of the East, but his influence was relatively limited. In Oregon, he was a highly controversial figure; his enemies called him "a monomaniac with Indian on the brain," and his friends did not contradict them for their own personal safety. In May, 1885, at the age of eighty-two, he was still offering his services for "aney usefull [sic] work which my experience and proclivities qualify me to do." In a letter to Indian Commissioner Price, he reiterated that, first of all, efforts were needed to elevate public sentiment so that the conscience of the people at large would demand the honest treatment of the Indians.[55] Beeson always had believed that reform of Indian policy must originate with an aroused public opinion, and his offers of service to the Indian Bureau nearly always included proposals for a truly evangelistic propaganda campaign throughout the nation. He had long been certain that the reform movement's success depended on the involvement of women. The Ladies' National Indian League, which Peter Cooper helped him organize in New York City in 1878, was one of the first of its kind. He was overjoyed at the success of the Women's National Indian Association and pleased to find that such an array of intellect and philanthropy had been organized for the protection of the Indians.[56]

Beeson's frequent requests for government funds to carry out

54. Newspaper clipping in Wendell Phillips, "Scrapbook."
55. John Beeson, letter to Hiram Price, May 19, 1885, Bureau of Indian Affairs, Letters Received.
56. Ibid.

his periodic suggestions for the improvement of Indian relations had always been refused since early in the Grant Administration, but he had seldom let these rebuffs discourage him. In 1885, he once more asked for an appropriation of $1,000 to finance a series of public Indian-rights meetings in the major cities of the nation. If he were accompanied by a band of Indian singers and assisted by good speakers and free tracts, he thought, he could do more to aid the Indian than all other methods combined. "The speeches of Fred Douglass and the songs of the Hutchinson family, were a great power in the antislavery cause," he wrote Indian Commissioner Price, "and there is today, just as much need of the same kind of power as there was then. The Indians are worth as much, and deserve as well, as the Negroe [sic] all that our wisdom,—wealth,—and kindness can do."[57]

His last letters to the Indian Bureau in 1886 concerned a revival of claims from the Rogue River War. It was the problem that had brought Beeson to Washington in 1856. Then, he had publicized the fraudulency of these claims, and his success had marked the beginning of his career in Indian-rights work. The claims supposedly had been settled nearly thirty years before, and the sudden appearance of a bill in Congress to pay some of these claims in full was like a ghost out of the past. Beeson had mellowed considerably since 1856, and he told the new Indian Commissioner J. D. C. Atkins, "I now realize that there were some innocent persons who had to kill, or be killed during the war, who suffered losses . . . which should be paid by the government." On October 13, 1886, he called for a public meeting in Medford, Oregon, "to consider all necessary means to get the payment of just claims" for losses sustained in the Indian wars of southern Oregon. He offered his services and those of his son to determine the justice of the claims presented. "If any proposition is accepted," he wrote Atkins, "it will be a proper expression of the conscience of the people whom President Cleveland said in his inaugurel [sic] address 'demands the Just Treatment . . . of the Indians.' "[58] Government officials investigated these claims in 1886 and 1887, but less than half of the sums requested were approved for payment.

This accord between John Beeson and his Oregon neighbors, who as frontiersmen had tried to kill him, burned his home, and

57. John Beeson, letter to Hiram Price, May 26, 1885, *ibid*. The Hutchinsons were a well-known family of singers who toured New England and Europe and sang to Union troops during the Civil War. Their own "Emancipation Song" and "Good Time Coming" helped spread abolitionist sentiment.

58. John Beeson, letter to John D. C. Atkins, October 16, 1886, *ibid*.

driven him from the territory, was symbolic of a vast change taking place in the nation. By 1886, the old frontier, with its lack of law and order, its boisterous expansionism, and its belligerent Indian-white relations, was rapidly disappearing. In its place was a mature society patterned on Eastern models but bearing an unmistakable frontier imprint.

With the Indians gathered on reservations and the trigger-happy volunteers and state militia replaced by less emotional law enforcement agencies, race relations in the West were becoming less and less an issue. Furthermore, most Western congressmen had become more sympathetic to such basic principles of the Peace Policy as education, civilization, and humane treatment. Many freshmen had entered the Congress in the late 1870's, and most of them saw the Indians in a different context than their predecessors had. Also, the restoration of the agency patronage system helped to mellow the politicians. Finally, they realized that, although the Indians were no longer the menace they had been, they still had to be considered and that new measures were needed to make them self-supporting members of society.[59] Westerners and humanitarian reformers in the East could begin to view the Indians with increased objectivity.

59. Robert W. Mardock, "The Plains Frontier and the Indian Peace Policy, 1865–1880," *Nebraska History*, XLIX, 2 (Summer, 1968), 200.

12

America's Conscience Is Soothed

The idea of apportioning Indian lands to individual tribal members was not a novel one when Carl Schurz adopted it as a part of his Indian policy in 1877. Most missionaries to the Indians were promoting private land ownership early in the nineteenth century.[1] It had been recommended by Secretary of War William Crawford in 1816, by President Monroe in 1819, and by Secretary of War John C. Calhoun in 1822. During the 1830's and 1840's, the government occasionally distributed land, but allotment in severalty was not generally effected until Indian Commissioner George Manypenny incorporated it in a series of treaties in 1854.[2] Manypenny acted out of a popular conviction that individual ownership of land would greatly accelerate the Indians' progress toward civilization.

These early severalty measures did not always benefit the Indians, particularly those in less advanced tribes. Provisions prohibiting the sale of the allotted lands were seldom incorporated in the treaties, and within a few years, great numbers of Indians who did not understand the theory or practice of individual land ownership had disposed of their holdings for trifling sums. In the meantime, Congress frequently authorized the immediate sale of the unallotted sections of the original reservations; the net result was a growing number of landless paupers.[3] Despite this serious weakness, at least from the Indians' viewpoint, the popularity of the severalty idea increased during the early years of the postwar reform period. Most of the treaties after 1864 provided for allotment in severalty on an optional basis, but little was done at first to activate these provisions.[4]

Under Grant's Peace Policy, the idea of individual land ownership was accepted as a necessary prerequisite for full civilization of the wild Western tribes. In 1870, Commissioner of Indian Affairs Ely Parker urged a policy of "giving to every Indian a home that

1. Robert F. Berkhofer, Jr., *Salvation and the Savage*, 81.
2. Loring Benson Priest, *Uncle Sam's Stepchildren: The Reformation of United States Indian Policy, 1865–1887*, 177; D'Arcy McNickle, *They Came Here First*, 262.
3. Priest, *Uncle Sam's Stepchildren*, 178–79.
4. *Congressional Record*, 46th Cong., 3d sess., 1880–1881, XI, Part 2, 1060.

he can call his own."[5] First came the gigantic task of concentrating the numerous roving and warlike tribes on restricted reservations. This task required most of the thought and energies of officials, agents, and the participating religious denominations during the first few years of Grant's Indian policy.

At first, many of the reformers urged only that the reservation lands be held by the Indian tribes in the same inviolable manner by which the whites held their property. As Lydia Maria Child suggested in the spring of 1870, "They must have reason to feel perfectly secure about the possession of the land they cultivate."[6] During the 1870's, as the reservation system developed, many people came to believe that security of tribal ownership of reservation land was not enough; civilization could not take place until that "citadel of savagery," the tribal relationship, had been destroyed. Acceptance of allotments based on relinquishing tribal ties would be a major change from the habits of nomadic barbarianism.

Provisions for allotment in severalty had been part of many of the treaties made with the Western tribes from 1865 to 1868, and upon the inauguration of the Peace Policy in 1869, these measures were immediately enacted. In 1869, Quaker Superintendent Samuel Janney told his Omaha charges, "One of the most important subjects for you to consider is the allotment of your lands." Two years later, he reported to the Indian Commissioner that individual land ownership, education, and religious instruction were necessary factors in preventing eventual extinction of the Indians.[7] In 1876, Bishop Whipple suggested to President Grant, "Whenever an Indian in good faith gives up his wild life and begins to live by labor give him an honest title by patent of 160 acres of land and make it inalienable."[8]

Although the actual division of reservation lands among individual tribesmen proceeded slowly because of insufficient appropriations, impracticable treaty stipulations, and resistance by skeptical Indians, the idea itself soon grew to the point that it threatened to dominate Indian policy. Carl Schurz, after taking office as Secretary of the Interior in 1877, observed, "The enjoyment and pride of the individual ownership of property [is] one of the most effective civi-

5. McNickle, *They Came Here First*, 263.
6. Lydia Maria Child, "The Indians," *The Standard*, I, 1 (May, 1870), 5.
7. Samuel M. Janney, *Memoirs of Samuel M. Janney*, 260, 281.
8. Bishop Whipple, letter to President Grant, July 31, 1876, Bureau of Indian Affairs, Letters Received.

lizing agencies."[9] In his annual reports for 1877, 1878, and 1879, Schurz outlined the Indian policy that was to be pursued under the Hayes Administration. It included the allotment "of land to the Indians in severalty," giving them "individual title to their farms in fee, inalienable for a certain period." When settlement in severalty had been accomplished, the plan was "to dispose, with their consent, of those lands on their reservation which are not settled and used by them, the proceeds to form a fund for their benefit." The opening of these unallotted lands to white homesteaders would also serve to mitigate the growing problem of encroachment. The final step would be to "treat the Indians like other inhabitants of the United States under the laws of the land." Schurz was certain that this program, and the education of the youth to "civilized ideas, wants and aspirations," would gradually solve the Indian problem without injustice to the Indians and without obstructing the development of the nation.[10]

The Indian-rights humanitarians could find little fault with this program, and most of them gave it their full support. The exceptions were the Ponca-rights advocates of Boston. Schurz's " 'infamous' severalty bill . . . would have, as White Eagle said of it, 'plucked the Indian like a bird,' " Helen Hunt Jackson wrote in 1881. She thought that the Indians did not want severalty, "as Schurz contends."[11] Except Mrs. Jackson and a few others, the opponents of Schurz ultimately supported the allotment policy as a means of achieving their primary objective of full citizenship for the Indians. Alfred Love's Universal Peace Union also encouraged the adoption of individual ownership of land as a way of ending the forcible reservation system.

The first general allotment bills were introduced in Congress in January, 1879—one each in the House and the Senate. Both were favorably reported in their respective legislative bodies, but no action was taken. Schurz again strongly recommended passage of a severalty bill in November, 1879, and this time the issue suddenly received national attention. The Ponca controversy was a sordid affair

9. Secretary of the Interior, *Annual Report of the Secretary of the Interior*, 45th Cong., 2d sess., 1877–1878, House Exec. Doc. No. 1 (Serial 1800), xi.

10. Secretary of the Interior, *Annual Report of the Secretary of the Interior*, 46th Cong., 2d sess., 1879–1880, House Exec. Doc. No. 1 (Serial 1910), 5.

11. Helen Hunt Jackson, letter to Henry Wadsworth Longfellow, March 2, 1881, Helen (Fiske) Hunt Jackson Papers, 1830–1885.

as far as governmental-reformer relationships were concerned, but it did publicize Schurz's Indian policy. It, more than any other experience, convinced government officials, congressmen, and Indian-policy reformers of the absolute need for cooperation. In 1868, Red Cloud's Sioux War and the Peace Commission report aroused humanitarian activity; in 1879, it was the Ponca removal and the Ute Indian War. The first brought the inauguration of Grant's Peace Policy; the second, a new phase of the original Peace Policy that culminated in the passage of the Dawes severalty act in 1887.

The allotment program received widespread support during the winter of 1879–1880. The Board of Indian Commissioners asserted that the only solution to the Indian problem was the distribution of lands in severalty with inalienable titles.[12] The General Assembly of the Presbyterian Church sent a committee headed by William E. Dodge to Washington to present a memorial asking that a policy of individual ownership of lands be granted the Indians. The committee repeated this mission the following year and interviewed President Hayes, who assured them of his sympathy with the policy.[13] In its annual meeting in Chicago, the American Missionary Association resolved to press Congress to secure for the Indians the ownership of land in severalty.[14] Even in Boston the Ponca-inspired Merchants Committee recommended that individual Indians have the privilege of selecting allotments with titles that would be inalienable for twenty-five years.[15] This recommendation was Schurz's proposal almost to the letter.

Negotiations with the Ute delegation in January, 1880, for the establishment of new reservations gave Schurz an opportunity to force through Congress a provision for the division of the lands as a part of the Ute agreement. The debates about this provision clearly indicated a serious division among the legislators. However, in March, they did pass the Ute bill with the severalty provision intact, but since many congressmen voted for it as an alternative to war, their acceptance was not proof that they would support it as a separate bill.[16]

The pressure of other business and the belief that the Indians

12. Clinton B. Fisk, letter to Secretary Schurz, January 29, 1880, in Carl Schurz Letters, Carl Schurz Papers, Vol. 58.

13. D. Stuart Dodge, *Memorials of William E. Dodge*, 179; *Congressional Record*, 46th Cong., 3d sess., 1880–1881, XI, Part 1, 620.

14. Clinton B. Fisk, letter to Carl Schurz, December 22, 1879, in Carl Schurz Letters, Carl Schurz Papers, Vol. 56.

15. The Boston Merchants Committee on the Removal of the Ponca Indians, *The Indian Question*, 26.

16. Priest, *Uncle Sam's Stepchildren*, 189–90.

were not prepared to support themselves in a competitive white economy, that they would lose their lands, or that they opposed severalty prevented the passage of an allotment bill in 1880 and again in 1881. Senator Henry M. Teller (Republican, Colorado) opposed the bill because he thought there was an "inherent objection in the Indian mind against land in severalty. . . . You cannot make any Indian on this continent . . . while he remains anything like an Indian in sentiment and feeling, take land in severalty," for they still clung to the old Indian idea that the land belongs in common.[17] Others, like Representative Charles E. Hooker (Democrat, Mississippi) maintained that allotment in severalty would cause the Indians to lose their land "and all the proceeds from the sale of it by fraud, force, or violence," but he agreed that they should be allowed to determine the matter for themselves.[18]

In his first annual message in December, 1881, President Arthur said there was "imperative need for legislative action" if the present efforts to civilize the Indians were to be successful. He recommended enacting "a general law permitting the allotment in severalty, to such Indians, at least, as desire it, of a reasonable quantity of land secured to them by patent, and for their own protection made inalienable for twenty or 25 years." This provision, he asserted, together with the extension of law over the Indian reservations and liberal appropriations for the Indian schools, would permit the gradual absorption of the Indians "into the mass of our citizens."[19]

During the 1880's, congressional opposition to the growing cost of the Indian program had increased. Congressmen of both parties were becoming impatient with an expensive program that had not made the majority of the Indians self-supporting. In March, 1882, during debates on the Indian appropriation bill, Senator George F. Hoar (Republican, Massachusetts) argued, "This country has expended and lost since Washington took the oath of office fully a thousand million dollars which it would have saved if our 210,000 Indians had been ordinary self-supporting farmers or mechanics." His solution was to continue spending for Indian education "for a few more years," which would make them self-supporting and end further expense to the government, except in fulfillment of existing treaties.[20]

17. *Congressional Record*, 46th Cong., 3d sess., 1880–1881, XI, Part 1, 780.
18. *Ibid.*, 499.
19. Henry Steele Commager, ed., *Documents of American History*, II, 107.
20. *Congressional Record*, 47th Cong., 1st sess., 1881–1882, XIII, Part 2, 2415.

Education for self-support gained considerable backing during the early 1880's, but most congressmen believed that it was too early to adopt a severalty policy. The severalty bill of 1881 had been brought before Congress by Senator Richard Coke (Democrat, Texas) and had passed the Senate in April, 1882, but the House took no action. The Senate approved an amended version in the spring of 1884, but in spite of the House Indian Affairs Committee's favorable report, there was still insufficient support for passage. By 1885, the sentiment began to shift away from the idea that education alone would produce self-supporting Indians to the idea that individual ownership of lands might provide a quicker and cheaper solution.

The land-hungry settlers, speculators, railroad builders, and congressmen who favored these interests considered the revised Coke bill unsatisfactory because it provided the tribes with an inalienable title to their reservations for twenty-five years. This stipulation nullified one of the most desirable results of allotment—the opening of surplus reservation lands to settlement. As Representative John J. O'Neill (Democrat, Missouri) explained it, a severalty program should solve the problems of the Indians, the poor whites, and the colored people. After the Indians received their individual allotments, the unallotted reservation lands should be made available to workers who had lost their jobs to labor-saving machinery and to other landless people, black and white.[21]

This viewpoint gained support among some Indian-rights workers who were now becoming convinced that a severalty bill would never pass Congress unless it satisfied the land interests. Herbert Welsh's Indian Rights Association concluded that a realistic approach was needed and began to support a new allotment-in-severalty bill. Senator Dawes introduced a bill in the Senate in February, 1886, that differed from the Coke bill only in a provision that allowed the Secretary of the Interior to purchase from the Indians any part of their reservations not needed for allotment. This provision was the appeal to the "land-grabber" that would activate many otherwise reluctant public officials.[22]

The Senate passed the Dawes severalty bill in record time and sent it to the House. Representative Bishop W. Perkins (Republican, Kansas), in reporting that the House Committee on Indian Affairs

21. *Ibid.*, 48th Cong., 2d sess., 1884–1885, XVI, Part 1, 867.
22. James B. Thayer, "The Dawes Bill and the Indians," *The Atlantic Monthly*, LXI (March, 1888), 318. In his autobiography, Thomas H. Tibbles claimed that the Boston Indian Citizenship Committee asked him to draw up a severalty bill that would express his ideas and that "in the long run that rough draft of mine became the backbone of the famous Dawes Severalty Act of 1887." Thomas Henry Tibbles, *Buckskin and Blanket Days*, 295.

favored the bill, explained that they wished to take from the Indians
the scalping knife and give to them the pruning hook. The committee also desired, he added, that the

> sun-dance shall be stricken down, and that in its stead we shall
> have industrial schools; that the commune shall give way to the
> dignity and rights of American citizens; that the heathen idols
> shall give place to the Christian altars, and the tribal organiza-
> tion broken up, and the individuality of the Indian encouraged
> and developed, and the lands unnecessarily reserved for them
> opened to the pioneer, that intelligence and thrift may find
> lodging there.[23]

All these objectives, the committee believed, could be accomplished
through the application of the Dawes bill.

Meanwhile, the humanitarian forces had received a setback that
made them determined to give all the support they could muster to
the Dawes bill. The case of *Elk vs. Wilkins* had been submitted to the
District Court of Nebraska by the Omaha Ponca Committee as a test
case to determine the Indians' citizenship status under the Fourteenth Amendment. This civil case was heard by the Supreme Court,
which handed down a decision in 1884. The Supreme Court justices
came to the same conclusion that the Senate Judiciary Committee
had reached in December, 1870: Although the Indians were born in
a geographical sense in the United States, they were no more born
in the United States and subject to its jurisdiction within the meaning of the first section of the Fourteenth Amendment than were "the
children of subjects of any foreign government born within the
domain of that government, or the children born within the
United States, of ambassadors or other public ministers of foreign
nations." However, the Court did leave the way clear for legislative
action by upholding the right of Congress to confer citizenship on
the Indians.[24]

After the announcement of the decision, the Indian-rights
groups began pressing the next session of Congress to take immediate measures to qualify the Indians for citizenship. Senator Dawes
declared that the *Elk vs. Wilkins* ruling was the strangest, if not the
wickedest, decision since the fugitive slave cases, and he responded to
the reformers' demands by introducing a citizenship bill.[25] It proposed designating every Indian who had been born in the territorial
limits of the United States, who had voluntarily taken up his residence

23. *Congressional Record*, 49th Cong., 1st sess., 1885–1886, XVII, Part
4, 2273.
24. Laurence F. Schmeckebier, *The Office of Indian Affairs: Its History, Activities, and Organization*, 65.
25. Priest, *Uncle Sam's Stepchildren*, 207.

"separate and apart" from any Indian tribe, and who had adopted "the habits of civilized life, to be a citizen of the United States, and entitled to all rights, privileges and immunities of such citizens."[26]

The advocates of Indian rights welcomed this measure, which most reformers had come to accept as a necessary move to clarify the enigmatic civil status of the tribes. A few humanitarians had been demanding citizenship for the Indian since early in the postwar reform movement. In 1868, Wendell Phillips had argued that the Indians were already citizens and that the government should recognize the fact. On the other hand, Alfred Love and the Universal Peace Union, noting that the Constitution excluded "Indians not taxed" from citizenship, demanded an amendment abolishing the restrictive clause. Most of the churches had adopted a more cautious approach that was in keeping with government policy and had looked toward Indian citizenship as a goal after the Indians were civilized. These moderates, who were decidedly in the majority, included such influential bodies as Peter Cooper's United States Indian Commission and individuals like Lydia Maria Child and William E. Dodge. In 1862, John Beeson had envisioned a "free and distinct" Indian nation and nationality, but later he proposed a territorial plan wherein the Indians would be represented in Congress by their own elected delegates until such time as they were prepared and disposed to become citizens.[27]

The Indian-rights associations that were organized in 1879 and throughout the early 1880's included in their statements of objectives citizenship for the Indians. This measure now ranked with individual ownership of land as one of the fundamental objectives of the reformers. The Supreme Court's consideration of *Elk vs. Wilkins* rallied reform forces behind the Fourteenth Amendment. The Universal Peace Union made the most notable change. It dropped its request for an amendment to the Constitution and demanded "that our fellow citizens of Indian birth be accorded the citizenship, suffrage and justice, whereto they are entitled by the Fourteenth Amendment to the Federal Constitution."[28]

The Secretary of the Interior and the Commissioner of Indian

26. Commissioner of Indian Affairs, *Annual Report of the Commissioner of Indian Affairs*, 1885, *Annual Report of the Secretary of the Interior*, 49th Cong., 1st sess., 1885–1886, House Exec. Doc. No. 1 (Serial 2379), vii–viii.

27. John Beeson, letter to President Lincoln, November 18, 1862, Secretary of the Interior, Letters Received; John Beeson, Memorial to Congress and the President, April 12, 1864, Senate, Letters Received.

28. "Resolutions passed at the Massachusetts Peace Convention," August 22, 23, 1883, Bureau of Indian Affairs, Letters Received.

Affairs opposed the Dawes citizenship bill because it would confer civil rights on many Indians who were not ready to assume the duties and responsibilities of citizenship. In December, 1885, President Cleveland noted the general concurrence about the proposition that the Indians be granted citizenship, but he advised caution before applying either severalty or citizenship.[29] In criticizing the Dawes citizenship bill, Indian Commissioner Atkins said that the Indians must first be so educated that citizenship would be an advantage to them. Most Indians, he added, were not sufficiently advanced in civilization "to make it safe, and to their best interest, to give them citizenship and title to their lands with unrestricted power of alienation."[30] Despite the Interior Department's opposition to citizenship, the Dawes severalty bill, as passed by the Senate in February, 1886, included the citizenship provision, but it was restricted to those Indians receiving allotments inalienable for twenty-five years.

The Dawes severalty bill, during the House debates on its provisions in 1886, gradually picked up support as the best way to solve the Indian question. Representative Joseph G. Cannon (Republican, Illinois), in arguing for its passage, said that because the progress made in civilizing the Indians was not sufficient, the policy must be changed. The tribal relation must be broken up, the Indians taught to work for self-support, and the surplus reservation lands opened for settlement. The industrious, civilized white families who took over these lands would provide the Indians with a good example that would help them become more rapidly civilized.[31] The majority of congressmen had accepted these principles by the spring of 1886, but they could not agree on the details of the final bill.

In his December, 1886, message to Congress, President Cleveland declared that "the more rapid transition from tribal organizations to citizenship" of those Indians capable of civilized life was now "pressing in its importance." He recommended that the tribes be persuaded to take up lands in severalty and that the "inequalities of existing special laws and treaties should be corrected and some general legislation on the subject should be provided."[32]

The President's firm advocacy of the Republican severalty measure opened the way for bipartisan support in the House, which now had a majority of Democrats. Cleveland's clear signal for action re-

29. James D. Richardson, ed., *A Compilation of the Messages and Papers of the Presidents*, 1897–1917 ed., X, 4940, 4942.

30. *Annual Report of the Commissioner of Indian Affairs*, 1885, viii.

31. *Congressional Record*, 48th Cong., 2d sess., 1884–1885, XVI, Part 2, 2273–78.

32. Richardson, *Messages and Papers*, 1897–1917 ed., XI, 5105–6.

ceived the enthusiastic support of Indian Commissioner Atkins, who had accepted the citizenship provision because of his desire for the allotment system. In the fall of 1886, Atkins called for the "true friends of Indian progress everywhere" to unite and to press "with zeal, determination, and all practicable dispatch the allotment system among the Indian tribes."[33]

Commissioner Atkins' request for aid was not really needed; advocates of Indian rights were already publicizing the merits of the Dawes bill. The effective lobbying of Dr. C. C. Painter of the Indian Rights Association brought the organization a share of the credit for securing its final passage.[34] Many of Herbert Welsh's forty-four public addresses on Indian policy during 1886 dealt with the severalty bill and related matters, and the Indian Rights Association printed 50,000 pamphlets on the subject that year.[35] The severalty bill also had the strong support of the Lake Mohonk Conference reports and the Women's National Indian Association.

Ethnologist Alice C. Fletcher also made a significant contribution to passage of the Dawes act. In 1882, her efforts to prevent the removal of the Nebraska Omaha tribe to the Indian Territory brought an act of Congress that gave the Omahas patents to their lands in severalty. Miss Fletcher was placed in charge of helping the tribe carry out the provisions of the act.[36] Indian Commissioner Atkins praised her for "having furnished a practical demonstration of the disposition and ability of the Indian to support himself."[37] In addition, she had furnished evidence that allotment in severalty might work for all Indians.

In January, the House passed the Dawes severalty bill, and a few days later, the Senate approved it. On February 8, 1887, President Cleveland signed it into law. The Dawes act provided for allotting

33. Commissioner of Indian Affairs, *Annual Report of the Commissioner of Indian Affairs*, 1886, *Annual Report of the Secretary of the Interior*, 49th Cong., 2d sess., 1886–1887, House Exec. Doc. No. 1 (Serial 2467), xx.

34. Dr. Painter closely watched other legislation affecting the Indians at the same time. For instance, when the House Committee on Indian Affairs decided to favor the location of Indian schools near the reservations rather than in the Eastern states, Painter presented Congress with such an array of evidence demonstrating the vital importance of the existing Eastern schools that the reservation school proposal was overwhelmingly defeated in the House. Indian Rights Association, *Fourth Annual Report*, 1886, 13.

35. *Ibid.*, 4–6.

36. Alice C. Fletcher, "Personal Studies of Indian Life," *The Century Magazine*, XLV, 3 (January, 1893), 454.

37. *Annual Report of the Commissioner of Indian Affairs*, 1886, xx.

160 acres of land to each head of a family living on a reservation. The government would hold in trust each allotted portion for the sole use of the new owner for a period of twenty-five years. At that time, he would receive the title to the land. Upon the completion of the allotments, each Indian who received an allotment would become subject to the laws of the state or territory in which he lived. Finally, every Indian born in the United States who received an allotment, who had separated himself from the tribe, and who had adopted the habits of civilized life would be declared a citizen with all rights, privileges, and immunities. After all lands had been allotted to a tribe, any surplus lands left within their reservation would be opened to white settlers under the homestead laws.[38]

The majority of the Indian-rights advocates agreed with the Indian Rights Association that the passage of the Dawes act was the "beginning of a new order of things" in Indian policy, but a dissatisfied minority soon made itself heard.[39] The proponents of immediate citizenship for all Indians condemned the act as too restrictive. The most outspoken critic was Theodore Bland, Meacham's successor as editor of *The Council Fire* and founder of the National Indian Defense Association. Bland contended that the government should withdraw completely from its wardship over the Indians in order that they might have full cultural freedom. Those who were convinced that citizenship should be granted on a much more gradual basis also objected, and others criticized the provision for disposal of unallotted reservation lands. This same objection had been raised about the prewar treaties containing allotment provisions, but Congress had not withheld these unallotted lands from settlement.

The Indians, too, were split over the issue. The Civilized Tribes in the Indian Territory, whose economy was well rooted in the tribal system, opposed any change. Most of the more progressive members of the less advanced tribes were agreeable to allotment, while the more conservative Indians often were adamantly against any proposal that would destroy the tribal organization. Some tribes, like the powerful Sioux, were not yet ready to accept the new order of things. However, the Indians did have a choice under the act. If and when

38. Commissioner of Indian Affairs, *Annual Report of the Commissioner of Indian Affairs, 1887, Annual Report of the Secretary of the Interior,* 50th Cong., 1st sess., 1887–1888, House Exec. Doc. No. 1 (Serial 2542), iv–ix. The Burke Act of 1906 provided that citizenship should not be granted until the expiration of the trust period and the issuance of the patent in fee. However, by the act of June 2, 1924, citizenship was conferred on all Indians born within the territorial limits of the United States. Schmeckebier, *Office of Indian Affairs,* 80, 90.

39. Indian Rights Association, *Fourth Annual Report,* 1886, 9.

the President decided to have a reservation surveyed, the actual allotments were to be made only after the Indians concerned voluntarily applied. If, after four years from the time allotments were made available, there were any resident Indians who had not claimed their share of land, the Secretary of the Interior was authorized, though not required, to compel all reluctant Indians to take an allotment.[40] Thus, the voluntary provision was limited, and in practice, the government vigorously encouraged Indians to participate in the severalty plan.

In his report of 1879, Secretary Schurz had explained why he believed that selling unallotted reservation lands would help both whites and Indians. The proceeds from the sale, he had said, would form a fund, the interest from which would be used to "gradually relieve the government of the expenses" of supporting the tribes. Furthermore, selling the land would open "to progress and improvement large districts now held by the Indians, which will then be of no real advantage to them and are now to nobody else."[41] The Indians would have their individual plots and the extra income from their investment, while the land-hungry whites, who already were invading Indian reservation lands at every opportunity, would be able to homestead the relinquished areas. Obviously, the pressure for a settlement of that nature was tremendous, especially from constituents in the border areas.

Despite the critics, most Indian-rights advocates and the public in general accepted the Dawes severalty act as a sensible and practical solution to a vexing racial problem that had been thwarting the best-laid plans of government officials for decades. Its success seemed only a matter of time, for the belief had developed that the traditional system of individual holdings must replace the costly agency-reservation program, with its vast holdings of unused land. Few reformers, government officials, or citizens thought the Indian tribal system encouraged progress or civilization. Pride of ownership, they believed, would generate individual initiative and provide the incentive that would bring both material and cultural advancement. The Dawes severalty act appeared to have fulfilled that need. At the same time, it created a definite and comprehensive Indian policy that could be practically applied and that had visible results.

Among the problems left for the reformers was the popular belief that the Indian question had been solved for all time. Harvard Law Professor James B. Thayer, a member of the Boston Indian Citizenship Committee, described the act as so "great, far-reaching,

40. Thayer, "The Dawes Bill and the Indians," 317, 320.
41. *Annual Report of the Secretary of the Interior*, 1879, 5–6.

and beneficent" that "there is danger lest the greatness of the present achievement should lead good men and women to slacken their vigilance, and to forget that much yet remains to be done."[42] The advocates of Indian rights knew that continued work and additional specific reforms were necessary. Herbert Welsh's Indian Rights Association praised the adoption of the Dawes act as "one of the greatest achievements of the friends of Indian rights," but it warned that the enactment of the law did not, in itself, change the condition of a single Indian. The work of selecting the men who would put its provisions into effect and the task of devising the plans to help the tribes progress from their present condition to the new order of things would be difficult. The association asserted that the results would be worth every effort, for "our Indian countrymen" would soon become self-supporting farmers and stock men after they left the reservations and the "fatal tribal bonds" that shut them from "all wholesome contact with our civilization."[43]

Besides concentrating on the Dawes bill, the association was pressuring Congress for the passage of Senator Dawes's Sioux bill and a bill for the relief of the Mission Indians of California. The Sioux bill called for dividing a portion of the Great Sioux Reservation of Dakota Territory into separate, smaller reservations. The remainder of the Sioux lands would then be available for settlement. The Indian Rights Association consistently favored opening all surplus reservation land for settlement, but at the same time, it insisted that the Indians be assured sufficient lands for self-support and eventual allotment in severalty. A case in point was that of the Mission Indians, whose lands were being appropriated by white settlers. The association paid for the legal counsel for these Indians and also brought the case before the California Supreme Court. In 1888, the court decided in favor of the Mission bands, and Indian-rights workers hoped the decision would form a precedent that would prevent similar aggressions elsewhere.[44]

In March, 1887, busy Herbert Welsh personally investigated the condition of Indian prisoners held by the government in Florida. These Indians were Geronimo's Apache band that had surrendered to the Army in 1885 and had been imprisoned at Fort Marion. Captain Pratt's Carlisle Indian school had accepted 44 of them the previous year, but over 400 remained in the crowded prison. Welsh advised the War Department that they be moved at once to a more suitable locality for their education. Thwarted in his attempts to see

42. Thayer, "The Dawes Bill and the Indians," 315.
43. Indian Rights Association, *Fourth Annual Report*, 1886, 9–10.
44. Indian Rights Association, *Sixth Annual Report*, 1888, 30–31.

President Cleveland and Secretary of War W. C. Endicott, Welsh gave the story of the intolerable prison conditions to the press. The resulting controversy brought a Cabinet meeting and the action Welsh had suggested. The Apaches were moved to a much larger and more healthful environment at Mt. Vernon Barracks, Alabama.[45]

The Dawes act had not remedied the lack of courts and a system of law for the Indians that was satisfactory by civilized standards. Immediately after Congress passed the act, the Boston Indian Citizenship Committee and the Indian Rights Association collaborated in drawing up a bill extending the law of the land to Indian reservations and establishing courts. They planned to have the bill introduced during the current congressional session.[46]

Meanwhile, Bright Eyes Tibbles was lecturing in Cambridge and Boston on the necessity of making the Indians equal with white men before the law, even to giving them the ballot, a goal that Wendell Phillips would have enthusiastically applauded.[47] Equality before the law was one thing, but the absorption of the Indians into the general mass of the population was quite another.[48] A number of deeply entrenched prejudices and misconceptions about the Indians persisted. It was a popular belief that the Indians were not really capable of civilized labor, that they were worthless and lazy by white standards.[49] Many thought that the program of Indian education was thus far a costly failure[50] and that Indians could not be educated in the Euro-American tradition, while others contended that the young educated Indians were unable to live among their own people unless they cast off the veneer of white civilization and reverted to savagery. Congressmen debated the issue at length when they considered appropriations for education. The Indian-rights workers did all the petitioning and pamphleteering they could to support education funds, usually with some success. However, congressional appropriations for education were always inadequate for the task, and even with the money from religious denominations and Indian-rights organizations, the funds had to be spread too thin.

After 1887, most of the active Indian-rights workers believed that final success was within reach, but Harriet Beecher Stowe may have been speaking for many of the veteran workers for human rights

45. Indian Rights Association, *Fifth Annual Report*, 1887, 27–32.
46. *Ibid.*, 6–7.
47. *The Boston Evening Transcript*, March 1, 1887.
48. *Ibid.*
49. Howard M. Jenkins, *The Indians as Workers*, 1.
50. Charles C. Painter, *Extravagance, Worth and Failure of Indian Education*, 19.

when she told the Connecticut Indian Association that the Indian policy would not be perfect until that time when "Christ's kingdom shall come, and his will be done *on earth as it is in Heaven.*"[51]

By 1887, very few veteran Indian-rights workers were alive. Bishop Whipple, who was sixty-five, still worked for his White Earth Reservation Chippewas and the Minnesota Sioux. John Beeson, the "oldest liveing pionere [*sic*] of Southern Oregon," had retired to his Talant, Oregon, farm, where he wrote occasional letters on Indian policy until his death in 1889.[52] Samuel Tappan and Cora Daniels were not as active in Indian-policy reform work during the 1880's as they had been earlier. Their marriage dissolved in 1876, and Cora had remarried, moved to Chicago, and resumed her lectures on spiritualism. Tappan and Wendell Phillips had kept in close touch during the 1870's, but Tappan had eventually moved to Washington, D. C., where he returned to his career as writer and newspaper correspondent. As his role in the Indian-rights movement diminished, so did his journalistic success and his financial well-being. John B. Sanborn visited Tappan in 1897 and found him in a cheap boarding house and "very near if not quite of the dead-beat class."[53] Alfred H. Love, who had achieved international recognition as the successful editor of his peace journal and as president of the Universal Peace Union, continued his work for women's rights, international arbitration, Indian rights, and the abolition of capital punishment.

Most of the uncompleted labor for the Indians fell to such capable reformers as Herbert Welsh and Charles C. Painter of the Indian Rights Association, Alice C. Fletcher, and the various branches of the Women's National Indian Association. The post-1887 reformers faced a different set of conditions than those that confronted the Peace Policy during the chaotic 1860's. With the exception of the Sioux Ghost Dance uprising and the Battle of Wounded Knee, hostilities were over, the Army was no longer needed, and there was no significant discussion of transfer. Furthermore, the conflict between Eastern reformers and Westerners was noticeably mellowing, which facilitated national cooperation on Indian policy. William Barrows, Secretary of the Massachusetts Home Missionary Society of the Congregational Church, saw the border, "where the two races meet," as

51. Harriet Beecher Stowe, letter to Mrs. Sara T. Kinney, March 2, 1888, in Ellen Terry Johnson, *Historical Sketch of the Connecticut Indian Association*, 63.

52. John Beeson, letter to John D. C. Atkins, October 16, 1886, Bureau of Indian Affairs, Letters Received.

53. John B. Sanborn, letter to George W. Martin, March 9, 1903, John B. Sanborn Papers.

the pivotal point on which the new policy "will turn for good or evil." People living on the border, where the severalty policy must be "wrought out practically," could easily veto its success. Western bordermen must become "tolerant and neighborly and patient and enduring with their inferior neighbors," while the Indians' friends should be ready to give those tribes adopting the Dawes act "a network of protective influences."[54]

In 1893, when Herbert Welsh spoke to a "large and intelligent" audience in Denver about the work of civilizing the Indians, he saw an illustration of the swift change that had taken place in the West. When he had last visited Denver in 1873, it had been a frontier town of 12,000 and only recently removed from the danger of hostile Indian attack. Within twenty years, it had become a city of 120,000, whose people were "so changed in sentiment to support an active Indian Society and listen to an advocacy of Indian Rights."[55] By 1887, all the tribes were on reservations and were being subjected to at least the rudiments of the civilization program. Some tribes had made considerable progress; the children were going to school, and the adults were learning how to farm. Others, like the western Sioux, had accomplished very little.

The direct influence of humanitarian reform activity on the improvement of Indian policy in the postwar era cannot always be measured precisely. However, similarity between the demands and proposals that the reformers made and the actual changes that the government incorporated over the years is striking. After Peter Cooper founded the United States Indian Commission in 1868, reform influence was direct and persistent.

President-elect Grant and his Seneca Indian aide, Ely Samuel Parker, had worked closely with the Quakers and other Indian-rights advocates to formulate an Indian policy that was basically humanitarian in concept. Humanitarians proposed the Board of Indian Commissioners and chose its members. From 1868 to 1887, the Indian Bureau usually made it clear that the active support and cooperation of church and human-rights organizations was vital for implementing the humane Indian policy. Their support of the Peace Policy probably saved it from collapse after the Modoc tragedy in 1873.

Publicity and pressure from reformers several times forced the government to discharge dishonest or uncooperative Indian commissioners and agents, to tighten up purchasing methods, and to stop

54. William Barrows, *The Indian's Side of the Indian Question*, 191, 192, 194.
55. Herbert Welsh, *Civilization Among the Sioux Indians*, 58.

corrupt practices. The reformers frequently influenced the appointment of Indian agents and other officials who would support the
Peace Policy. Reform groups encouraged abolition of the treaty system in 1871 and passage of the Indian Homestead Act in 1875. Most
legislation and activity concerning Indian policy after 1868 bore the
imprint of humanitarian ideas and demands. The reformers strongly
opposed transfer of the Indian Bureau to the War Department, "the
antithesis to peace and civilization." The transfer issue and such incidents as the Piegan Massacre inspired attacks on the Army by Wendell Phillips, Peter Cooper, Lydia Maria Child, and Alfred Love. It
was essentially an alliance between the humanitarians and the Senate
that defeated transfer legislation.

The Indian-rights organizations helped to persuade several of
the visiting Indian delegations that the Peace Policy was to their best
interests. The Indians gained confidence in the humanitarians after
humanitarian efforts to secure clemency for the convicted Kiowa and
Modoc leaders were successful. Reformers also helped to prevent
border settlers from invading and usurping Indian lands. The Indians' realization that not all white men were bent on seizing their
lands and destroying their race greatly encouraged their cooperation
with the government.

The humanitarians opposed concentration of the Western tribes
on a few large reservations, and after they especially objected to the
forcible removal program, the original plan was modified. Criticism
of the Ponca removal to the Indian Territory also aroused widespread support for a second wave of Indian-policy reform that began
in 1879.

During this second phase, the reformers exerted as great an
influence as they had in the first years of Grant's Peace Policy. The
passage of the Dawes severalty act in 1887 was a major triumph for
the reformers. Although it did not embody all the humanitarian
ideals that had been fought for, it did move toward the ends sought.

The Indian-rights workers usually could see only one side of the
Indian question. The exaggerations and half-truths frequently found
in humanitarian lectures, literature, and memorials were more the
result of ignorance and enthusiasm than willful misrepresentation.
Most of the people who worked for Indian rights considered the
problems and viewpoints of the white settlers and the harassed Army
detachments only as they affected the Indians. Since the settlers and
the Army seemed to foment the wrongs and injustices done to the
Indians and to advocate extermination, they were often castigated.

The frontier settlers and the Army felt unjustly censured and
resented, or even feared, the reformers' meddling in Indian affairs.

They retaliated by strongly opposing the Peace Policy and the reformers. The consequent lack of mutual respect, and the absence of common viewpoints and objectives between East and West, impeded the over-all success of any humanitarian policy until the 1880's.

Though motivated by idealistic principles, the reformers held concepts that were not always based upon thorough study of the problem and that were not always sufficiently tempered with realism and practicality. Also, they were reluctant to compromise or even to pay lip service to the other side of the question. Lydia Maria Child recognized this characteristic when she said that Thomas Paine had no tact: "he goes to work on a hard and knotty moral log, with might and main, but he is prone to drive in the wedge butt end foremost. It is a common defect with reformers."[56] Such traits, perhaps, made it more difficult to formulate and maintain a consistent Indian policy, but the controversy they created raised the Indian problem to the level of a national issue—a usual prerequisite for any major reform legislation. In 1884, Senator Dawes told his colleagues that the reformers "have waked up the nation; they have forced the government into this work. . . . to them the nation will yet acknowledge its debt of gratitude for having led it to abandon the cruel and merciless and profitless processes by which they had undertaken hitherto to deal with the Indian and to take him as they have the colored man and treat him as a man."[57]

The advocates of Indian rights were confident that true justice could be attained by means of humanitarian Federal legislation and through the application of Christian principles. That they were able to realize most of their goals is significant, and they believed that the reforms had substantially improved the condition of the Indians in their time and for the future.

56. Lydia Maria Child, letter to Sarah Shaw, April 8, 1876, Lydia Maria Child Papers, Houghton Library.
57. *Congressional Record*, 48th Cong., 1st sess., 1883–1884, XV, Part 4, 4071.

Bibliography

MANUSCRIPT MATERIAL

Beecher, Henry Ward, Papers, 1838–1878. Library of Congress.
———, Letters. Miscellaneous Personal Papers, Library of Congress.
Child, Lydia Maria, Papers. Boston Public Library.
———, Papers. Houghton Library, Harvard University.
———, Letters to John Greenleaf Whittier, 1857–1876. Library of Congress.
———, Letters. Giddings-Julian Papers, 1863–1899, Library of Congress.
———, Letters. John C. Underwood Papers, Library of Congress.
———, Letters. Miscellaneous Personal Papers, Library of Congress.
Cooper, Peter, Letters. Cooper-Hewitt Papers, Library of Congress.
———, Letters. Miscellaneous Personal Papers, Library of Congress.
Cushman, Charlotte, Letters. Charlotte Cushman Papers, Library of Congress.
Garrison, William Lloyd, "Antislavery Letters Written by William Lloyd Garrison, 1866–1870," Vol. 7, No. 95. Boston Public Library.
Grant, Ulysses S., Letters. George Hay Stuart Papers, Library of Congress.
Harvey, James M., Correspondence Received, Subject File: Indians, 1869–1872. Kansas State Historical Society.
———, Correspondence Received, 1869–1873. Kansas State Historical Society.
Jackson, Helen (Fiske) Hunt, Papers, 1830–1885. Houghton Library, Harvard University.
———, Letters. Carl Schurz Papers, Library of Congress.
———, Letters. Miscellaneous Personal Papers, Library of Congress.
Kansas House of Representatives, House Concurrent Resolution No. 26. Kansas State Historical Society.
Lamberton, Berenice, "A Biography of Lydia Maria Child." Unpublished Ph.D. dissertation, University of Maryland, 1953.
May, Samuel, Papers, 1864–1869, Vol. 10, No. 10. Boston Public Library.
Peaslee, John B., Letters. John B. Peaslee Papers, Library of Congress.
Phillips, Wendell, Papers, 1843–1884. Library of Congress.
———, Papers. Houghton Library, Harvard University.
———, Letters. Miscellaneous Personal Papers, Library of Congress.
———, Letters. Giddings-Julian Papers, 1863–1899, Library of Congress.
———, Letters. George Hay Stuart Papers, Library of Congress.

————, "Commonplace Book." Boston Public Library.
————, Miscellaneous Lectures and Other Notes. Boston Public Library.
————, "Scrapbook." Boston Public Library.
————, Letters. Homer Baxter Sprague Papers, Library of Congress.
Sanborn, John B., Papers. Kansas State Historical Society.
Schurz, Carl, Letters. Carl Schurz Papers, Vols. 7–61, Library of Congress.
————, Letters. Miscellaneous Personal Papers, Library of Congress.
Stowe, Harriet Beecher, Papers. Library of Congress.
————, Letters. John C. Underwood Papers, Library of Congress.
————, Letters. Miscellaneous Personal Papers, Library of Congress.
Tappan, Lewis, Letters. Lewis Tappan Papers, Library of Congress.
Tappan, Samuel F., Papers. Kansas State Historical Society.
————, "Autobiography." Manuscript. Samuel F. Tappan Papers, Kansas State Historical Society.
————, Letter, April 17, 1859. Thomas W. Higginson Collection, Kansas State Historical Society.
————, Letter, January 12, 1859. Charles Robinson Papers, Kansas State Historical Society.
Ticknor, Benjamin H., Letters. Benjamin H. Ticknor Papers, Library of Congress.
Whittier, John Greenleaf, Collection. Library of Congress.
————, Letters. Lewis Tappan Papers, Library of Congress.
————, Letters. Miscellaneous Personal Papers, Library of Congress.
————, Letters. John B. Peaslee Papers, Library of Congress.
————, Letters. Charlotte Cushman Papers, Library of Congress.
————, Letters. Benjamin H. Ticknor Papers, Library of Congress.

U. S. GOVERNMENT DOCUMENTS

Secretary of the Treasury, Annual Report of the Secretary of the Treasury. 1848.
Secretary of War, Annual Report of the Secretary of War. 1865–1887.
————, Report on the Sand Creek Massacre. Senate Exec. Doc. No. 26. 39th Cong., 2d sess., 1866–1867.
————, Letter transmitting the report of Brevet Colonel Baker, upon the late expedition against the Piegan Indians, in Montana. House Exec. Doc. No. 197 (Serial 1418). 41st Cong., 2d sess., 1870.
Secretary of the Interior, Annual Report of the Secretary of the Interior. 1862–1887.
————, Letters Received and Letters Sent, 1862–1887. National Archives.
————, Commissioner of Indian Affairs, Annual Report of the Commissioner of Indian Affairs. 1860–1887.
————, Bureau of Indian Affairs, Letters Received and Letters Sent, 1865–1887. National Archives.
————, Board of Indian Commissioners, Incoming Correspondence, 1869–1890. National Archives.

————, "Summary of the Work and Recommendations of the Board of Indian Commissioners from the Annual Reports, 1869–1915." Manuscript, April 1, 1916. National Archives.

Congress, Joint Special Committee, *Condition of the Indian Tribes.* Senate Report No. 156. 39th Cong., 2d sess., 1866–1867.

House of Representatives, Letters Received, 1865–1887. Records of the Legislative Branch (Congress), National Archives.

————, *Official Modoc War Correspondence.* House Exec. Doc. No. 122 (Serial 1607). 43d Cong., 1st sess., 1874.

Senate, Letters Received, 1862–1887. Records of the Legislative Branch (Congress), National Archives.

————, *Report to the Senate on the Origin and Progress of Indian Hostilities on the Frontier.* Senate Exec. Doc. No. 13 (Serial 1308). 40th Cong., 1st sess., 1867.

————, *Report to the Senate Transmitting All Correspondence Concerning the Ute Indians in Colorado.* Senate Exec. Doc. No. 31 (Serial 1882). 46th Cong., 2d sess., 1879–1880.

————, *Testimony Before the Select Committee on Removal of Northern Cheyennes as to the Removal and Situation of the Ponca Indians.* Senate Miscell. Doc. No. 49 (Serial 1944). 46th Cong., 3d sess., 1880–1881.

————, Committee on the Judiciary, *The Effect of the Fourteenth Amendment upon the Indian Tribes.* Senate Report No. 268 (Serial 1443). 41st Cong., 3d sess., 1870.

Congressional Globe, 38th Cong.–42d Cong.

Congressional Record, Vols. 1–20.

Statutes at Large, Vols. 12–32.

NEWSPAPERS

The Boston Daily Advertiser, 1865–1889.
The Boston Daily Globe, 1872–1890.
The Boston Evening Transcript, 1865–1890.
The Boulder (Colorado) *News,* 1869–1878.
The Christian Register (Boston), 1878–1879.
The Daily Colorado Herald (Central City), 1868.
Daily Colorado Miner (Georgetown), 1869–1873.
The Daily Colorado Times (Central City), 1867.
Daily Colorado Tribune (Denver), 1867–1871.
The Daily Press (Philadelphia), 1870–1886.
The Denver Daily Times, 1872–1882.
The Denver Weekly Times, 1873–1880.
The Evening Bulletin (Philadelphia), 1872–1876.
Independent (New York), 1868–1870.
The Junction City (Kansas) *Union,* 1864–1873.
The Junction City (Kansas) *Weekly Union,* 1867–1876.
Kansas Daily Tribune (Lawrence), 1866–1876.
Kansas State Record (Topeka), 1866–1875.
The Leavenworth (Kansas) *Daily Conservative,* 1866–1868.

The Leavenworth (Kansas) *Daily Times,* 1866–1867.
The Manhattan (Kansas) *Independent,* 1868.
The Marysville (Kansas) *Enterprise,* 1866.
The National Anti-Slavery Standard (New York). This publication appeared as a weekly newspaper from May, 1868, to April, 1870. In May, 1870, it became *The Standard,* a periodical. On July 30, 1870, it was once again changed to a weekly newspaper, *The National Standard,* and appeared from July 30, 1870, to December 30, 1872.
The Olathe (Kansas) *Mirror,* 1867.
The New York Semi-Weekly Tribune, 1869–1870.
The New York Times, 1865–1890.
The Press (Philadelphia), 1870–1886.
The Weekly Colorado Herald (Central City), 1870.
The Weekly Press (Philadelphia), 1872–1886.
Western Observer (Washington, Kansas), 1869.

ARTICLES AND PERIODICALS

Beeson, John, ed. *The Calumet,* I, 1 (February, 1860), 1–32. (Only one issue was published.)
Child, Lydia Maria, "The Indians." *The Standard,* I, 1 (May, 1870), 1–6.
Colyer, Vincent, "Vincent Colyer's Reply to General Sheridan, February, 1870." *The Bond of Peace,* III, 4 (April, 1870), 42.
Conway, Moncure D., "Wendell Phillips." *The Fortnightly Review,* XIV, 43 (July 1, 1870), 59–73.
Curtis, George Ticknor, "Reminiscences of N. P. Willis and Lydia Maria Child." *Harper's New Monthly Magazine,* LXXXI, 485 (October, 1890), 717–20.
Enochs, James C., "A Clash of Ambition: The Tappan-Chivington Feud." *Montana Magazine,* XV, 3 (Summer, 1965), 58–67.
Evans, Robert K., "The Indian Question in Arizona." *The Atlantic Monthly,* LVIII (August, 1886), 167–76.
Fletcher, Alice C., "Personal Studies of Indian Life." *The Century Magazine,* XLV, 3 (January, 1893), 441–55.
Garfield, Marvin H., "The Indian Question in Congress and in Kansas." *The Kansas Historical Quarterly,* II, 1 (February, 1933), 29–44.
"General Grant's Indian Policy." *The Nation,* XXVIII (January 9, 1879), 22.
Hayter, Earl W., "The Ponca Removal." *North Dakota Historical Quarterly,* VI, 4 (July, 1932), 262–75.
Howard, Oliver O., "The True Story of the Wallowa Campaign." *The North American Review,* CXXIV (July, 1879), 53–64.
"The Indian Delegation." *The Standard,* I, 3 (July, 1870), 177–78.
"Indian Department." *The Voice of Peace,* I (July, 1874), 62–64.
"Indian Department." *The Voice of Peace,* II (February, 1876), 165–66.

"Indians in Washington and Their Interview." *The Voice of Peace,* V (February, 1879), 164.
"Interview of the Peace Society with the Modoc and Klamath Indians." *The Voice of Peace,* II (May, 1875), 21–24.
Jenness, Theodora R., "The Indian Territory." *The Atlantic Monthly,* XLIII (April, 1879), 446–52.
"Justice for the Indians." *The Voice of Peace,* V (May, 1878), 29–30.
Julian, George W., "The Land Question." *The Standard,* I, 1 (May, 1870), 33.
King, Henry, "The Indian Country." *Century Magazine,* XXX, 8 (August, 1885), 599–606.
Lewis, Eleanor, "Letters of Wendell Phillips to Lydia Maria Child." *The New England Magazine,* V, 6 (February, 1892), 730–34.
Love, Alfred H., "The Indians." *The Bond of Peace,* I, 12 (December, 1868), 3.
————, "We Must Avenge the Dead." *The Voice of Peace,* VI (November, 1879), 139.
"Lydia Maria Child." *The Atlantic Monthly,* L, 6 (December, 1882), 840–44.
Mardock, Robert W., "The Antislavery Humanitarians and Indian Policy Reform." *The Western Humanities Review,* VII, 2 (Spring, 1958), 131–46.
————, "Irresolvable Enigma? Strange Concepts of the American Indian Since the Civil War." *Montana Magazine,* VII, 1 (Winter, 1957), 36–47.
————, "The Plains Frontier and the Indian Peace Policy, 1865–1880." *Nebraska History,* XLIX, 2 (Summer, 1968), 187–201.
"A National Disgrace." *Harper's Weekly,* XX, 1023 (August 5, 1876), 630–31.
Painter, Edward, "Friends Among the Indians." *The Standard,* I, 1 (May, 1870), 15–17.
"The Peace Movement." *The Voice of Peace,* VI (January, 1880), 171.
Pennsylvania Peace Society, "Third Annual Report of the Executive Committee." *The Bond of Peace,* III, 1 (January, 1870), 8.
————, "Official Report of the Twelfth Anniversary Meeting." *The Voice of Peace,* V (January, 1879), 145–58.
Phillips, Wendell, "Extracts from an Address by Wendell Phillips, at the Academy of Music, Philadelphia." *The Voice of Peace,* II (December, 1875), 141–43.
————, "The New Powers of Congress." *The Standard,* I, 2 (June, 1870), 101.
————, "Wendell Phillips to the United States Indian Commission, May 17, 1870." *The Standard,* I, 2 (June, 1870), 114–15.
"Public Action of the Universal Peace Union." *The Voice of Peace,* V (April, 1878), 13–14.
"The Recent Change in the Indian Bureau." *The Nation,* XIII (August 17, 1871), 100–101.

"Report of the Convention of the Indian Commission in New York." *The Nation*, X (May 26, 1870), 329.

"Report of the Executive Committee of the Universal Peace Union." *The Bond of Peace*, I, 12 (December, 1868), 7.

Shenandoah, "The Massacre of the Piegans." *The Standard*, I, 2 (June, 1870), 90–91.

"Sitting Bull." *The Voice of Peace*, VI (September, 1879), 86–87.

Stoddard, R. H., "John Greenleaf Whittier." *Appleton's Journal*, V, 107 (April 15, 1871), 431–34.

Tappan, Samuel F., "Our Indian Relations." *The Standard*, I, 3 (July, 1870), 161–66.

Thayer, James B., "The Dawes Bill and the Indians." *The Atlantic Monthly*, LXI (March, 1888), 315–22.

Universal Peace Union, "Official Report of the Eighth Annual Meeting." *The Voice of Peace*, I (June, 1874), 36.

————, "Official Report of the Twelfth Anniversary Meeting." *The Voice of Peace*, V (July, 1878), 49–60.

————, "Official Report of the Thirteenth Anniversary Meeting." *The Voice of Peace*, VI (June, 1879), 33–46.

————, "Public Action of the Universal Peace Union." *The Voice of Peace*, V (April, 1878), 13–14.

"U.S. Indian Policy." *The Pall Mall Gazette* in *Littell's Living Age*, I (January 4, 1873), 145.

Walker, Francis A., "The Indian Question." *The North American Review*, CXVI, 239 (April, 1873), 329–88.

Welsh, Herbert, "The Indian Question Past and Present." *The New England Magazine*, III, 2 (October, 1890), 257–66.

BOOKS AND PAMPHLETS

Albree, John, ed., *Whittier Correspondence from the Oak Knoll Collections, 1830–1892*. Salem, Massachusetts: Essex Book & Print Club, 1911.

Athearn, Robert G., *William Tecumseh Sherman and the Settlement of the West*. Norman: University of Oklahoma Press, 1956.

Austin, George L., *The Life and Times of Wendell Phillips*. Boston: Lee & Shepard, 1888.

Baer, Helen G., *The Heart is Like Heaven*. Philadelphia: University of Pennsylvania Press, 1964.

Bancroft, Frederic, ed., *Speeches, Correspondence and Political Papers of Carl Schurz*. New York: G. P. Putnam's Sons, 1913. 6 vols.

Bancroft, George, *History of the United States of America*. Boston: Little, Brown, and Company, 1876. 6 vols.

Barrows, William, *The Indian's Side of the Indian Question*. Boston: D. Lothrop Company, 1887.

Bartlett, Irving, *Wendell Phillips, Brahmin Radical*. Boston: Beacon Press, 1961.

Battey, Thomas C., *The Life and Adventures of a Quaker Among the Indians.* Boston: Lee & Shepard, 1875.

Beadle, J. H., *The Undeveloped West; or Five Years in the Territories.* Philadelphia: National Publishing Company, 1873.

Beecher, William C., and Reverend Samuel Scoville, *A Biography of Henry Ward Beecher.* New York: Charles L. Webster & Company, 1888.

Beeson, John, *A Plea for the Indians.* New York: n.p., 1858.

Belden, George P., *Belden, the White Chief; or, Twelve Years Among the Wild Indians of the Plains.* Cincinnati: C. F. Vent, 1872.

Berkhofer, Robert F., Jr., *Salvation and the Savage.* Lexington: The University Press of Kentucky, 1965.

Berthrong, Donald, *Southern Cheyennes.* Norman: University of Oklahoma Press, 1965.

Bland, Theodore A., *Life of Alfred B. Meacham.* Washington: T. A. & M. C. Bland, 1883.

Boston Merchants Committee on the Removal of the Ponca Indians, *The Indian Question.* Boston: F. Wood, Book and Job Printer, 1880.

Bowles, Samuel, *Our New West.* New York: Hartford Publishing Company, 1869.

Carrington, Col. Henry B., *History of Indian Operations on the Plains.* (50th Cong., 1st sess; Senate Exec. Doc. No. 33 [Serial 2504].) Washington: Government Printing Office, 1888.

Carrington, Margaret I., *Ab-Sa-Ra-Ka, Land of Massacre.* Philadelphia: J. B. Lippincott & Company, 1879.

Child, Lydia Maria, *An Appeal for the Indians.* New York: William P. Tomlinson [1868].

————, *Letters from New York, 1st and 2d Series.* London: F. Pitman, 1879.

————, *Letters of Lydia Maria Child.* Boston: Houghton, Mifflin, and Company, 1883.

Clum, Woodworth, *Apache Agent: The Story of John P. Clum.* Boston: Houghton Mifflin Company, 1936.

Colyer, Vincent, *Bombardment of Wrangel, Alaska.* (41st Cong., 2d sess.; Senate Exec. Doc. No. 67.) Washington: Government Printing Office, 1870.

Commager, Henry Steele, ed., *Documents of American History,* 5th ed. New York: Appleton-Century-Crofts, Inc., 1949. 2 vols.

Connelley, William E., *A Standard History of Kansas and Kansans.* Chicago: Lewis Publishing Company, 1918. 5 vols.

Cooper, Peter, *Letter from Peter Cooper to the Delegates of the Evangelical Alliance.* New York: Baker, Godwin & Company, 1873.

Crawford, Samuel J., *Kansas in the Sixties.* Chicago: A. C. McClurg & Company, 1911.

Curti, Merle, *Peace or War: The American Struggle, 1636–1936.* New York: W. W. Norton & Company, 1936.

Dodge, D. Stuart, *Memorials of William E. Dodge.* New York: Anson

D. F. Randolph and Company, 1887.

Dodge, Grenville M., *The Battle of Atlanta and Other Campaigns.* Council Bluffs, Iowa: The Monarch Printing Company, 1910.

Dodge, Richard I., *Our Wild Indians.* Hartford: A. D. Worthington and Company, 1890.

Fletcher, Alice C., *Indian Education and Civilization.* (48th Cong., 2d sess.; Senate Exec. Doc. No. 95, II, Part 2 [Serial 2264].) Washington: Government Printing Office, 1888.

Fritz, Henry E., *The Movement for Indian Assimilation, 1860–1890.* Philadelphia: University of Pennsylvania Press, 1963.

Fuess, Claude Moore, *Carl Schurz, Reformer.* New York: Dodd, Mead and Company, 1932.

Gabriel, Ralph Henry, *The Lure of the Frontier, A Story of Race Conflict.* Vol. II, Pageant of America Series. New Haven: Yale University Press, 1929.

Garrison, Wendell P., and Francis J. Garrison, *William Lloyd Garrison, 1805–1879: The Story of His Life Told by His Children.* New York: The Century Company, 1885–1889. 4 vols.

Glassley, Ray Hoard, *Pacific Northwest Indian Wars.* Portland, Oregon: Binfords & Mort, 1953.

Goodale, Francis A., ed., *The Literature of Philanthropy.* New York: Harper & Brothers, 1893.

Gossett, Thomas F., *Race: The History of an Idea in America.* Dallas: Southern Methodist University Press, 1963.

Hare, Lloyd Custer M., *The Greatest American Woman: Lucretia Mott.* New York: American Historical Society, 1937.

Harmon, George Dewey, *Sixty Years of Indian Affairs: Political, Economic, and Diplomatic, 1789–1850.* Chapel Hill: The University of North Carolina Press, 1941.

Harrison, J. B., *Latest Studies on Indian Reservations.* Philadelphia: Indian Rights Association, 1887.

Hebard, Grace Raymond, and E. A. Brininstool, *The Bozeman Trail.* Glendale, California: Arthur H. Clark Company, 1960. 2 vols.

Hibben, Paxton, *Henry Ward Beecher: An American Portrait.* New York: George H. Doran Company, 1927.

Higginson, Thomas Wentworth, *Contemporaries.* Boston: Houghton Mifflin Company, 1899.

———, *John Greenleaf Whittier.* New York: The Macmillan Company, 1911.

Hollowell, Anna Davis, ed., *James and Lucretia Mott. Life and Letters.* Boston: Houghton, Mifflin and Company, 1884.

Hoopes, Alban W., *Indian Affairs and Their Administration: With Special Reference to the Far West, 1849–1860.* Philadelphia: University of Pennsylvania Press, 1932.

Indian Rights Association, *Annual Report.* Philadelphia: Indian Rights Association, 1883–1889. 6 vols.

Jackson, Helen Hunt, *A Century of Dishonor.* New York: Harper & Brothers, 1881.

————, *Ramona*. Boston: Little, Brown and Company, 1931.

————, and Abbot Kinney, *Report on the Condition and Needs of the Mission Indians of California*. Washington: Government Printing Office, 1883.

Janney, Samuel M., *Memoirs of Samuel M. Janney*. 4th ed. Philadelphia: Friends Book Association, 1890.

————, *Report to the Convention on Indian Affairs of Friends, October 29, 1871*. New York: Publishers for the Yearly Meeting, 1871.

Jenkins, Howard M., *The Indians as Workers*. Philadelphia: Indian Rights Association, 1892.

Johnson, Ellen Terry, *Historical Sketch of the Connecticut Indian Association*. Hartford: Fowler and Miller Company Press, 1888.

Julian, George W., *Political Recollections, 1840–1872*. Chicago: Jansen, McClurg & Company, 1884.

Kappler, Charles J., *Indian Affairs, Laws and Treaties*. Washington: Government Printing Office, 1929.

Keiser, Albert, *The Indian in American Literature*. New York: Oxford University Press, 1933.

Kelsey, Rayner Wickersham, *Friends and the Indians, 1655–1917*. Philadelphia: Associated Executive Committee of Friends on Indian Affairs, 1917.

Korngold, Ralph, *Two Friends of Man*. Boston: Little, Brown and Company, 1950.

Kroeber, A. L., *Anthropology*. rev. ed. New York: Harcourt, Brace and Company, 1948.

Kuhlman, Charles, *Legend into History*. Harrisburg, Pennsylvania: The Stackpole Company, 1952.

Lamar, Howard Roberts, *Dakota Territory, 1861–1889. A Study of Frontier Politics*. New Haven: Yale University Press, 1956.

Larson, T. A., *History of Wyoming*. Lincoln: University of Nebraska Press, 1965.

Lester, Charles Edwards, *Life and Character of Peter Cooper*. New York: J. B. Alden, 1883.

Lewis, Lloyd, *Captain Sam Grant*. Boston: Little, Brown and Company, 1950.

Love, Alfred H., *An Appeal in Vindication of Peace Principles, and Against Resistance by Force of Arms*. Philadelphia: Maas and Vogdes, Printers, 1862.

————, *A Brief Synopsis of Work Proposed, Aided and Accomplished by the Universal Peace Union During the Last 31 Years, 1866–1897*. Philadelphia: n.p., 1897.

Lowitt, Richard, *A Merchant Prince of the Nineteenth Century*. New York: Columbia University Press, 1954.

Mack, Edward C., *Peter Cooper, Citizen of New York*. New York: Duell, Sloan & Pearce, 1949.

MacMahon, Richard R., *The Anglo-Saxon and the North American Indian*. Baltimore: Kelly, Pict & Company, 1876.

McNickle, D'Arcy, *They Came Here First*. Philadelphia: J. B. Lippincott Company, 1949.

Manypenny, George W., *Our Indian Wards*. Cincinnati: Robert Clarke & Company, 1880.

Martyn, Carlos, *Wendell Phillips: the Agitator*. New York: Funk & Wagnalls, 1890.

May, Samuel Joseph, *Memoirs of Samuel Joseph May*. 3d ed. Boston: American Unitarian Association, 1890.

Meacham, Alfred B., *Wigwam and War-Path; or the Royal Chief in Chains*. 2d ed., rev. Boston: John P. Dale & Company, 1875.

Mumford, Thomas J. *Memoir of Samuel Joseph May*. Boston: Roberts Brothers, 1873.

Nevins, Allan, *Abram S. Hewitt: with Some Account of Peter Cooper*. New York: Harper & Brothers, 1935.

Newman, Henry Stanley, *Memories of Stanley Pumphrey*. New York: Friends' Book & Tract Committee, 1883.

New York Indian Peace Commission, *A Thorough Digest of the Indian Question*. [New York: n.p., 1876.]

Nye, Russell B., *William Lloyd Garrison and the Humanitarian Reformers*. Boston: Little, Brown and Company, 1955.

Odell, Ruth, *Helen Hunt Jackson*. New York: D. Appleton, Century Company, 1939.

Osgood, Phillips Endicott, *"Straight Tongue"*. Minneapolis: T. S. Denison and Company, 1958.

Painter, Charles C., *Extravagance, Worth and Failure of Indian Education*. Philadelphia: Indian Rights Association, 1892.

Parker, Arthur C., *The Life of General Ely S. Parker*. Buffalo Historical Society Publications, XXIII. Buffalo: Buffalo Historical Society, 1919.

Partington, Frederick E., *The Story of Mohonk*. New York: Morrill Press, 1911.

Pearce, Roy H., *The Savages of America*. Baltimore: The Johns Hopkins Press, 1953.

Peebles, J. M., *Around the World*. 2d ed. Boston: Colby and Rich, 1875.

Philadelphia Yearly Meeting, *A Brief Sketch of the Efforts of The Philadelphia Yearly Meeting of the Religious Society of Friends, to Promote the Civilization and Improvement of the Indians; Also, of the Present Condition of the Tribes in the State of New York*. 2d ed. Philadelphia: Friends Book Store, 1879.

Phillips, Wendell, *Christianity a Battle, Not a Dream*. London: Cherry & Fletcher, 1869.

————, *The Freedom Speech of Wendell Phillips, Faneuil Hall, December 8, 1837*. Boston: Wendell Phillips Hall Association, 1891.

————, *The People Coming to Power*. Boston: Lee & Shepard, 1871.

————, *Review of Webster's Speech on Slavery*. Boston: American Anti-Slavery Society, 1850.

————, *Speeches, Lectures, and Letters*. Boston: Lee and Shepard, 1892.

Pratt, Capt. Richard H., *How to Deal With the Indians*. n.p., 1891.

Priest, Loring Benson, *Uncle Sam's Stepchildren: The Reformation of United States Indian Policy, 1865–1887*. New Brunswick: Rutgers University Press, 1942.

Quinton, Amelia S., *Proceedings of the Third Annual Lake Mohonk Conference of Friends of the Indian*. Philadelphia: Sherman & Company, 1885.

Rahill, Peter J., *Catholic Indian Missions and Grant's Peace Policy, 1870–1884*. Washington: The Catholic University of America Press, 1953.

Raymond, Rossiter W., *Peter Cooper*. Boston: Houghton, Mifflin and Company, 1901.

Richardson, James D., ed., *A Compilation of the Messages and Papers of the Presidents, 1789–1902*. Washington: Government Printing Office, 1908. 10 vols.

————, *A Compilation of the Messages and Papers of the Presidents*. New York: Bureau of National Literature, 1897–1917. 20 vols.

Rockwell, Wilson, *The Utes, A Forgotten People*. Denver: Swallow Press, 1956.

Rushmore, Elsie Mitchell, *The Indian Policy During Grant's Administrations*. Jamaica, New York: The Marion Press, 1914.

Rusling, James F., *Across America: or, the Great West and the Pacific Coast*. New York: Sheldon and Company, 1874.

Sargent, Mrs. John T., ed., *Sketches and Reminiscences of The Radical Club of Chestnut Street, Boston*. Boston: James R. Osgood and Company, 1880.

Schmeckebier, Laurence F., *The Office of Indian Affairs: Its History, Activities, and Organization*. Baltimore: The Johns Hopkins Press, 1927.

Sears, Lorenzo, *Wendell Phillips, Orator and Agitator*. New York: Doubleday, Page & Company, 1909.

Shenstone, N. A., *Anecdotes of Henry Ward Beecher*. Chicago: R. R. Donnelley & Sons, 1887.

Sherwin, Oscar, *Prophet of Liberty: The Life and Times of Wendell Phillips*. New York: Bookman Associates, 1958.

Slattery, Charles Lewis, *Felix Reville Brunot, 1820–1898*. New York: Longmans, Green and Company, 1901.

Spalding, Charles S., *Peter Cooper: A Critical Bibliography of His Life and Works*. New York: New York Public Library, 1941.

Sprague, Marshall, *Massacre: The Tragedy at White River*. Boston: Little, Brown and Company, 1957.

Stewart, Edgar I., *Custer's Luck*. Norman: University of Oklahoma Press, 1955.

Stuart, George Hay, *The Life of George Hay Stuart*. Philadelphia: J. M. Stoddard & Company, 1890.

Swanton, John R., *The Indian Tribes of North America*. Washington: Government Printing Office, 1952.

Tatum, Lawrie, *Our Red Brothers and the Peace Policy of President Ulysses S. Grant*. Philadelphia: J. C. Winston and Company, 1899.

Textor, Lucy E., *Official Relations Between the United States and the Sioux Indians*. Palo Alto, California: Leland Stanford, Jr. University Publications, 1896.

Thomas, John L., *The Liberator: William Lloyd Garrison*. Boston: Little, Brown and Company, 1963.

Tibbles, Thomas Henry, *Buckskin and Blanket Days*. (1905.) Garden City: Doubleday & Company, 1957.

———, *Hidden Power, A Secret History of the Indian Ring*. New York: G. W. Carleton & Company, 1881.

Turner, Katherine C., *Red Men Calling on the Great White Father*. Norman: University of Oklahoma Press, 1951.

Twain, Mark, *Roughing It*. New York: Harper and Brothers, 1913. 2 vols.

Underwood, Francis H., *John Greenleaf Whittier*. Boston: James R. Osgood & Company, 1884.

United States Indian Peace Commission, *Papers Relating to Talks and Councils Held with the Indians in Dakota and Montana Territories in the Years 1866–1869*. Washington: Government Printing Office, 1910.

Welsh, Herbert, *A Brief Statement of Aims, Work, and Achievements of the Indian Rights Association*. Philadelphia: Indian Rights Association, 1886.

———, *Civilization Among the Sioux Indians*. Philadelphia: Indian Rights Association, 1893.

Welsh, William, *Indian Office: Wrongs Doing and Reforms Needed*. Philadelphia: n.p., 1874.

Whipple, Henry Benjamin, *Lights and Shadows of a Long Episcopate*. New York: The Macmillan Company, 1899.

Whittier, John Greenleaf, *The Works of John Greenleaf Whittier*. Boston: Houghton, Mifflin and Company, 1892. 7 vols.

Wilson, Robert F., *Crusader in Crinoline: The Life of Harriet Beecher Stowe*. London: Hutchinson & Company, 1942.

Women's National Indian Association, *An Earnest Petition Needed*. n.p. [1879].

Wynkoop, Col. Edward W., *Address Before the Indian Peace Commission of the Cooper Institute, New York, December 23, 1868*. Philadelphia: A. C. Bryson, 1869.

Zachos, John C., *A Sketch of the Life and Opinions of Mr. Peter Cooper*. New York: Murray Hill Publishing Company, 1876.

Zylyff [Wendell Phillips], *The Ponca Chiefs*. Boston: Lockwood, Brooks & Company, 1880.

Index

242